Canine Nutrition

FOOD, FEEDING AND FUNCTION

Dr Jacqueline Boyd

Canine Nutrition

FOOD, FEEDING AND FUNCTION

THE CROWOOD PRESS

First published in 2023 by
The Crowood Press Ltd
Ramsbury, Marlborough
Wiltshire SN8 2HR

enquiries@crowood.com
www.crowood.com

British Library Cataloguing-in-Publication Data
A catalogue record for this book is available from the British Library.

ISBN 978 0 7198 4183 5

Cover photo of cocker spaniel Byrbwll Nugget by Andrew Robinson

Acknowledgements
This book could not have been written without the help and support of so many friends, family, colleagues, students and clients – two- and four-legged! You have all continually supported me, shouted at me (when needed), taught me, inspired me and understood when I said I couldn't do something because I was 'chained to my desk'.

Special thanks to my mum and dad for always supporting me and absolutely (mostly!) allowing me to indulge in my animal-related passions from an early age – I can never thank you enough.
Big hugs to my bestie Sarah who has always been my cheerleader and has the best skill of saying the right thing to make me feel less of an imposter at the right time (I don't think you even know you do it!).
Special spaniel snogs to Hannah – for just being the perfect pal always!

To everyone at Crowood for their help, support, guidance, and confidence – I will be eternally grateful for this opportunity.

Finally, to my little cocker spaniel team, past and present. Every single one of you has inspired me and made me a better person, scientist, teacher and canine caregiver. Not a day goes by when you don't make me think 'I wonder…' and off I go exploring another avenue of canine science. You have also been constant companions during long hours at the computer, made me get up for walks, runs and cups of tea. You have even been brilliant models for photos! You are the best.

Photographs all by the author except for the following: Andrew Robinson of Whaupley Gundogs: pp.49, 66, 126 and 136; Adam Scott: pp.87 and 124; Pixabay/congerdesign: p.86; Pixabay/jagdprinzessin: p.88; Pixabay/Jeanette 1980: p.20 (bottom); Pixabay/Julie C: p.2; Pixabay/No-longer-here: pp.54 and 84; Pixabay/Rebecca Scholz: p.10; Pixabay/Viola: p.62 (bottom); Unsplash/Hermes Rivera: p.20 (top left); Unsplash/Natalie Spehner: p.48; and Unsplash/Ayla Verschueren: p.89.

Typeset by Simon and Sons

Cover design by Sergey Tsvetkov

Printed and bound in India by Replika Press Pvt Ltd

Contents

Introduction

The Domestic Dog

The dog is one of the earliest domesticated species and one of our most commonly kept companion animals. For thousands of years, we have shared our environment, living spaces, diet and sometimes even our beds with them. Dogs have become an integral part of human society around the world. Some dogs exist in a feral, semi-feral or pariah state, their degree of integration with human community and culture varying depending on culture, religion and social status. These dogs survive with a level of dependence on humans for their nutrition, largely by scavenging human waste and left-overs. They demonstrate feeding strategies and preferences based on food availability.

Conversely, the domestic dog that lives as a companion, working colleague, assistance/therapy animal or in the myriad of other roles that dogs find themselves in, is typically entirely dependent upon their human caregiver(s) for their complete nutritional provision, care, management and wellbeing. These dogs are typically cared for in a way to support them 'thriving', not just 'surviving', and nutrition is a significant part of that. 'You are what you eat' is an oft-quoted adage, highlighting the importance of nutrition in overall health, and while it can sometimes over-simplify the relationship between food and the animal eating the food, there is little doubt that diet can play a significant role in supporting health, activity and promoting longevity.

OPPOSITE: Let's look forward into the world of canine nutrition and feeding.

Feeding Our Dogs

What and how we feed our dogs is easily one of the most debated and discussed subjects by canine enthusiasts around the world. As dogs have become increasingly recognised and described as family members, and the humanisation of dogs has become more common, dietary choices made by caregivers have become more diverse and increasingly humanised. Added to this is a multibillion-dollar international industry in the form of pet food production, distribution and marketing. Consequently, canine nutrition and feeding have significant human and commercial interest.

In animal nutrition, we refer to the animal feed industry, while the food industry is that which produces and supplies products for human consumption. The food and feed industries are linked. The feed industry benefits from by-products from the food industry, and supplies animal-derived products back into the food industry for human consumption. When it comes to our pets, however, we have humanised the terms we use, referring to 'pet food' and 'dog food'. To avoid confusion, in this book, the term 'food' will be used when talking about what we feed our dogs and what they choose to eat, while acknowledging that the pet food industry is a significant (and growing) part of the global animal feed industry. The term 'diet' will also be used for the food we feed to our dogs, not necessarily indicating any restriction of food for weight control – the more typical 'human' use of the term.

Why This Book?

The concept for this book first took root when I was lecturing degree-level, animal science students. We were exploring nutrition fundamentals and examining the nutritional requirements and feeding standards for the domestic dog. In that discussion, 'the human factor' was mentioned and we considered the impact that we have on dietary choices for dogs in our care.

In a class of undergraduate students, well versed in critical analysis and assessing scientific evidence, it was clear that the biases, beliefs, traditions, the approaches taken to feeding their own dogs and how they would advise others, varied significantly. Some felt that domestic dogs should be fed like wolves. Others felt that sustainability and ethical considerations meant that companion dogs should be fed vegetarian or vegan diets. The diversity of views in that class was a microcosm of the wider, global dog-caregiver community.

I realised a slightly different approach was needed to how I both taught and advised canine nutrition. Yes, science and an evidence base were essential to ensure that what was being fed would supply the nutrients needed in a suitable amount and form. However, there was a significant variable that had both dramatic and subtle impacts – the human(s). Luckily, I also have more than a passing interest in anthrozoology – the science that explores the interactions between humans and non-human animals. Combining nutritional science with the science of human – animal interactions has underpinned much of my nutrition work since.

By examining how we view our dogs and our relationships with them, and exploring the diversity of those relationships, we can start to understand the choices and decisions made by individuals for their dogs. Combined with knowledge and understanding of the dogs' nutritional needs, we can start to make logical, rational and appropriate dietary choices – ones that are mutually acceptable and beneficial. It can also help us have confidence in our own decisions and support others who might seek advice with compassion and respect.

But, in exploring canine nutrition and feeding, identifying fact from fiction can be difficult and, for some, a source of much stress. Who to trust? What is safe? What does my dog really need? What is the best diet for my dog? These are all valid and frequent questions when it comes to feeding our dogs.

Feeding Our Dogs with Science, Sense and Sensibility

A golden rule in animal nutrition is to always 'feed the animal in front of you'. I now add to that, 'and ensure that whatever you feed that animal, also meets with the human needs'. This does not mean sacrificing an evidence-based and well-formulated diet for an animal to suit the whims and desires of their human caregiver. It is about balancing the needs of both parties and finding the 'best fit' – like so many other things in life, nutrition is a compromise, but it can be a good compromise!

This book aims to explore how to meet this nutritional 'best fit' for dog and human. If you are interested in how to navigate the world of canine nutrition, and how to make effective, evidence-based choices that support your dog's health, wellbeing, longevity and activity level, then this book is for you.

We will explore the essentials of canine nutrition through the biology of the dog, their nutritional requirements and how these differ in different circumstances and situations. We will examine some of the hot topics in the dog world and consider how what we feed our dogs can impact on the environmental challenges the world faces, all with an evidence base. In order to enhance accessibility and readability, references have not been referred to explicitly within the text. However, where information has come from a key scientific resource, the full reference information is available at the end of the book, should you wish to access the original, primary material to learn even more.

This book is not intended to tell you there is one single way to feed your dog(s), nor will it vilify different options, ingredients, diet types or pit commercially produced dog food against 'natural' or home-prepared diets. Instead, we will examine current evidence and apply that to how we might best feed our dogs for our individual circumstances and situations. The majority of dogs eat a mixed diet through their lifetime. Situations change, economics alter, ingredient availability changes and a host of other variables affect the food and feed industries. Being able to be responsive, dynamic and informed about how to make decisions can then become a useful skill.

This book will help you do exactly that, no matter what your budget or situation is.

I am hugely privileged to share my life with my own dogs and want to make the world a better place for dogs and their people. Thanks for joining me on this part of my mission and I hope that this book will help shape your knowledge, understanding and application of nutritional science to the benefit of you and your dog(s). Whether you live with one dog or many, occasionally care for others' dogs or are just interested in learning more, let's go for a walk into the world of feeding the domestic dog.

PART ONE

Navigating Nutrition: The Essentials of Canine Nutrition

CHAPTER 1 The Dog

Introduction to Canine Nutrition and Feeding

Deciding what, when and how to feed your dog can be difficult. Canine nutrition is easily one of the most debated subjects in the dog world and a topic that can easily become polarised. Everyone who has ever cared for a dog will have experienced the variety of food options available, as well as the varied consequences and the results of using them. Some people swear by particular food types, forms, ingredients and even manufacturers. Others will have had to vary approaches and explore alternatives because of convenience, veterinary and health concerns, performance, availability, individual preference and a range of other factors that affect our dietary decision-making for our dogs.

In this chapter, we are going to explore the evolutionary history of our domestic dogs and what that means for their nutritional ecology – essentially, where our dogs have come from and how that affects what and how we feed

Even dogs of the same breed have individual nutritional requirements.

them. We will consider the digestive anatomy, physiology and feeding behaviour of dogs and examine what a dog needs, and even wants, from their food. The role of you, your dog's caregiver/owner/partner/handler is also important, because you make the decision as to what to buy and feed your dog(s). This will help us to understand the fundamentals of canine nutrition and to identify key factors to consider when we make nutritional choices for our dogs.

An Individual Approach to Feeding

The reality is that in nutrition a 'one size fits all' approach rarely works – an individual approach needs to be taken. Nutritional guidelines are available and are wonderful, evidence-based starting points in formulating diets, but every individual animal is unique and nutritional individuality is important. When feeding dogs, an individual approach is as much about the person(s) caring for the dog, as it is about the dog itself. We must feed the animal in front of us and fully acknowledge that nutritional individuality. This is why nutrition can be sometimes a tricky subject – what works fantastically for one dog (and their person), may not work for another.

Our dogs should affect the choices we make – breed/type, size, activity level, health status and even their own taste preferences, will all impact on the dietary choices made. For example, my own dogs are all the same breed, and several are closely related, but my little 'family group' (I avoid the term pack as they do not function as a pack in the biological sense of the word) range in age, bodyweight and activity level. Consequently, while to the untrained eye they will all look very similar and there might be an assumption that they are all fed the same, there are subtle amends made for each, based on their individual needs. Nutritional individuality is an important concept for supporting a long, healthy life for our dogs.

Food Choices for Our Dogs

Wander down the aisle of any pet shop, pet section in your supermarket or even search your favourite online retailer for 'dog food' and you could well be overwhelmed by the variety of options on offer. On one hand, this variety means that selecting an option to suit your

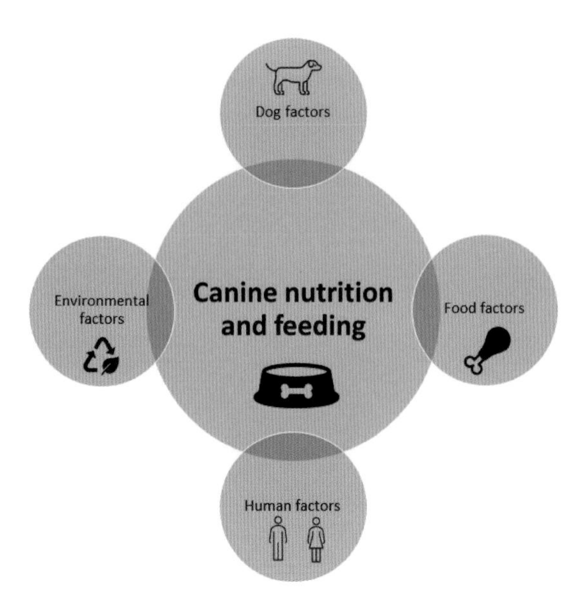

A number of overlapping factors affect the diet choices we make for our dogs.

individual dog and living situation should be easy. However, a significant problem comes when there is too much choice. Choice is not even just in the form and flavour of food that is available to feed our dogs. It comes from manufacturer, marketing claims and even nutritional support and guidance. Ingredients and different formulations increase choice further. Terms such as 'natural' and 'superfood' are common parlance in pet foods now, despite having little defined clarity of meaning.

When looking at dietary choices for our dogs, it is useful to consider distinct groups of influencing factors:

- Animal (dog) factors
- Food factors
- Human factors
- Environmental factors

While these factors can be viewed as distinct from each other, they overlap and all impact on the choices we make in feeding our dogs.

Animal factors relate to how an animal digests its food and what it eats. Food factors include nutrients and their bioavailability. Human factors are the choices we make and lifestyles we lead that impact on our dogs' diets. Environmental factors include aspects of sustainability, as well as the ability to source chosen foodstuff.

The Nutritional Ecology of the Domestic Dog

The domestic dog (*Canis lupus familiaris*) was one of the first species that humans domesticated and is one of the most commonly kept domestic species globally. Dogs are our companions, work colleagues, family members, therapists and exercise partners, and fulfil a whole host of other roles, both for and with us. Exploring our dogs' ancestry, their relationship with related species and what they have evolved to eat helps us understand what they prefer to eat, what they need to eat and what we choose to feed them. Let's explore the biology of our dogs that is relevant to their nutrition and feeding.

Nutritional ecology is the scientific understanding of how an animal relates to its environment through food and nutrition provided by that food. For our dogs, this means understanding their evolution, their nutritional requirements and the links between nutrition and health, wellbeing, reproduction and performance. These are essential points when thinking about making the best choices for what we choose to feed our own dogs.

The Ancestral Dog and a Common 'Wolf-Like' Ancestor

The domestic dog evolved from a common wolf-like ancestor – a now extinct population of wolves and ancestors to the modern grey wolf (*Canis lupus*). The early 'proto-dogs' were domesticated by living beside, and with, human populations, benefitting from human waste and left-overs, including excess food that we couldn't effectively use because of our own digestive and metabolic limitations. Archaeological evidence also indicates that early dogs were fed prepared diets, reflecting distinct roles in society. The preparation of specific dog food is thus not just a modern concept.

The Origin of the Domestic Dog

Over thousands of years (estimates range from 200,000 to 15,000 years), dogs have shared our environment, our living spaces and our diet. This means that while the modern dog and the grey wolf are closely related at the genetic level, there are subtle genetic differences meaning that dogs are not wolves – direct comparisons are scientifically inaccurate. These genetic changes have affected the physical appearance, metabolism, behaviour and nutritional requirements of our dogs. The exact origins of dogs are still under intense debate, but evidence

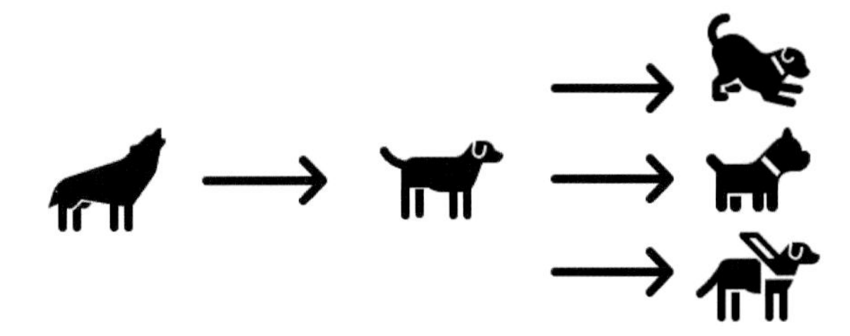

Our dogs evolved from a common wolf-like ancestor to produce the diversity in dogs we see today.

shows that intensive selection has occurred over the years of domestication. This selection has been both natural and artificial – natural selection occurring where individual animals had some advantage that supported survival and reproduction. This means that their genetics were more likely to be passed to future generations. Artificial selection is where humans deliberately selected individual animals from which to breed. These individuals had characteristics, such as appearance, size, behaviour, docility or trainability, considered useful, so there was a desire to keep those traits in subsequent offspring.

Dogs and humans have a deep evolutionary past. Dogs and humans show convergent evolution – two species evolving together over time and developing shared traits and abilities that are mutually beneficial. This has had some interesting consequences for the domestic dog, including their ability to recognise and respond to our facial expressions and pointing gestures. Dogs have developed anatomical changes, including alterations to their eye muscles, not seen in wolves, meaning that they are more able to adopt 'puppy dog eyes' in their interactions with us – a significant benefit to the human–dog relationship, especially when it comes to feeding them. But what does this mean about the diet of our dogs? What does the evolutionary history of dogs mean for how we feed them?

The Dog – a Carnivore?

Dogs are described as carnivores, referring to diet and their zoological classification. However, defining dogs as carnivores from a dietary perspective is an over-simplification. In a zoological sense, dogs are quite correctly called carnivores or, more specifically, carnivorans – they are members of the order Carnivora.

The order Carnivora is a large group of animals, including almost 300 distinct species that have biological characteristics that support the consumption of animal

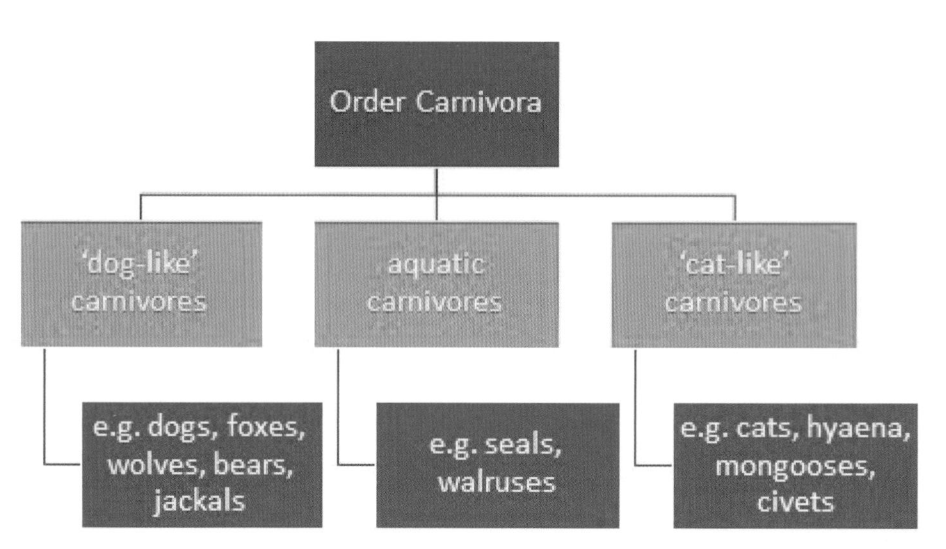

A simple representation of the order Carnivora, to which dogs belong.

tissues – carnivore translates as 'flesh-eating'. Members of the Carnivora include the 'dog-like' carnivorans, such as bears, dogs and weasels; the 'cat-like' carnivorans, such as felids, hyaena and mongooses; and the aquatic carnivorans, such as seals and walruses. These animals show a wide geographical distribution and diverse dietary intake.

Characteristics of the Carnivorans

The carnivorans all have a defining physical characteristic called the carnassial apparatus, irrespective of whether their diet is carnivorous, omnivorous (mixed plant and animal material) or mostly herbivorous. The carnassial apparatus is a modified fourth premolar tooth in the upper jaw and the first molar in the lower jaw. These teeth overlap and function like a pair of scissors to shear through flesh.

The carnivoran jaws are limited in their ability for lateral or side-to-side movement, meaning that the carnassial apparatus has enhanced strength and functionality in its vertical shearing motion. This also means that our dogs are not able to chew food in the same way as animals such as horses or sheep. This limits the amount of mechanical processing of food in the mouth and explains why dogs will often gulp or gorge their food.

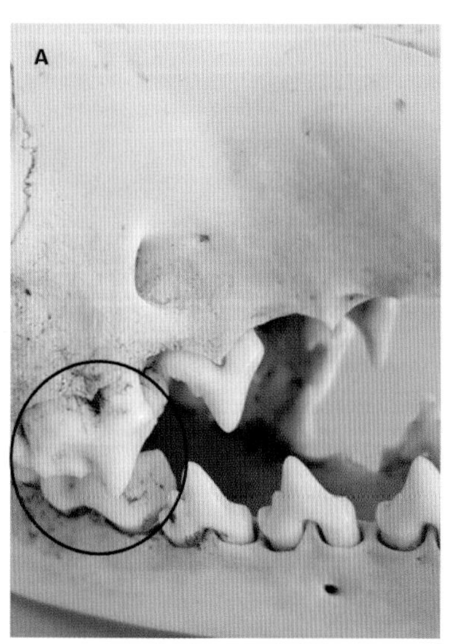

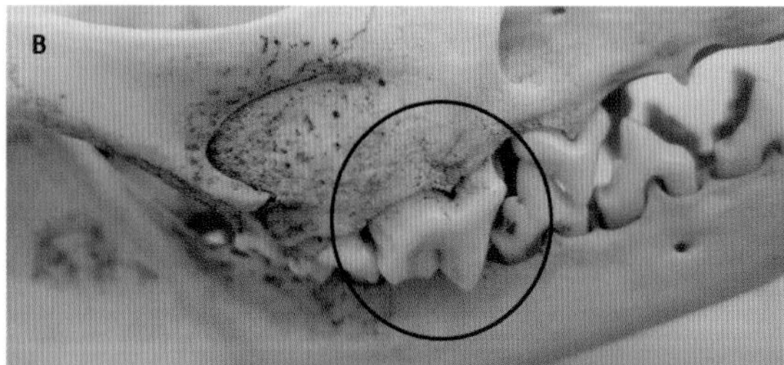

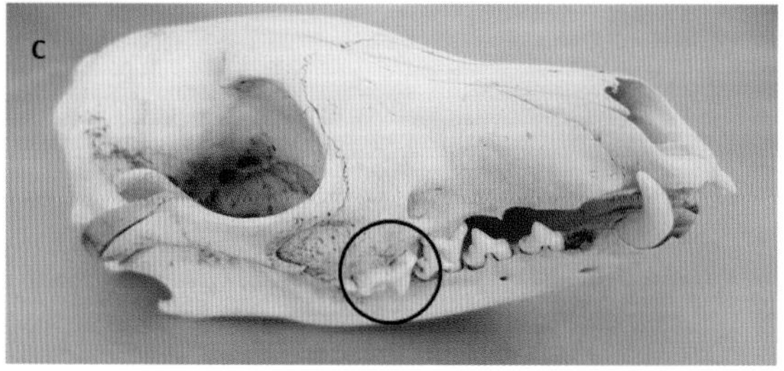

The carnassial apparatus in a canid skull. Note that the dentition is not complete, but the location of the carnassial apparatus is circled in each image. A, Jaws opened to show the upper premolar overlapping the lower molar. B, Jaws closed to show how the teeth are positioned in a closed mouth. C, Location of the carnassial apparatus in relation to the skull and other dentition.

There are strong attachments of jaw muscles to the skull in carnivore species. This is useful for catching and dispatching prey animals, as well as the processing of material for eating. While this is not as essential in our dogs as in ancestral or other related species, dogs do have significant jaw strength, although this is affected by differences in skull and jaw shape and size.

A general trend is that the carnivorans that consume a diet rich in animal-derived tissues, such as the true or obligate carnivores (e.g. cats), have fewer teeth in total than those with a more mixed dietary intake, such as the dog. Bears and dogs appear to have modifications to their premolars and molars that support an increased amount of grinding and processing of plant material, while those species that have an insect- or fish-based diet have distinct dental adaptations.

Our dogs retain many of the characteristics of carnivorans and it is correct to call them carnivores based on zoology and anatomy. However, the diet of dogs does mean that calling them carnivores from a nutrition perspective is less clearcut.

The Diet of Carnivorans

Many carnivorans are dependent on the consumption of animal tissues to supply essential nutrients that cannot be obtained from plant or other sources. The domestic cat (*Felis catus*) is a true or obligate carnivore, for example. In contrast to dogs, cats require animal tissues in their diet to supply pre-formed vitamin A, arachidonic acid and the amino acid taurine, in addition to other key nutrients. A dietary deficiency in any of these nutrients can be catastrophic for obligate carnivores.

Conversely, dogs can synthesise vitamin A and arachidonic acid from plant precursor compounds, and their need for a dietary supply of taurine appears to be less than cats. Indeed, dogs are capable of synthesising taurine if enough precursor substances are provided in the diet, although lately, taurine in dog diets has attracted attention. Consequently, dogs are commonly described as omnivorous or opportunistic/facultative carnivores.

Carnivorans have also adapted to alternative dietary ingredients. Predatory carnivorans are known to consume the partially digested gut contents of herbivore prey, while others scavenge and occasionally actively seek out plant and fungal matter to eat. Carnivorans demonstrate a dietary spectrum that ranges from ‘true’ carnivory through to a plant-based diet. The giant panda has a highly specialised diet of bamboo and has evolved certain dental and digestive adaptions to deal with this

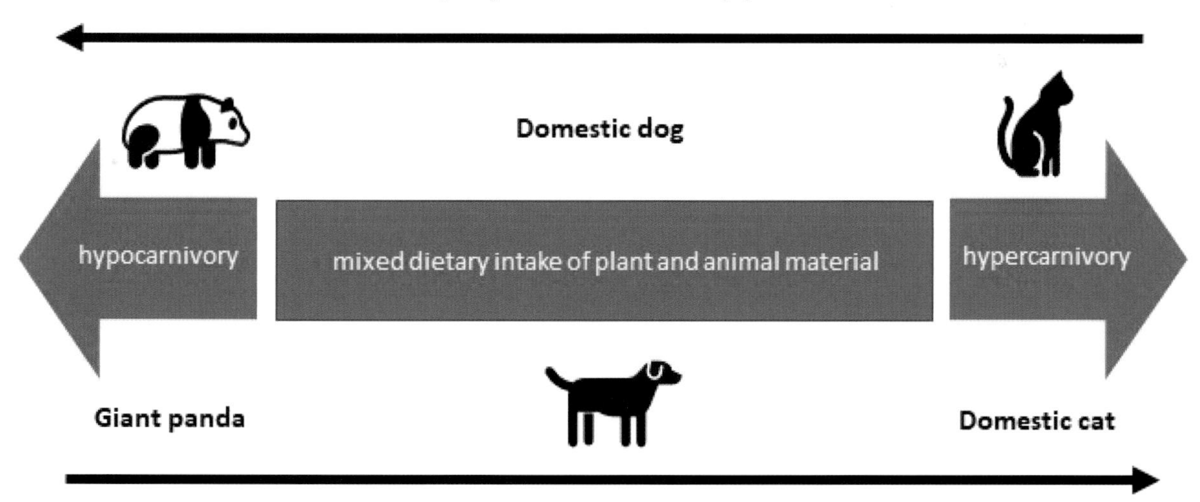

The spectrum of carnivory, from the hypercarnivorous, true/obligate carnivores to species that have a plant-based diet. The domestic dog has evolved to survive on a diet consisting of mixed plant and animal-derived material and is often described as an opportunistic/facultative carnivore or as an omnivore.

foodstuff. Seals and other aquatic species have teeth that are adapted for a diet mostly consisting of fish. Dogs have also developed genetic changes that support a dietary intake of mixed animal and plant material. A notable adaptation is the ability to digest starch carbohydrate, thanks to the presence of amylase enzymes that aid the breakdown of starch in the digestive tract. This means that dogs, unlike wolves, are able to thrive on a starch-rich diet, providing the starch is appropriately cooked.

In fact, genes that encode proteins involved in digestion and metabolism appear to have rapidly evolved as dogs developed, strongly supporting a role of diet in domestication. Research suggests that different dog breeds have different capabilities to digest starch. These findings further add to our understanding of the importance of nutritional individuality when feeding our dogs.

The Dog – a Canid

So, while the dog is classified as a carnivore, in common with other members of the order Carnivora, dogs have additional physical and other biological characteristics indicating a mixed diet is consumed. The 'dog-like' carnivorans include a number of families of related species. Dogs belong to the family Canidae, which includes three subfamilies, two of which are now extinct – the Hesperocyoninae and the Borophaginae. The third is the Caninae subfamily, members of which are referred to as canines and include wolves, jackals, foxes, the domestic dog and other 'dog-like' species. Caninae members have a diverse range of diets – some are hypercarnivorous and animal-derived material is the majority of their dietary intake. Others are hypocarnivorous and specialise in other dietary ingredients, such as plants and insects.

Broadly, canids range from opportunistic scavengers, to omnivores, to general carnivores, with many showing substantial dietary flexibility. Some species will scavenge or hunt individually, while others show group hunting or scavenging behaviours. Feral dogs have been recorded as group-hunting medium-sized prey. In some rare but slightly disturbing cases, humans have been hunted by dogs. Because of their wide dietary adaptations, dogs and their canid relatives are naturally found on every continent, with the exception of Antarctica. Indeed, domestic dogs are banned from Antarctica for fears that they could introduce and transmit diseases to other resident species.

Smaller canids tend to be hypocarnivorous or even omnivorous, with their diets often consisting of up to 70 per cent animal-sourced material and the remainder consisting of seeds, fruit, plants and sometimes insects. Being able to be flexible in the food consumed is a distinct survival advantage for any species, especially where there may be significant seasonal or other environmental changes. This could well in part account for the success of the dog. The extinction of many large hypercarnivorous species, such as the dire wolf (*Canis dirus*), is considered linked to their dependence on prey species. When the abundance of prey species fell, the ability of species dependent on them for food to survive also fell.

The Diet of Dogs

Dogs are a highly successful species, thanks to the development of skills, characteristics and behaviours that we

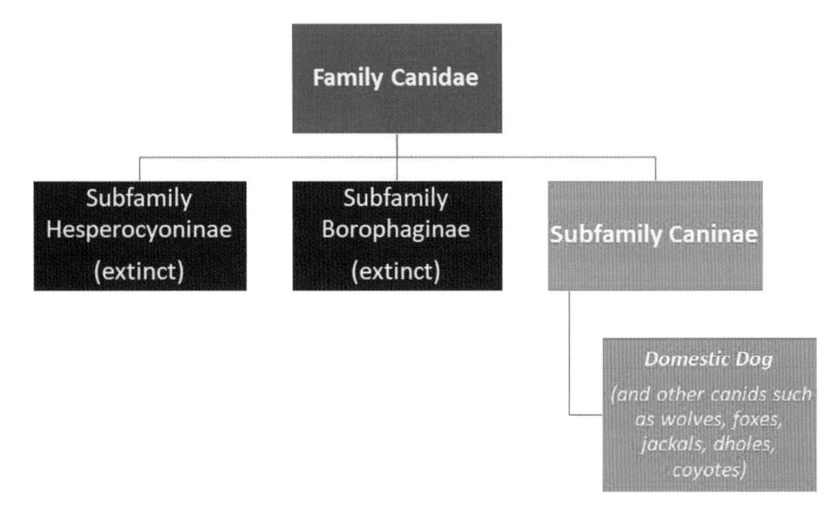

A simplified representation of the subfamily members of the family Canidae, the dog-like carnivorans. Two subfamilies are now extinct and exist only in the fossil record. Dogs belong to the subfamily Caninae.

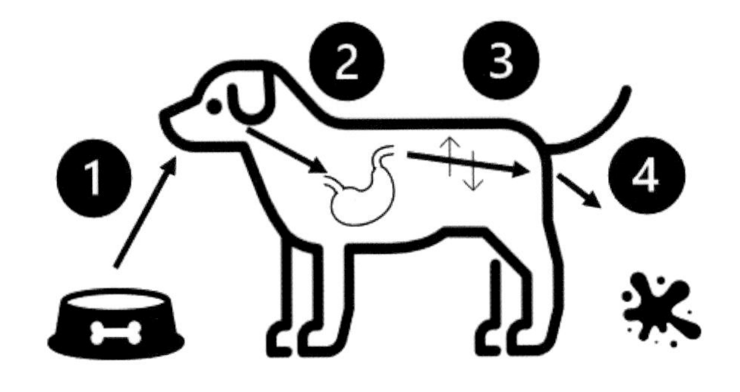

The digestive process in the dog. 1, Ingestion of food via the mouth. 2, Digestion of food begins in the stomach and continues in the small intestine. 3, Absorption of the nutrients liberated by digestion in the small intestine. 4, Elimination of indigestible material and waste as faeces.

like and find useful, as well as their dietary flexibility. The domestic dog that we know and love, has evolved as an opportunistic scavenger, with a taste preference for animal-derived material. This preference for animal-tissue will come as no surprise to anyone who uses food rewards in training. However, our dogs also retain many scavenger-like characteristics and can be opportunists in how they acquire food, as well as the material they choose to consume – some of which is less than appealing to human sensitivities.

How our dogs eat, what they eat, the structure of their digestive system and how it functions, all descend from their evolutionary ancestry. It is useful to think about this when considering the nutrition of our own, modern dogs. We also have to remember that domestication and selective breeding has meant there are some significant changes in the domestic dog that are also relevant when considering their nutrition and how we can best provide it.

Digestive Anatomy and Physiology of the Dog

Digestive anatomy refers to the organs and structures that comprise the digestive system. Physiology is how the system works. In biology, structure and function are closely linked, so examining structure (anatomy) and physiology (function) means we can consider the digestive system of the dog from start to finish and how it works to support the digestion of food.

The Digestive Process

Digestion has four stages, all supported by the anatomy and physiology of the digestive system. The first stage is *ingestion* where food is consumed and, initially, mechanically processed in the mouth with the aid of the dog's teeth. The next stage is *digestion*, where the food ingested is broken down and processed to liberate nutrients and make them available to the body. Digestion is achieved by mechanical and chemical processes. Once digestion has begun, the process of *absorption* occurs, where the products of digestion are absorbed from the digestive system and transported around the body. The final stage is *elimination*, where any material that has not been digested or absorbed, plus waste and indigestible matter, is excreted as faeces.

Mechanical and Chemical Digestive Processes

Mechanical digestion begins in the mouth when the teeth alter the shape and size of ingested food particles by shearing, crushing and grinding. This reduces the size of food for ease of swallowing and increases the surface area of ingested material for later digestive processes. However, dogs have limited ability to chew, and mechanical processing is restricted to some shearing and tearing of material, rather than prolonged grinding and chewing, as seen in other species. This also means that the time spent eating by the average dog is short and characterised by rapid ingestion of food. Mechanical digestion is aided by muscular contractions (peristalsis) of the digestive system that moves food along the digestive tract, mixing it with various secretions during its digestive journey.

Unfortunately, some dogs are prone to consuming, intentionally or accidentally, indigestible foreign bodies that are not altered in shape or size by mechanical processing. Examples include stones, large pieces of bone, toys, clothing or household items. These are described as 'dietary indiscretions' and occasionally require surgical intervention to remove the offending item and to prevent severe damage to the dog's digestive system.

Chemical digestion is where secretions from tissues and organs along the digestive tract break down nutrients. This process is termed hydrolysis and is helped by specialised substances called enzymes. Enzymes are biological catalysts that work to speed up reactions and are critical for normal metabolic and digestive functioning. There are a number of different enzymes involved

Examples of enzymes involved in the dog's digestive system, the nutrients they digest and end products produced

Enzyme	Nutrient targeted	End product of enzymatic digestion
Amylase	Carbohydrate – starch amylose	Glucose
Sucrase	Carbohydrate – sucrose	Fructose and glucose
Maltase	Carbohydrate – maltose	Glucose
Lactase	Carbohydrate – lactose	Glucose and galactose
Lipase	Lipid/fat	Glycerol, free fatty acids, monoglycerides, diglycerides
Trypsin	Protein	Polypeptides, individual amino acids
Pepsin	Protein	Polypeptides, individual amino acids
Peptidases	Protein – peptides	Dipeptides, individual amino acids
Chymotrypsin	Protein	Polypeptides, individual amino acids

in digestion, each specifically breaking down an individual nutrient into smaller end products, suitable for absorption. These enzymes are released from digestive organs and tissues at various points along the length of the digestive system.

The Digestive System

Digestion starts in the mouth and ends with the elimination of faeces. The transit time for material from being eaten to elimination is rapid, typically taking between six and twelve hours. The digestive system (sometimes called the alimentary canal or gastrointestinal tract) is a short, simple tube that runs from mouth to anus and involves a number of different structures, tissues and organs. It has intimate links to other body systems. An important recognition is that the health of the digestive system and the population of microorganisms that live within it, the microbiome, can all have significant effects on the rest of the body, from the immune system to the nervous system. While most research currently focuses on the human microbiome and how it differs between individuals and its impact, we are learning about the role of the canine microbiome in our dogs' health and wellbeing.

The Mouth

Digestion starts in the mouth. Food is acquired, partially mechanically processed by the teeth and mixed with saliva. When a dog sees and smells food, saliva is secreted. Indeed, the work of Pavlov has made this fact standard in our understanding of classical conditioning. Anyone caring for dogs will be familiar with the 'drool' reflex when treats, food or even the dinner bowls appear – even the anticipation of food can cause salivation.

Saliva

The dog has several salivary glands that secrete saliva in response to stimuli. Major salivary glands are found around the jaw and base of the ears. Minor glands are found in the mouth and around the tongue. Saliva production varies based on diet and other factors, but a medium-sized dog (approx. 20kg) may produce up to a litre of saliva per day. Saliva is key in the early stages of digestion. It acts as a lubricant, by aiding chewing and swallowing. It also contains substances that have antibacterial effects, potentially limiting the risk of consuming pathogenic bacteria. However, canine saliva also contains allergens that humans may react to and can contain bacteria potentially dangerous to humans, making dog bites a significant infection risk.

Unlike many other species, dogs have negligible digestive enzymes in their saliva. These enzymes start the digestion of some substances, particularly carbohydrates, almost immediately after eating in humans, for example. However, this is limited in dogs and while some evidence suggests there might be some alpha-amylase in dog saliva, its importance for digestion is likely to be limited.

Saliva enhances taste by solubilising water-soluble components of food that are detected by the olfactory system and taste buds. Dogs can detect compounds commonly found in animal-derived tissues (typically nucleotides, amino acids and some organic acids), meaning there is a dietary choice preference for foods rich in these substances, aided by smell and taste.

Taste Buds

Dogs have a limited number of taste buds on their tongue and in their mouth. The number of taste buds is often quoted as around 1,700. This is fewer than seen in grazing animals, such as cattle, where an enhanced ability to detect different tastes is important in the selection of safe material to eat. Dogs do not show an increased preference for saltiness like many grazing species. But dogs can detect specific flavours, including sweetness, and appear to prefer sweet to bitter tastes. This could be why dogs sometimes select sweet plant material to eat and their occasional (as well as potentially dangerous) ingestion of sweet human foods, such as chocolate. Interestingly, cats appear unable to detect sweet flavours, further supporting their dietary classification as obligate carnivores, in contrast to the more omnivorous dog.

Dogs have taste receptors that detect sweetness which might account for their interest in potentially dangerous human foods such as chocolate. Note – no dog was allowed to consume chocolate for this image!

Dentition

Dogs have enlarged canines, a carnassial apparatus and more teeth than many obligate carnivores. For example, the domestic cat has thirty teeth, while the dog has forty-two. This increased number of teeth is associated with subtle changes suggesting a gradual move away from a hypercarnivorous diet and towards alternative dietary components. The significant alterations in skull shape and size in many dog breeds have altered the position of teeth and, in some cases, created dental overcrowding issues. This is nutritionally important as some dogs may be limited in their ability to ingest and process food. Brachycephalic dogs that have significantly shortened muzzles, such as bulldogs, may struggle to eat from narrow food bowls or to process food easily because of their tooth positioning. This is in distinct contrast to dogs with moderate-length muzzles (mesocephalic or mesaticephalic), such as the Labrador retriever, or dogs with elongated muzzles (dolichocephalic) like the borzoi. Bite force is also related to the size and shape of the skull, jaws and bodyweight. Consequently, what might be suitable for a golden retriever to eat, might be less than ideal for a pug.

The Oesophagus

Ingested material leaves the mouth and moves to the stomach via the oesophagus, which has a muscular structure that supports rapid swallowing – the movement from mouth to stomach takes seconds. Mucus helps to lubricate the oesophagus and aids swallowing. Food travels down the oesophagus and enters the stomach through the cardiac sphincter, a tight ring of muscle that controls entry to (and exit from) the stomach.

The Stomach

The dog's stomach is small and simple in relation to their body size but is capable of significant expansion and can function as a food store. This means that dogs can consume large quantities of food in short periods of time and supports opportunistic scavenging and

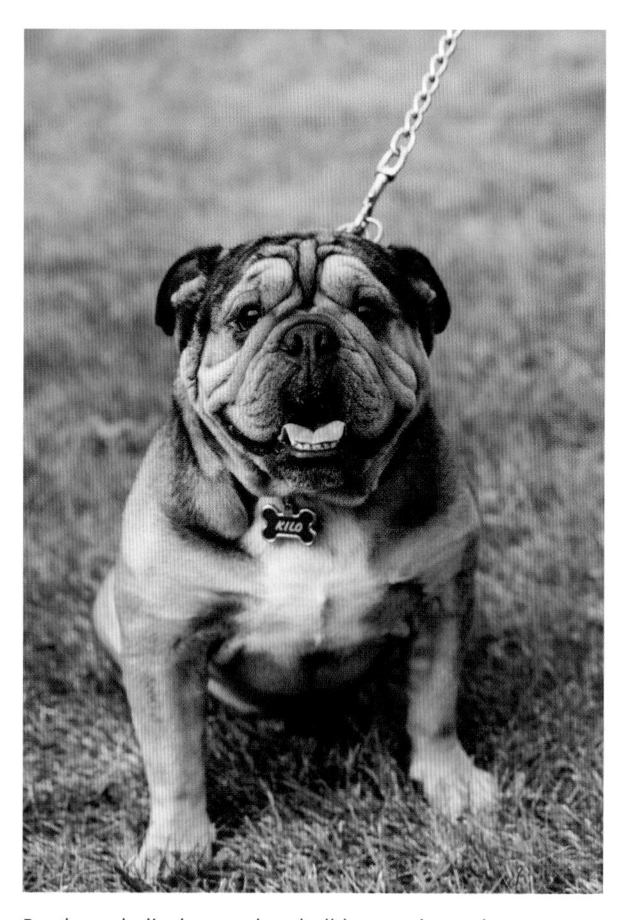

Brachycephalic dogs such as bulldogs and pugs have shortened muzzles.

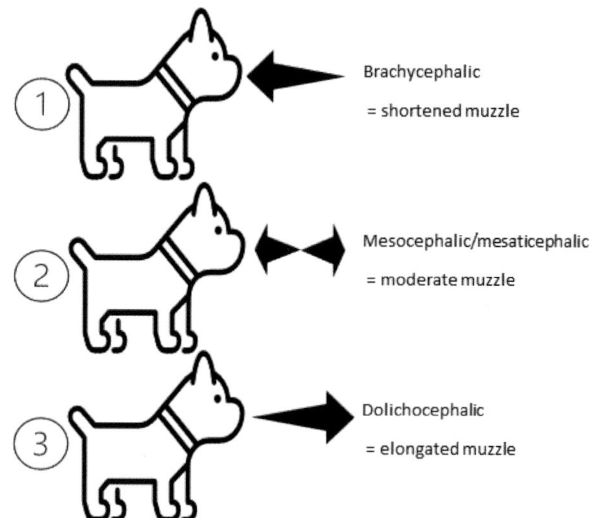

Skull shape and size will affect a dog's bite force and tooth positioning. 1, Brachycephalic dogs have shortened muzzles and often have altered tooth positions. 2, Mesocephalic (or mesaticephalic) dogs have moderate muzzle lengths and are more reminiscent of ancestral dog-types . 3, Dolichocephalic types have very elongated muzzles that may also affect tooth position.

gorge-feeding. Chemical digestive processes to break down dietary protein start in the stomach, although most digestion of fats/lipids, carbohydrates and proteins occurs in the small intestine.

In the stomach, food mixes with gastric secretions, including digestive enzymes and hydrochloric acid

Dolichocephalic dogs such as the borzoi have elongated muzzles.

(HCl). This means that the stomach contents are highly acidic, which promotes digestion and can help to protect dogs from potentially pathogenic microorganisms. It is often reported that the dog's stomach has a pH much lower than other species, although evidence does not always support this. The stomach regularly contracts, mixing its contents and preparing them for release into the small intestine via the muscular pyloric sphincter. This opens in short bursts to move stomach contents into the small intestine.

The activity of the stomach is controlled by hormones and the nervous system. A number of factors can affect its physiology. The presence of food activates neural signalling to promote the functioning of the stomach. Anxiety, fear, illness and stress can affect how the stomach and the rest of the digestive system work. This may have a negative effect on the overall digestion and digestive health of our dogs.

Food characteristics can affect how the stomach processes its contents and empties. Large meals are retained for longer than small meals and solid food is removed much more slowly than liquid. Diets high in fat leave the stomach slowly, as do diets with high levels of soluble dietary fibre, although insoluble and indigestible dietary fibre tend to increase stomach emptying.

The Small Intestine

The small intestine has three distinct regions – the duodenum is the first part, followed by the jejunum, which is the longest portion of the small intestine, and the ileum, which empties into the large intestine. The small intestine is where most carbohydrate and fat digestion occur. Some proteins will have been partially digested in the stomach, but protein digestion continues in the small intestine, where enzymes continue to break them down into polypeptides and individual amino acids. Peristalsis helps to move digesta along and continues the mechanical processing of it. Mucus is secreted into the small intestine and helps to lubricate and protect its lining, as well as aiding the passage of digesta through the small intestine to the large intestine.

A number of digestive secretions are released into the small intestine from the pancreas and other glands in the lining of the small intestine. These secretions are rich in enzymes to digest fats, proteins and carbohydrates. The pancreas also secretes bicarbonates salts into the small intestine – important for neutralising acidic digesta and ensuring that the pH allows digestive enzymes to function. The liver produces bile, which is stored in the gall bladder and released into the small intestine when needed. Bile works to emulsify dietary fat, in order to make it available to lipase enzymes for digestion and absorption.

Nutrient Absorption in the Small Intestine

Digestion is completed in the small intestine. Once nutrients are broken down into their constituent parts, they are absorbed through the cells that line the small intestine. The small intestine has a large surface area available for the absorption of substances thanks to modifications on the surface of cells lining its digestive surface. These modifications are called villi and are 'finger-like' projections from the cell surface. The villi have further microscopic projections called microvilli, further increasing the available surface area for absorption.

Vitamins and minerals are also absorbed in the small intestine. The small intestine is the major site for the absorption of nutrients following digestion. Once the products of digestion are absorbed, they are transported to the liver and other tissues via the blood and lymphatic systems. Once at the liver, nutrients are processed further, metabolised or transported to other body locations.

Absorption of nutrients occurs via different processes. Some are simple and work passively via concentration gradients, with substances moving from an area of high concentration to an area with a lower concentration. Other products of digestion are actively transported and require specific carrier substances. Vitamin B12 requires a substance called intrinsic factor for absorption. If a diet has adequate vitamin B12 but there is an issue with intrinsic factor, deficiency can still occur. Equally, if the small intestine is damaged, irritated or inflamed, normal digestion and absorption of nutrients can be affected.

There is also a significant microbial population resident in the small intestine. This population, combined with that found in the large intestine, constitute the dog's intestinal microbiome. In the small intestine, this microbial population works to competitively exclude potentially disease-causing organisms from colonising the area and produces various substances that are beneficial for the overall health of the dog and the microbiome, notably short-chain fatty acids (SCFAs).

Microbiome health can be supported by including ingredients in the dog's diet, such as prebiotic fibres like MOS (mannanoligosaccharides) and FOS (fructooligosaccharides). The intestinal microbiome is also responsible for the synthesis of vitamin K and many B vitamins. These can then be directly absorbed from the intestine.

As digesta move through the small intestine, anything that can be broken down and digested is, and the resulting nutrients are absorbed. If there are still indigestible materials, these continue passing through the small intestine, eventually reaching the large intestine.

The Caecum

The small intestine joins the large intestine at the ileocecal valve, through which any material that has not been digested or absorbed passes into the colon. Where the large and small intestine join, there is a blind pouch called the caecum. The caecum is where there is substantial microbial digestion (fermentation) of material in some species. Horses and rabbits have significantly enlarged caeca and are dependent on microbial fermentation to digest their plant-rich diets, dogs much less so.

In carnivores and omnivores, the caecum is much smaller than in hind-gut fermenters, and there is less reliance upon microbial fermentation of dietary fibre. However, the dog has a caecum that is larger (relative to body size) than the cat and some fibre digestion does occur. The microbial population within the caecum also contributes to the microbiome of the large intestine and is linked to both intestinal and whole animal health. There is also some microbial digestion of fibre in the rest of the large intestine. The by-products of microbial digestion include compounds that give faecal matter its colour and smell, and impact on the form, consistency and output of faeces. If material passes into the large intestine that has not already been fully digested, it can be fermented and various gases produced, some of which are unpleasant when released as flatulence. Sudden dietary changes or dietary ingredients (poor-quality sources of protein, indigestible fibre and some other carbohydrates) can cause excess microbial gas production and offensive flatulence and faecal smells. Indeed, any disturbance to the microbiome population can result in digestive changes. This is why any dietary changes should ideally occur slowly, to minimise the impact on the microbiome population.

The Large Intestine (Colon)

The caecum is continuous with the large intestine, also known as the colon, which leads to the rectum and then the anus. The dog's colon is short compared to herbivorous species, but it has a key role in resorbing water and electrolytes (sodium especially) from digested material. Unlike the small intestine, the colon has no villi or microvilli to increase surface area, and absorption is passive rather than active. If there is inflammation or irritation of the colon (colitis) then the resorption of water and electrolytes is affected. This results in loose stools, or diarrhoea in extreme cases. In these situations, it is critical to ensure adequate hydration for dogs, and sometimes provide electrolytes also, especially if the diarrhoea is prolonged.

Faecal Output from the Digestive System

Material that reaches the rectum is eliminated as faeces. The amount, consistency, colour, texture and smell of faeces are all affected by the diet and health of the dog. Frequency of defecation is affected by diet quantity and quality, as well as the proportions of individual ingredients. Diets high in indigestible fibre (plant or animal-derived) will result in larger faeces than more digestible diets, which will produce smaller, less frequent faeces. Faecal monitoring is a simple daily health check for any caregiver to undertake and is also important if dietary amends have been implemented. Faecal scoring charts are a useful way of recording the quality of faeces and usually work on a numerical scale. If there are significant and persistent changes in a dog's faecal output, further investigation is important to ensure any digestive or other health issues are identified promptly and can be managed.

Healthy 'Poop'

Normal, 'healthy' dog faeces are often described as formed, 'sausage-like' with surface cracks, but are easily collected and leave little residue where excreted. Faecal output that is very small and hard can indicate constipation. A liquid consistency also indicates digestive disturbance and possible infection. Time of defecation can impact on faecal consistency, with afternoon faeces often having higher water content than those passed in the morning. The colour and consistency of faecal output can be a sign of dietary ingredients. Historically, dogs often produced faeces that were white, crumbly and chalky. This was indicative of high levels

White, chalky, crumbly dog 'poop' is a sign of lots of bone or other minerals in the diet.

of bone or bonemeal in dogfood and is still occasionally seen after dogs have been fed large quantities of bone or a diet that is high in minerals that are not bioavailable and are excreted. Diets rich in poultry tend to produce lighter, yellow-coloured faeces than diets rich in beef or lamb. Occasionally, faeces will be very dark in colour and sometimes with a tar-like consistency. This can be a sign of intestinal bleeding from illness or injury and should be investigated by a veterinary surgeon. This occasionally also occurs in highly active dogs and is reminiscent of gastrointestinal bleeding that can occur in human and equine athletes.

What a Dog Needs and What a Dog Wants from their Food

Our dogs need food to survive and to thrive, but for our companion, sporting and working dogs, food is more than just survival. Nutrition is without doubt one aspect of our dogs' lives on which we can have a significant impact, and so nutrition is described as a controllable variable. Good nutrition means different things to different people, in different situations, but a nutritionally balanced and appropriate diet goes a long way in supporting the health, wellbeing and lifespan of our dogs.

When we think about what any food that we feed to our dogs needs to do, we must consider our dogs, what they need and want from their food. We must acknowledge the ancestry of the dog and their fundamental biology, including digestive anatomy and physiology. We must consider what they prefer to eat, as well as what we know they will benefit from eating. We must review whether our dogs' diets supply the nutrients needed to support their overall biology, as well as their activity level and lifestyle, and whether those nutrients are in the forms and amounts needed.

Nutrient Supply

Food needs, first, to supply energy to our dogs. Energy is effectively the fuel that food provides to support everything that the body does, from day-to-day maintenance and repair, through to high levels of activity. Food supplies the macronutrients, protein, carbohydrate and fat, which provide that energy. Food also supplies nutrients that support the body and its functioning in other ways. Food also supplies micronutrients in the form of vitamins and minerals, and although they are needed in much smaller quantities than the macronutrients, micronutrients are essential for normal bodily function. When nutritionists talk about complete and balanced diets, they are referring to the need for a diet to supply all nutrients in the correct amount and form for our dogs, avoiding potential risks of nutritional inadequacy through excess or deficiency.

Food as Enrichment and Reward

Beyond basic nutrition, food is important in other ways. Food can be environmentally enriching, and we can strategically use food to support training and behaviour management as rewards. Food can support positive behavioural activity via food-activity toys or devices that can encourage movement and problem-solving. These items can provide stimulation or distract dogs who might otherwise be tempted to show less than desirable behaviours, and to promote preferable ones.

Food Safety

Our dogs also need food to be safe. Any food fed should not cause injurious harm or illness. This means that food should not be contaminated by bacteria or other potentially pathogenic organisms, toxic substances or problematic items. Ironically, the scavenging behaviour of dogs does mean that dietary indiscretions, or the consumption of food and other material that could be harmful, is remarkably common.

Food can be enriching for our dogs. Cow hooves stuffed with mashed potato and vegetables make for a tasty treat.

Food Acceptability and Palatability

Food must also be acceptable and palatable – our dogs need to want to eat it. The best formulated or prepared diet in the world is of absolutely no value if a dog will not eat it. Sometimes dogs can be food neophobic – they may dislike novelty or new foods/ingredients based on palatability or prior experience. Sometimes our dogs are exceptional in their ability to train us, and food refusal or reticence is less about palatability and more about knowing that their behaviour around food may well influence our behaviour around their food and its provision – basically we end up giving them what they want!

Summary

- The domestic dog has evolved as an opportunistic scavenger with diverse dietary habits.
- Dogs have the digestive anatomy, physiology and dentition of a carnivore, as well as a dietary preference for animal derived material but can digest starch and eat a wide range of dietary material.
- We make dietary choices for our dogs based on key influencing factors relating to the dog, the food, the humans (us) and the environment.
- Digestion has four stages – ingestion, digestion, absorption and elimination – our dogs have specific adaptions to support these stages.
- Dogs need a diet that is nutritionally adequate, safe, palatable and acceptable – we make choices based on our needs and those of our dogs.

CHAPTER 2 The Caregiver

The Human at the End of the Lead

How many times have you been asked, or have asked someone else, 'What do you feed your dog?'. This is quite possibly one of the most frequent questions asked in those dog-related chats – in the park, at training, at events, your neighbour who thinks your dog looks extra shiny, your friend at training class, your vet, your trainer, on social media – the list goes on. The problem is that what you feed your dog and what I feed my dog are likely to be as diverse as our individual lives. Our own situations in terms of finances, family, living situation, time, need for convenience (or not), health, morals and a whole host of other variables, all impact on the choices we will and need to make. Combine this with our dog and their specific, individual needs, then the possible diet choices for each individual situation are immense.

In this chapter we will explore the factors that impact on the dietary choices we make for our dogs and focus on the 'human at the end of the lead'. This is critical because it is us, the people caring for dogs, who actually purchase the food that we will feed to them. Indeed, companion animal nutrition is quite fascinating as an industry, because all the marketing is targeted to appeal to the person, not the actual consumer of the product – the animal; in this case, the dog.

Let's explore how to make decisions, who to seek advice from and who to trust for that advice. The individuality of dog and person is also critically important – one size rarely fits all and we must always feed the animal in front of us. Finally, we will examine what we need and want from the food we feed to our dogs, as a way to help support you in your decision-making process and to be confident in the decisions you make for you and your dog.

The Relationship between Dogs and People

The human–dog relationship has a profound impact on the food choices we make for our dogs. Lifestyles also

Each dog is an individual and the relationships we have with our dogs affects what we choose to feed them.

The majority of the world's dogs are free-living, feral or pariah dogs, living on the edges of human society.

affect what we choose to feed our dogs. There is a stark difference between the feeding choices made by someone looking after multiple dogs, all living in a kennelled environment and on a daily food budget per dog, and someone caring for a single dog, living a life of luxury, viewed as a close family member and where every need and whim is catered for. Of course, there are variations between these extremes, from family pet who 'moonlights' as a working gundog once a week, to dogs working as assistance or therapy animals, and competing in competitive disciplines. All have their own needs and requirements, and the nutritional choices will often reflect these. Recognising that there is diversity in canine caregiving, in addition to nutritional individuality, is important in all aspects of canine care and management.

What About Dogs Without People?

It is easy to forget that the dogs that live in proximity with us, are cared for by us and share our lives, are a small proportion of the global population of dogs. Most dogs live as feral, semi-feral, stray, very lightly managed or even pariah dogs. They exist on a mixed diet of scavenging, occasional food provided by humans and some hunting. The diet of these dogs is interesting in terms of composition, but does not cause the same level of debate as that

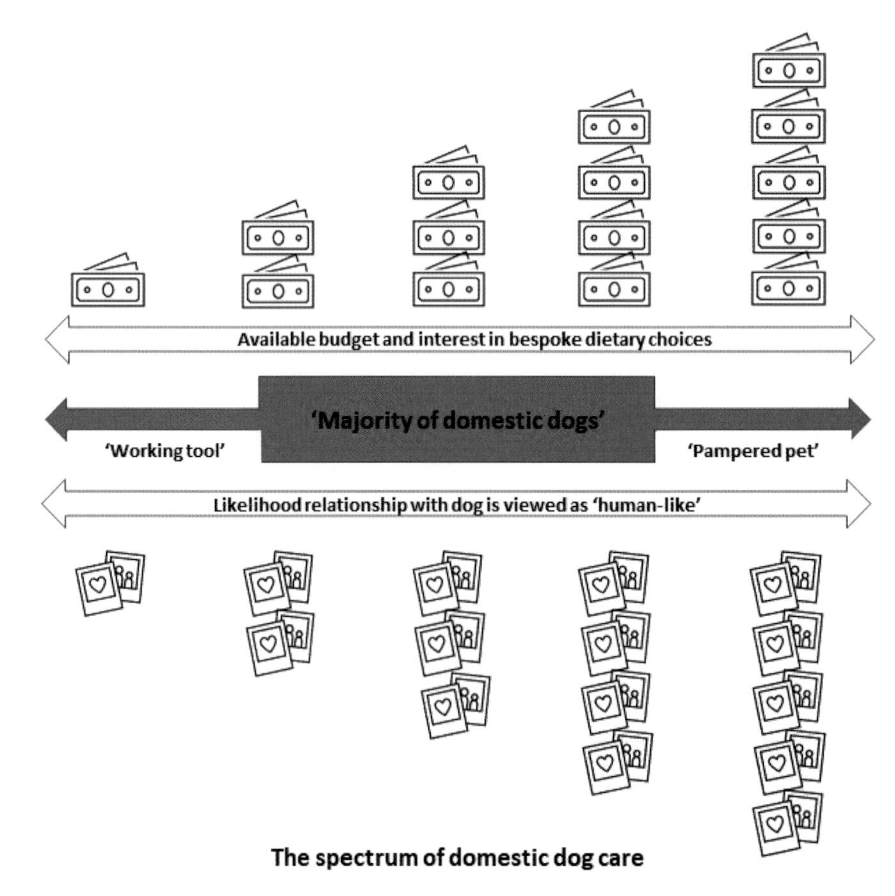

There is a wide spectrum of how managed domestic dogs are viewed by people, from working tool to pampered pet. This affects the choices made by caregivers for diet, healthcare and other aspects of care. The more a dog is viewed as a family member rather than as a working 'tool', the more likely that budget and interest in a tailored or bespoke diet is enhanced.

seen when talking about what the average, managed companion dog gets fed.

The Spectrum of Canine Caregiving

For dogs that are proactively managed and cared for by humans, there is a wide spectrum of how dogs are viewed, cared for and fed. I have met dogs viewed purely as working tools. These dogs are usually fed on a basic, functional level, often on a least-cost basis. Their care and wellbeing are important, but from a functionality and work-capability perspective – pragmatism being a common theme.

At the other end of the spectrum are dogs who are living in environments and fed diets that would exceed the living situations and standards of many people. Equally, there are working dogs who are viewed and managed as pampered pets, and there are dogs apparently living a 'life of luxury' but who lack deep connection with a human. The more 'human-like' that the relationship between a person and their dog is, the more likely it is that the available budget, interest and desire to mimic a human lifestyle for them will be. This also extends to what the dog will be offered to eat by their caregiver(s).

Do We Overcomplicate Feeding Our Dogs?

Ask ten people with dogs what they feed to their dogs and you will get ten different answers. You'll also get many more reasons for their choices. In the dog world, opinions and beliefs about feeding are strongly held, passionately shared and vigorously defended. Because we have close bonds with our dogs, and increasingly view them as close family members, their care, management and diet are becoming more humanised. Expectations are evolving and because nutrition is a variable that can be managed and altered to have a direct bearing on our dogs, it attracts real interest.

However, it is easy to overcomplicate feeding our dogs. We can focus too much on ingredients, forgetting about the nutrients that are needed. We might avoid certain manufacturers or suppliers. We often explore the latest fads and fashions in feeding – supplements or entire diet choices. We might feel guilty about aspects of our dogs' care (perhaps leaving them at home while we go to work) and overcompensate by feeding to excess. The emotions we feel for our dogs have a profound effect on the choices we make for them.

External peer pressure exerts an impact too, whether via marketing messages from dog-food businesses, social media 'influencers' or even trainers, friends and family. It makes me sad when people say that they have been made to feel bad about what they feed their dog, especially if they are limited in the choices they can make. If we genuinely care for dogs, we should also extend that care and compassion to their people and avoid making judgemental comments or statements about anyone's diet choices for their dog(s). Instead, we can support people in making the best choice for their individual situation, while ensuring that a good level of nutritional science is also applied.

Most domestic dogs live sedentary lives. They live in centrally heated homes, have good healthcare and low to moderate levels of exercise. Consequently, the average dog needs a diet that supplies nutrition in an acceptable and palatable form to support health and wellbeing. With this as a starting point, we can then explore what additional requirements we might have, to meet the individual needs of us and our dogs. Sometimes those needs are essential, such as increased nutrient supply to support growth. Sometimes they are because we want to home-prepare food for our dogs or explore alternative dietary ingredients, such as insects or plant-based options for lifestyle or sustainability choices.

However, there is a huge amount of conflicting information, discussion and debate that is freely available about how best to feed dogs. Some of that information can be quite scary, or judgemental, suggesting that certain choices are harmful. Sometimes it suggests that your dog's care is not uppermost in your mind. It is unsurprising that many caregivers question what they are doing and lose confidence in their dietary choices for their dogs. So, how do you decide and who should you trust?

Decision-Making for Your Dog's Diet

Dietary decision-making for your dog is best done on an evidence base. This means sourcing information, confirming its legitimacy and assessing how it fits with the needs of you and your dog. The problem is knowing who and what information to trust.

Modern canine nutrition has come a long way from the first commercial dog-foods. We now know far more about the biology of the dog and their nutritional requirements. Nutritional science is a good place to start

Cognitive biases can affect our decision-making. When it comes to choosing what to feed our dogs, a number of factors need to be considered and it can be difficult to decide what is most important.

in your decision-making, although science is a continual process and knowledge is constantly being acquired as more research is undertaken. The scientific process means that as evidence is acquired and new knowledge gained, practices and advice evolve. Canine nutrition is no different. Where views, advice and practices change as a result of new evidence, this indicates that the scientific process is working.

Beware the Cognitive Bias

Cognitive biases are ways of thinking that can be highly efficient but can also lead to ineffective decision-making. Feeding our dogs is not immune to cognitive biases. Common biases include the 'bandwagon effect' where feeding trends become commonplace because everyone decides to try them, especially if some people have raved about the success they have had. This is why feeding fashions often wax and wane. Naturalistic fallacy is another, where there is a bias towards anything deemed to be, or labelled as, 'natural' and a presumption that this means it is safer or somehow better than alternatives. Beware of your biases and be alert to the effect they may have on your decision-making, especially when seeking advice or looking at marketing material. You might see words and phrases such as 'superfood' or 'natural' that tap into your cognitive biases and manipulate your decision-making.

How to Choose What to Feed Your Dog

The dietary choice you make for your dog depends as much on you as it does on your dog. Whatever and however you decide to feed your dog, at the very least, it needs to supply enough energy and essential nutrients for survival. It will support the maintenance of good health and a long life. If your dog is active, growing, pregnant or lactating, nutrition needs to support this too. Your dog needs to want to eat it and you need to want to feed it. It needs to fit with your lifestyle and ability to afford and prepare it. You need to be able to get the food too – if supply or availability of ingredients or even the whole diet is difficult, then keeping your dog's diet consistent might be tricky. If a diet does not fully address any of these points, then it is unsuitable and unsustainable for you both. Working through a simple checklist of questions is often an excellent, evidence-based starting point, from which further choices can be made. This process can also help challenge your biases and remove some emotion from your decision-making.

Who Should I Trust for Nutrition Advice?

Sometimes extra nutritional advice and support is needed. Many people will initially turn to social media, and while there is some excellent advice available there, there is also some fundamentally incorrect and even dangerous advice. How can you decide what is good advice and what is less good about feeding your dog?

Your vet is often a good starting point for guidance, especially if your dog has a health issue that is nutrition-related or one that can be supported via nutrition. In serious clinical nutrition cases, referral to a suitably qualified veterinary nutritionist is recommended. Sometimes other professionals will be able to assist and always look for someone who is qualified (ideally to degree level in an appropriate subject area as a minimum) and insured to support you. Beware of 'miracle cures' or guarantees of changes in short spaces of time. Equally, it can be dangerous to explore some approaches without consulting your vet, especially if your dog has a diagnosed condition and is on medication. Anyone who suggests that they are an alternative to your vet, could be putting your dog in danger and could even be breaking the law – in the UK, only qualified and registered veterinary surgeons can diagnose and treat conditions. Ideally, your dog will have a

Checklist for Choosing a Diet for Your Dog

Use these questions and sub-questions as an evidence-based way to help you work out what type of diet might be a best fit for you and your dog:

1. What is your dog's daily energy requirements?
   a. Are they growing, pregnant, lactating or highly active?
   b. Do they need to maintain, gain or lose bodyweight?
   c. Are they a young puppy, a mature adult or a senior dog?
   d. Are they spayed or neutered?
   e. Where does your dog live – kennel or house?
2. Does your dog have any health issues, dental problems, preferences, sensitivities or allergies that mean that their diet needs to be amended?
   a. Are there nutrients that need managed/modified levels?
   b. Are there ingredients that need to be minimised or avoided?
   c. Does the form of the diet need consideration – wet, dry, raw?
   d. Does your dog have breed-/type-specific nutritional requirements?
   e. Does your dog prefer to eat certain flavours or ingredients?
3. What can you afford to feed your dog?
   a. What is your daily/weekly/monthly budget?
   b. Do you need to factor in supplements/rewards/chews to this budget?
4. Can you easily get regular access to your chosen dog food and can you store it?
   a. Do you need a regular supply or can you bulk buy/prepare meals and store/freeze?
   b. Do you have suitable alternatives in case of supply issues?
5. Do you (or any of your household members) have health issues or other concerns about certain foods or ingredients?
   a. Is anyone immunocompromised or on medication that might mean hygiene is extra important around dog food?
   b. Does anyone have an allergy or sensitivity to food components or ingredients, such as gluten, where exposure, even in dog food, might be an issue?
   c. Do you have concerns about the ethics, welfare or sustainability of dog-food ingredients?
   d. Are there manufacturers/suppliers that you wish to avoid?
6. What do you want to feed your dog?
   a. Is convenience important for you (dry or packaged food might be easier)?
   b. Do you enjoy home-cooking and home-preparation?
   c. Do you want to feed a less processed diet?
   d. Do you want to feed an alternative ingredient diet (e.g. plant-/insect-based)?

team of professionals to help you and them – or they will work together to ensure the best possible care for your dog. This could include your vet, trainer, behaviourist, nutritionist, veterinary physiotherapist and other canine professionals.

When seeking nutrition advice, it is sensible to ask why information is being provided. In most cases, advice and support is given with the best intentions – to help you and your dog. Sometimes, however, it can be biased. Is the information coming from a business or organisation that wishes to maximise profit and make a sale? While this is perfectly legitimate (everyone needs to make a living), some marketing practices can unfairly create fear, confusion and anxiety for caregivers. It could be that organisations with particular interests or agendas share information – promoting ethical, moral or other specific choices. Sometimes, information simply comes from individuals, who have good intentions, but the information provided is not backed up by knowledge and understanding of individual dog and caregiver circumstances.

Always Remember Nutritional Individuality

You and your dog are unique. Your situation and circumstances are too. It is important to remember this when choosing a diet for your dog – what works for your friend may not work for you (or your dog). This applies to their genetic make-up, as well as their living situation, health and activity level. Factor into this, the variation in individual caregivers and their needs, and it's clear why there are so many options available and such diversity in feeding practices.

In choosing a diet for your dog, you need to consider what your dog needs, what you need and what a food can provide. Somewhere, in the plethora of options available, will be the best choice for you and your dog. By thinking carefully what you need a diet to do, as well as what your dog needs from that diet, you can take an evidence-based and confident approach to your decision-making.

There is no best dog food, but there is a best dog food for each individual dog and their person.

Summary

- We have almost complete control over what and when our dogs eat – this means we have a responsibility to make suitable and appropriate diet decisions for them.
- There is a wide spectrum of the dog–human relationship and this impacts on the choices that will be made for individual dogs – the nature of each relationship will affect the financial and emotional investment a caregiver has with their dog.
- Every caregiver and dog's situation and needs are unique – this means nutritional choices often have to be tailored carefully to meet those needs.
- Most dogs on a balanced diet of any type will be perfectly healthy – we can sometimes overcomplicate feeding our dogs.
- Good nutrition is not just about the best food, it is about the best food for an individual dog.

CHAPTER 3 The Food

Food and the Essentials of Nutrition

Nutrition is how our dogs get the energy and resources needed to survive and thrive. Food supplies these in the form of nutrients. Nutrients are dietary components with specific roles in the body that support overall health and activity. Nutrients are defined as 'essential' or 'non-essential.' Essential nutrients must be supplied in the diet. Non-essential nutrients might be supplied in the diet but can also be produced in the body if suitable precursor substances are present – some of those precursors are the essential nutrients. There are six classifications of nutrients that must be supplied in a dog's diet – water, fat, protein, carbohydrate, vitamins and minerals. Food also supplies energy, which is not a nutrient but is provided via dietary fat, protein and carbohydrate – the energy-providing macronutrients.

The Components of Food

Food consists of dry matter (DM) and water. Food that is high in moisture (such as raw meat or tinned dog-food) will have much lower levels of DM in the same volume than dry food. The DM includes the nutrients. Food DM is broken down further to an organic and an inorganic fraction. These terms refer to the chemistry of the compounds within these groups – organic means the compounds contain the element carbon, inorganic means they don't.

The organic fraction of food DM includes fat, carbohydrate, protein, vitamins and minor nutrients, such as organic acids. The inorganic fraction includes the minerals, such as calcium and iron. It is this fraction that is often identified on pet food labels as 'ash' and creates confusion for caregivers. The ash is what is left after food has been chemically analysed and represents the minerals in the food and not that ash has been added to your dog's food.

Fat, protein and carbohydrate all supply a source of energy in the diet and are macronutrients because they are needed in larger quantities than the micronutrients. The micronutrients include vitamins and minerals, which are only needed in small amounts, but are essential for health. Laboratory tests are used to assess the nutrients and amounts supplied by a food and individual ingredients. If you are home-preparing your dog's food, you will probably use reference tables of this information in formulating the overall diet.

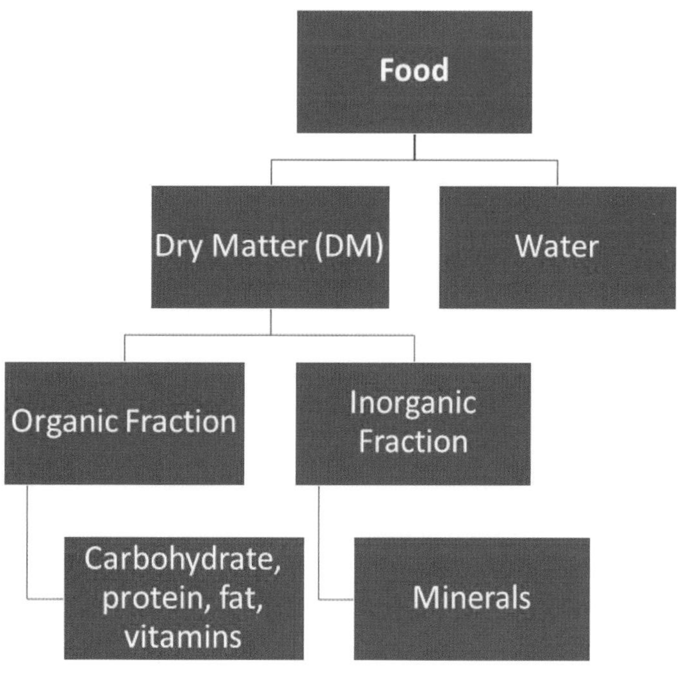

The components of food.

The Nutrients

Our dogs need nutrients, and different food ingredients supply nutrients, albeit in different forms and amounts. Understanding the nutrients provided by ingredients, how much and in what form, is important to formulate our dogs' diets. If you are using a commercially produced dog food, knowing about the ingredients included and their nutritional value can help your decision-making about what to feed. Looking at the provision of nutrients is a much better way of assessing a diet than simply looking at ingredients. If we focus too much only on ingredients, we can lose sight of the nutrition a diet provides, so taking a nutritional science approach means examining the nutrients required by our dogs and then assessing how best to supply them.

Food ingredients supply the nutrients our dogs need. Nutrients are supplied by different ingredients and nutrition can be tailored for individual dogs and circumstances by changing ingredient types or amounts included in a diet. If you are feeding a commercial dog-food, the ingredients included might affect your purchasing choices – you may wish to avoid particular ingredients for health, welfare, sustainability or even price concerns. If you are home-preparing food, you'll need an understanding of how different ingredients can be combined to supply a nutritionally balanced and suitable diet for your dog. Not all nutrients are equal. Different sources of protein will differ in their digestibility, for example. Fat might be sourced from plants or animals, affecting the overall composition. Carbohydrates can be soluble and rapidly digested and absorbed, or insoluble and indigestible.

Nutrients and Energy: Food as Fuel

As well as supplying essential nutrients to our dogs, food fuels our dogs. Food provides energy to allow them to do everything they need to do, and a constant source of energy is needed for survival. Energy itself is not a nutrient, but food must supply adequate levels of the energy-providing nutrients to support health and well-being. A dog's energy requirement is the first thing their diet must meet and between 50 and 80 per cent of their DM intake will be used for energy. Energy-providing nutrients will meet energy needs before they are used for any other purpose in the body. If insufficient energy is supplied in a diet, a dog will lose weight and body condition, sometimes breaking down their own muscle mass to obtain energy. Prolonged energy deficit will result in ill-health and will eventually be fatal. Conversely, excess dietary energy will result in a dog gaining weight and potentially developing overweight and obesity.

How Does Food Supply Energy?

The nutrients that supply energy in the diet are energy stores that function as a fuel source. At the most basic level, they store energy in their chemical structure and when that structure is broken down during digestion and absorption, energy is released. Our dogs use that energy to support maintenance of the body and activity output.

How Much Energy Does My Dog Need from their Food?

Dogs need different amounts of food energy based on their individual situations, such as age and activity level. Young, active dogs need more energy to support growth and exercise than more sedentary, mature dogs. Many caregivers will 'feed by eye' and simply increase or decrease the amount they feed their dogs based on how their dogs look and how they are performing. However, it is better to get an idea of how much energy our dogs are likely to need, and calculations allow us to make evidence-based dietary choices to supply that energy. Sometimes this will involve changing the amounts of individual nutrients in the diet to make it more or less energy-dense.

Energy Requirements of Different Dogs

It is possible to calculate estimated energy requirements for our dogs based on their bodyweight and activity level. This provides an idea of the energy that a diet must supply each day to support the maintenance of body tissues, as well as activity output.

For many companion dogs, their energy requirement is that of maintenance – enough energy needs to be supplied to support day-to-day maintenance of the body and little else. Most companion dogs have limited energy expenditure, are likely to be spayed or neutered, live in warm homes and might even have doggy clothing. Ironically, this same population of dogs is often provided with calorific treats and have other lifestyle factors that may predispose them to weight gain.

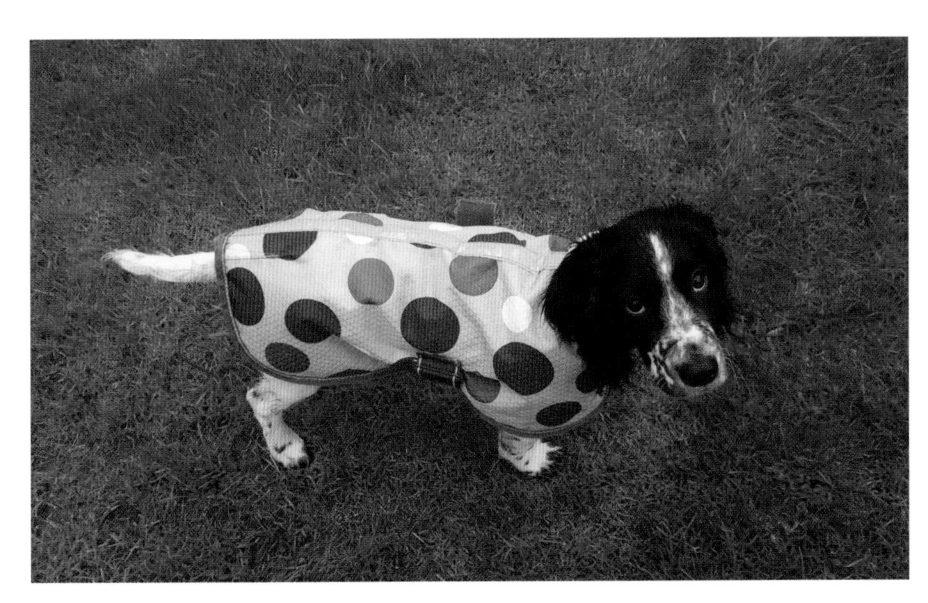

Dog coats are useful to keep them clean and dry, but also reduce their daily energy requirements.

Conversely, some dogs have increased energy requirements and their diet needs to reflect that. The age of your dog will affect their energy requirements through life. Young, growing dogs will have increased energy needs to support the growth process and the increased activity so common with younger animals. Puppies also have limited thermoregulation capacity and energy is also needed to support the generation of body heat. As maturity is reached, growth slows and body maintenance becomes more of a consistent turnover, repair and regeneration process that needs less energy than when actively growing. Voluntary activity often reduces with maturity too. Spay and neuter can also reduce the energy requirements of our dogs.

Illness, recovery and healing after injury or surgery also mean that the energy requirement of our dogs will increase. If illness has resulted in digestive upset and disturbance, there might be a protracted period of digestive limitation, meaning that a recovery diet is needed. Where tissues are being repaired or a dog is recovering after illness, a diet with increased energy provision can support the recovery process and mean that small but energy-rich and nutritious meals can be provided.

As dogs age, wear and tear on the body and the ageing process can affect activity levels, meaning that energy needs reduce even further. Where there is musculoskeletal pain, perhaps because of osteoarthritis, movement can become limited and weight gain becomes a real possibility without careful management of dietary energy intake. Ageing also often means that age-related changes to dentition and the digestive system can mean that food intake and energy acquisition from the diet are impaired.

Pregnant bitches will require an increased amount of dietary energy during the last weeks of pregnancy. She might also need increased frequency of meals, to compensate for the reduced capacity of the digestive system to cope with large volumes of food if a large litter is being carried. Lactation is immensely energy demanding and requires additional dietary energy to be supplied. For bitches nursing large litters, and typically when puppies are between three and five weeks old, milk production constitutes an incredible demand on the body. It is essential that the diet fuels the bitch's energy needs to support both her and her puppies.

Highly active and working dogs will need increased supply of energy via the diet. One of the most common nutritional queries is from handlers of hard-working or highly active dogs, reporting that their dogs don't maintain bodyweight during a working or competitive season. The pressures of hard work, high levels of daily activity and sometimes travel, competition stress and other factors, can mean that these dogs are physically incapable of eating and digesting sufficient calories each day to maintain body condition. Sled dogs competing

Pregnancy and lactation require additional dietary energy.

in long-distance races routinely lose a substantial percentage of their bodyweight during the race and are estimated to have a daily calorie requirement exceeding 10,000 kilocalories (kcal) per day. For context, the recommended daily calorie intake for an adult human female is approximately 2,000kcal per day.

Assessing an individual dog based on their age, breed/type, lifestyle, activity, health and other factors is essential to work out their energy requirements. If you would like to be more scientific about calculating their needs, Chapter 5 explores how.

Ingredients and Sustainability

When thinking about our dog's food, we have a responsibility to consider the nutritional value of the food, the energy and nutrients it supplies, as well as its wider environmental impact. Balancing these points against our own and our dogs' needs requires careful consideration. Awareness of the origin of ingredients is increasingly important from a sustainability perspective. Environmental and geopolitical challenges are making some ingredients difficult to source or very expensive. Ingredients that need to be transported across the world come with a significant carbon footprint. Animal-derived ingredients are particularly problematic in many cases as they can be environmentally damaging during production. Their use in dog food might also be competing against the human food-chain – a significant concern with the rise in use of 'human grade' material in dog food. As a result, we are seeing alternative ingredients being used, especially different proteins, such as insects. Evidence suggests these ingredients are nutritionally valuable and acceptable to our dogs, but there remains concern from some caregivers that diets including these ingredients are not appropriate for dogs. The debate about 'species-appropriate' feeding continues. Sustainability, availability and affordability are all factors that will impact on how and what we feed our dogs in the future.

Digestibility of Food

Another important aspect of food is how digestible it is for our dogs. The digestibility of food will affect if the nutrients are available and in what amount. No food is 100 per cent digestible and there is always material that is considered indigestible. This passes through the digestive system and is eliminated as waste. Much fibre is indigestible but is still beneficial for the health of the digestive system by providing material for the intestinal microbiome to feed off, for bulking stools and for removing old cells from the digestive tract.

Digestibility is affected by a number of factors, including level of processing, ingredients, fibre content, health and activity level of the dog. Dietary fat tends to be approximately 90 per cent digestible, whereas carbohydrate and protein are approximately 85 per cent and 80 per cent digestible, respectively. Not all forms of nutrients are the same though. Shoe leather is high in protein but is not very digestible, and while your dog might enjoy chewing on it, its nutritonal value is low. Raw meat is considered highly digestible compared to heavily processed diets. However, comparisons of different food-types suggest that lightly cooked/steamed chicken breast is more digestible than raw chicken, which in turn is more digestible than dry, chicken-based dog-food.

In general, high-quality, well-prepared and formulated diets tend to be more digestible than low-quality diets. This means that less needs to be fed of highly digestible diets to meet nutritional needs, although appetite and gut fill must also be considered – we don't want our dogs to continually feel hungry. A balance often needs to be struck between digestibility and the volume fed. Sometimes, highly digestible diets fail to make our dogs feel satisified because of the small, nutrient-dense volume fed. This might mean that alternatives are needed.

What about 'Fillers' in Dog Food?

Fillers are described as low-cost ingredients with no nutritional value in dog food. In reality, all ingredients have either a nutritional or processing role, so the term filler is rather inaccurate. Some ingredients, such as indigestible fibre, will be used to provide 'bulk' to a diet. This is useful in weight-management diets and can help to bulk stools and support anal gland emptying, for example. Water and air can be classed as fillers – both are effective at making a meal appear larger than it might otherwise be (think about the difference between popcorn kernels and popped corn). Both are used to aid feelings of 'fullness' for our dogs and, although water is an important nutrient, air is justifiably classed as a true filler.

The Importance of Water – the First Limiting Nutrient

Water is essential for supporting life and is one of the most basic requirements for any living organism. We often take water for granted and forget how critical it is. Water is described as the first limiting nutrient because deficiency will have rapid and significant impacts. Even mild dehydration will affect our dogs' ability to exercise, learn and support a safe body temperature. About 65 per cent of our dogs' bodyweight is water. A loss of 10 per cent body water can result in severe health consequences and a loss of up to 15 per cent can result in death.

Overall, water supports temperature regulation, waste removal and digestive function. It is called the universal solvent because many substances can be dissolved in it and metabolic reactions depend on water. The minimum daily water requirement for dogs varies, based on individual situations. Dogs continually lose water by evaporation from the respiratory system, urination and in their faeces. Dogs are negatively affected by a lack of water within hours, while a lack of food will take much longer to have a significant impact. For this reason, a constant supply of drinking water is recommended.

Sources of Water

There are three sources of water – drinking water, water in food and water produced as a by-product of metabolic reactions in the body – metabolic water. Drinking is the most significant source of water for most dogs. Food with high moisture content is a useful source of water and dogs fed 'wet' food often drink less than those on dry diets.

Drinking Water

Dogs will drink from a number of water sources, including places that are less than ideal and are sources of potential contamination, such as puddles. While

The three sources of water: 1, Drinking. 2, Food. 3, Metabolic

Dogs will often be less choosy about where they drink than we might like.

drinking from unclean sources should be discouraged and not relied upon as a source of drinking water, most healthy dogs show no ill effects, although there is a risk of ingesting disease-causing organisms such as *Leptospira* spp. (a bacteria typically spread by rats) and *Giardia* spp. (a parasite originating from livestock and infected dogs) that can cause illness. Providing a consistent and clean supply of drinking water, from a bowl that is large enough to allow your dog to safely fit their muzzle in and lap from, is a simple but essential aspect of canine care. While bowls are available in a number of materials, a stainless-steel bowl is easy to clean and sterilise, and less likely to harbour potentially pathogenic organisms, than other materials.

Water in Food

Raw or moist diets can be up to 80 per cent moisture, but drinking water is still needed. Water intake is much higher for dogs fed dry food. Soaking dry food can encourage water intake and support digestion and palatability. Dry foods are often coated with fats and oils that are liberated when water is added. This can enhance the smell, taste and acceptance for some dogs. Do not add boiling water to dry food as this can destroy heat-sensitive nutrients. Equally, soaked food should not be left uneaten at room temperatures for extended periods, as there is the risk of bacterial growth.

Metabolic Water

Metabolic water production is only a small proportion of the daily water requirement (between 5 and 10 per cent) and cannot be exclusively relied upon as a water source.

Practical Water Provision for Your Dog

Knowing your dog's typical daily water-intake is good practice. While this is likely to increase if temperatures are high or your dog has been active, unusual and unexplained increases in water consumption might suggest other problems. Seek veterinary advice if there are sudden changes to your dog's drinking habits. This is especially important for unspayed bitches, as increased drinking can be a sign of pyometra (infection of the uterus) and requires prompt veterinary attention. For older dogs, altered drinking might suggest age-related disease, so again, speak to your vet.

Lots of factors affect how much your dog will drink each day, including diet, temperature, exercise, age, health and sometimes individuality. Increased ambient temperatures, extreme exercise and high-fat, high-protein diets, all increase water-intake to support metabolism, cooling and waste removal. Pregnant, whelping and lactating bitches increase their water intake, notably if there is a large litter and at about weeks three to five after whelping, when milk production (and consumption) is at its highest.

A useful way to check your dog's hydration status is to assess their urine output, frequency of urination and the colour of their urine. If urine is very dark-coloured and passed only infrequently or in tiny amounts, this may signal a level of dehydration. Healthy urine should be lightly straw-coloured and not be excessively smelly. If

A fresh, clean supply of drinking water should be always available. Water bowls should be cleaned and refilled regularly.

there are significant changes to urine output, appearance or frequency, seek veterinary advice.

Keeping water bowls clean and (re)filled regularly with fresh, clean water is one of the simplest things we can do to support our dogs' overall health and wellbeing, in addition to feeding well.

The Importance of Dry Matter (DM) for Nutrition

To fully assess a food for nutritional value, the dry matter (DM) fraction and its water, or moisture, content is determined. Wet dog-food (including raw) has higher moisture content than dry dog-food (typically about 8 per cent moisture). The DM basis of a food is important in working out how much needs to be fed to meet a dog's nutrient needs. It is also important to be able to compare the nutrition provided by two different foods. If you look at labels of dog foods, you will see percentage values for protein, fat, fibre and ash declared under the heading 'analytical constituents'. The moisture content will be noted on labelling where it exceeds 14 per cent. However, nutrient values can only really be compared across several types of food effectively on a DM basis (DMB). This is because the 'values on labels' are based on total weight, which includes moisture, and are on an 'as fed' basis, meaning that is what your dog actually eats, moisture and all.

How Can I Calculate Nutrient Content on a DMB?

If you want to be able to compare the nutrition provided by different foods, you need to calculate the nutrient content of each food on a DMB. First, you need to know the values of nutrients declared on the label and the moisture content. If no moisture content is noted, as is common for dry food, assume a typical 8 per cent moisture content. A rule of thumb is that the calculated DMB value will be higher than that declared labelled nutrient value because of the removal of water from the calculation. For high-moisture foods, calculated DMB values will be higher than for dry diets. You can calculate the amount of a nutrient on a DMB by following these steps:

1. Calculate the dry matter content of the food by subtracting the moisture content from 100,
   e.g. a dry food with a moisture content of 8%:
   $$100 - 8 = \text{dry matter of } 92\%$$
2. Divide the percentage value of the nutrient of interest by the dry matter value,
   e.g. a dry food with 24% protein and dry matter of 92%:
   $$24 \div 92 = 0.26$$
3. Multiply the value from step 2 by 100 to give the DMB percentage,
   e.g. calculated 0.26 protein in step 2 (above):
   $$0.26 \times 100 = 26\% \text{ protein DMB}$$

By calculating nutrient levels on a DMB, you can compare the nutritional value of different types of food for your dog. For example, you might, on first glance, think that feeding a raw diet will reduce the amount of protein your dog is getting as the percentage of protein on pack will be lower than declared on a dry food. However, when calculated on DMB, you could actually be feeding even more protein that you thought. This is important in exploring food factors of importance in nutrition.

DMB calculation example – wet dog food

Analytical Constituents:
Crude protein12%
Crude fat 11%
Crude fibre 2%
Crude ash 3%
Moisture 68%

DM of food: 100-68 = 32%

DM of protein: (12/32) x 100 = 37.5%

DM of fat: (11/32) x 100 = 34.4%

Example of a DMB calculation for the protein and fat content of a wet dog-food.

What Do these Percentage Values for Nutrients Mean?

The analytical values on labels and those calculated on a DMB give you an idea of how much of a given nutrient is supplied in a specific amount of food. If protein is calculated to be 32 per cent DMB, this means that 32 per cent of what you feed on a DMB is protein, e.g. if you feed 100g of food DM, then 32g of that will be protein. Remember that not all of that protein will be available to your dog, however, as it will not all be digestible or bioavailable. These values are useful to work out if your dog's food is providing the right amount of nutrients, or for you to make dietary amends to meet your dog's needs.

Summary

- Dogs need nutrients, and food supplies those nutrients in different forms and quantities.
- Food consists of a dry matter (DM) fraction and water – different types of food can be compared on a dry matter basis (DMB).
- There are six classes of nutrients – proteins, fats, carbohydrates, vitamins, minerals and water.
- Protein, fat and carbohydrate are macro-nutrients that supply energy, in addition to other biological functions.
- Vitamins and minerals are micronutrients and are critical for normal body function.
- A dog's energy needs must be met by their diet before anything else and water is also essential for survival.

CHAPTER 4 The World of Dog Food

The History of Dog Food

Dogs have been human companions for thousands of years. Dogs, and their ancestors, have shared our left-overs, scavenged our waste and, sometimes, benefited from extra food that we didn't eat and gave to them. Modern dogs continue to have similar dietary choices. Even the most well-fed and exquisitely nourished pet dog may struggle to repress their scavenging traits – my own dogs (who I like to think are well fed and on a great nutritional strategy) have been known to empty the kitchen bin, counter surf and help themselves to items from the kitchen table. This is in addition to the occasional 'tasty' snack while out walking – the result of the toilet habits of the local cats or the left-overs by a less-than-tidy fellow human. Dogs are fundamentally omnivorous, opportunistic scavengers, with a preference for animal-derived tissues. This has important consequences for the food choices we make for our dogs.

While the origin of commercial dog-food is often attributed to James Spratt, who, in the 1860s, developed baked biscuits, originally sold for feeding to dogs during cross-Atlantic sailings, there is evidence that humans were developing specific diets for dogs long before. These dog foods were not commercially produced on the scale now seen, and nor were they backed up by robust nutritional science, but they represent a gradual evolution in the world of dog food and highlight the importance of the human–dog bond in its development.

Today, we can decide to feed our dogs commercially available dog-food (of all types, from dry to raw) or we can choose to home-prepare their diet. While there has been an increase in people exploring and feeding alternatives to dry food, such as raw, cold-pressed, home-cooked and so on, most dogs are still fed commercially produced dog foods. The dog-food market is now a global, multibillion-dollar industry, growing year-on-year. With the pet-dog population increasing, the demand for safe, nutritious and acceptable (to dog and person) dog food represents a significant market, although concerns about health, environmental sustainability, processing and nutritional suitability means that many caregivers are exploring other food options for their dogs.

Our dogs have a range of food options available.

The Food and Feed Industries – What Do They Mean for Our Dogs' Food?

Animal and human nutrition are closely linked. Indeed, the commercial animal nutrition world is interested in nourishing animals and humans – lots of animals are fed to produce meat, milk or other products, for human consumption. The *feed* industry is concerned with feeding animals. The *food* industry is concerned with human nutrition. The feed industry is, in part, driven by human consumer demands for the food industry, with a focus on cost, nutrition, health and, increasingly, concern and interest in the welfare of animals producing food products. Consequently, the feed industry is closely aligned with the food industry. Notably, when talking about companion animal nutrition, while technically they fall within the feed industry category, the term 'pet food' is much more commonly used – this means we call what our dogs eat 'dog food' and highlights the humanisation of the human–dog relationship.

By-products from the food industry often find their way into animal feed while also complying with national and international regulations concerning what can, and what cannot, be fed to animals. Animals destined for human consumption, or producing substances that humans eat, have very specific regulations permitting the raw feed ingredients and additives that can be added to their diets. This limits the origin and sources of feed ingredients. Regulations maintain the safety and integrity of the human food-chain, but also impact on the nutrition of other animals, such as our dogs, which are never intended to enter the food chain.

Each industry also benefits from advances in knowledge and technical innovations. Our dogs' food, whether the main dietary components or as treats, comes from the feed and food industries, unless you are producing ingredients yourself. Most large commercial dog-food manufacturers are owned by parent companies and corporations that retain an active commercial interest in the human food industry. This is unsurprising, especially in the historical context that waste or left-over products from the food industry were re-purposed for use in companion animal diets – for example, the portions of slaughtered animals that, for reasons of preference or culture, are not typically desirable for human consumption. The use of these in food developed for dogs and cats makes economic and environmental sense.

The Evolution of Dog Food

For as long as we have lived with dogs, we have fed them. Archaeological evidence suggests that dogs were fed specifically prepared diets for much longer than the existence of the dog-food market. However, significant commercial production of dog food really commenced in the early 1900s with biscuits first being produced and then tinned food appearing in the 1920s. Tinned dog-food was popular until the 1940s, when war meant that metal and food was rationed, and dry dog-foods started to increase in popularity. After rationing ended, tinned food again become a popular choice, although the development of extrusion technology in the 1950s meant that dry dog-food became commonplace and remains a popular dog-food choice. Recently, the variety of dog food available has quite literally exploded. From budget to premium brands, raw to home-prepared, the choices and types of dog food available are as diverse as individual dogs and their caregivers. Some of the new ways of preparing dog foods are the result of nutritional and technological innovations, as well as meeting the increased demands of critical canine caregivers. Awareness of the relative differences between food types, and the pros and cons of each, can aid your decision-making. Fundamentally, your first decision is whether to go commercial, home-prepared or a mix of the two.

Commercial vs. Caregiver-Prepared Dog-Food – How to Decide?

Whether you decide to purchase commercially available dog-food (of any type) or prepare your own dog food (raw, fresh or cooked), it is important that the food is nutritionally adequate and formulated to account for your dog's nutritional needs. Because storage and even preparation can impact on nutrient levels and bioavailability, these also need to be considered. Commercial manufacturers will undertake this through formulation and end-product analyses. Independently or home-formulated diets will

Common dog food choices include wet or dry, although there is a huge range of different ways to provide nutrition to our dogs.

often rely on data tables and associated resources to devise nutritionally complete diets.

Commercial Dog-Foods

For many caregivers, the convenience and economy of manufactured diets of all types is attractive. In addition, because commercial animal-food production is tightly regulated, there can be a degree of confidence in nutritional adequacy, safety and additional support, if needed. However, there are disadvantages to commercially produced foods. Nutritional individuality is not always easy and sometimes individual situations need a more tailored approach. While safety of food and ingredients is under regulatory control, mistakes and accidents do occur: foreign bodies can by-pass quality control processes, nutrient levels can be accidentally too high or too low and other contamination, including with potentially pathogenic organisms such as *Salmonella*, is possible for all dog-food types.

Most companies have excellent quality control and assurance processes and procedures, allowing early detection and reaction to possible problems via recalls and customer alerts. Others, however, are less diligent, and the lack of a recall history is not necessarily a sign of quality – it could simply mean that problems are not looked for or detected. There have been multiple cases globally of significant recalls, contamination concerns (some resulting in illness and death) and problems with ingredients and formulation. This has happened with all types of commercial dog-food, from extruded to raw. It is important to balance the incidence of these events with the size of the global dog-food industry and the number of dogs fed without incident – this is seen in the human food industry too.

A practical approach many caregivers take is to rotate commercial diets. That is, identify diets that meet dog and caregiver requirements but are manufactured by different companies and then regularly rotate their use. You can even mix different types of food and combine commercial and home-prepared or add toppers and additional ingredients, if you are concerned about excessive use of processed food or food from a single source. The only caveat is that you should ensure what you feed is balanced to meet nutrient requirements.

Extruded Dog-Food

Most dry dog-food is extruded and often described as kibble. Extrusion was an important development in the dog-food world as it permitted mass production of food that was convenient, cost-effective and could be stored for long periods without significant deterioration in nutrition or quality. The process of extrusion uses specialised machinery that mixes ingredients together, cooking the resulting mixture and effectively forcing it through a pressure cooker – the extruder. The process is similar to baking bread and produces small 'biscuits' that can be coated with fat to enhance palatability and nutritional value.

A wide range of extruded dog-foods are now available, meeting the nutritional needs of different canine life-stages, health and activity levels. The quality of extruded products differs in terms of ingredients used, level of

An example of a dry, kibble dog food, uniform in shape and size.

processing and even quality control. Traditionally, extruded products used meat meals as a key ingredient. Grain ingredients are also important for both nutritional and functional processing roles, the carbohydrate content aiding the formation of the extruded kibble. Modern extruders can use fresh meat (usually in the form of a slurry or paste) and work at lower temperatures than older versions, as well as being less reliant on grain or rice for carbohydrate. This has meant that a range of ingredients can be included, as well as improving the digestibility and quality of the end product. A significant growth area in dog food has been the development of 'grain free', dry, extruded foods, where the key carbohydrate ingredient is often potato or sweet potato instead of the traditional grains.

How Does Processing Affect the Nutritional Value of Dog Food?

A concern about extruded dog-food is that processing at high temperatures leads to a loss of nutritional value, because of nutrient destruction. Many processed foods (not just extruded kibble) add vitamins, minerals and other ingredients to replace those lost during processing and to account for those likely to degrade during storage. Indeed, all foods will degrade over time and a balance needs to be struck between level of processing/cooking for safety (by destroying potentially dangerous microbes) and for improved digestibility (because cooking will liberate some nutrients and enhance the bioavailability of others). The use of preservatives, natural or artificial, is also common in the end-product dog-food, but also in some of the raw ingredients, to ensure nutritional stability over time. There is often concern about the use of preservatives, especially artificial ones such as BHT (butylated hydroxytoluene), but they are useful to minimise deterioration of food, rancidity and maintain nutritional quality during storage. Many companies now use natural preservatives, such as rosemary extract or vitamin E instead.

What About the Nutritional Value of Commercial Dog-Food?

The production of companion animal food is tightly regulated in terms of nutrition, but legislation and regulatory bodies differ in different geographical locations and jurisdictions. This applies to production, ingredient sourcing, marketing and labelling, among other things. A general approach is taken within this book and where specifics are noted, they have a UK/European-centric approach. For readers in other locations, you are advised to confirm what local regulatory and legislative frameworks might apply. If you home-prepare your dog's food, fewer regulations apply beyond those that affect your sourcing and supply of raw ingredients.

The nutritional value of commercial food is often debated, sometimes very passionately in the dog world, and it will differ based on the type of food, quality of ingredients and level of processing. Striking a balance between processing to liberate nutrients and support digestibility of some ingredients, while acknowledging others will be negatively impacted, is needed.

Processing and cooking at high temperatures can produce compounds that may have negative health-effects. These compounds include AGEs (advanced glycation end-products) that are associated with increased oxidative stress and inflammation if ingested at high levels. AGEs form as a result of chemical reactions between sugars and proteins during cooking via a process called the Maillard reaction – typically seen when toasting bread. These compounds give browned food its distinctive taste and smell. Animal-derived products are also high in AGEs and new ones can form during cooking, making highly processed dog food a significant potential source of these compounds. AGEs also form as a result of normal metabolic processes in the body, but when levels of AGEs become excessive, problems may arise. There is increased awareness of the long-term impacts of feeding

The browning of bread when making toast is the result of the Maillard reaction.

(or eating) processed foods and this must be balanced against other factors. Reducing the amount of highly processed food fed can limit exposure to AGEs in human and canine nutrition.

Raw or fresh diets have less concern with processing issues, but some nutrients can be less bioavailable than in processed foods. Poor formulation can result in nutritional inadequacy. There is a risk of microbial contamination, including from antibiotic-resistant bacteria that have been found in some raw dog-foods, so careful hygiene needs to be maintained during storage, preparation and feeding to minimise this risk to both dogs and people. However, fresh foods are good to incorporate in your dog's diet, even if you usually feed processed meals, as treats or meal toppers.

Dry, Wet or Raw Dog-Food?

Broad classifications of dog food include dry (kibble/biscuit), wet (tinned or other packaging) and raw. There are also semi-moist diets, cooked and a host of other options available, including dehydrated and freeze-dried. Each has their own merits and disadvantages, some of which are discussed (*see* Table). Convenience and cost are major factors for many caregivers, as well as supplying adequate nutrition.

Dry food is convenient, has a reasonable shelf-life, is easy to source and store, and is acceptable for many dogs in terms of palatability and nutrition. Wet (or even semi-moist) foods are often highly palatable and can be useful for supporting water intake for some dogs but will have a shorter shelf-life (when opened) than dry food, for example. Raw diets can also support fluid intake and tend to be highly palatable and acceptable to many dogs but can be limited by caregiver convenience and storage. For some, the cost, preparation and planning of raw/fresh feeding can be a significant limitation.

Sadly, in the dog-food world, the debate about dry versus raw feeding has become intensely polarised and instead of being based on evidence and reality, much discussion centres on ideas and comment, some of which are inaccurate. Aside from nutritional individuality, there remains little robust evidence to categorically state that one diet type and choice is superior to another overall. The huge number of variables encountered in our dogs, from activity to health, breed, type, size and living situation, all make a simple 'this diet is better than the alternative' statement difficult and, in truth, unlikely ever to be confirmed completely. Remembering the nuances of dog

Some examples of the range of dog food types available and their characteristics

Dog-food type	Description and key characterisitcs
Extruded kibble	Dry kibble produced by high-temperature 'cooking'. Convenient, economical, easy to store. Range of quality, ingredient types and nutritional specification available. Can be fed dry or soaked. Requires carbohydrate content to support extrusion process. Meat meal or fresh meat can be used based on extrusion technology used. Widely acceptable to dogs and caregivers. Digestibility and nutritional value vary.
Baked biscuit	Dry, baked biscuits. Low moisture content. Less common than extruded. Convenient and easy to store. Often used as a 'mixer' with meat. Widely acceptable to dogs and caregivers. Digestibility and nutritional value vary.
Freeze-dried	Food ingredients are mixed and frozen in a process where water is removed. Convenient, easy to store, fed rehydrated with warm water. Can be expensive but acceptable to fussier eaters and nutritional value may be greater than some alternatives because of reduced levels of processing. Easy to store.
Dehydrated	Ingredients and mixed and water removed, usually via gentle cooking during dehydration process. Lightly cooked so nutrients often more complete and digestibility is good. Expensive but palatable, especially if fed rehydrated with warm water. Easy to store – usually as a meal or powder.
Cold-pressed	Ingredients are mixed in water and 'pressed' at low temperatures to form pellets. Nutrients are less damaged by processing and may be more digestible than alternatives. Slightly higher moisture content than other 'dry' foods, so shorter shelf-life and expensive.
Raw, coated	Biscuit or kibble is spray-coated with raw or cooked ingredients to produce a palatable, convenient dry food that straddles the desire to feed raw/cooked with the convenience of dry. Shorter shelf-life than fully extruded or biscuit varieties.
Semi-moist	Semi-moist food and treats are usually in the form of small nuggets/pellets and has higher moisture content (25–40%) than traditional baked or extruded food. Palatable and often less nutrient damage, as processed at lower temperatures than extrusion. Shorter shelf-life and more expensive than other dry foods. Can be high in sugars due to humectants (substances that bind water) used to maintain the semi-moist characteristics.
Wet/moist	Usually tinned or in other packaging (trays, cartons, etc.) with approximately 70% moisture content. Mixed ingredients but mostly animal-derived products. Usually cooked in pack and level of cooking varies. Palatable and attractive. Can be mixed with dry food/mixers or fed as a complete diet. Digestibility and nutritional value vary. Easy to store with long shelf-life unless opened.
Raw and fresh	Uncooked, fresh ingredients – meat, organs, bone, eggs, vegetables and fruit. Meat will be frozen so needs storage and preparation. Different variations of ingredients and presentations possible – grinds, minced, blends, whole carcass, etc. Can be freshly sourced, homemade, DIY or commercially prepared. Palatable and attractive. Can be unbalanced if not well formulated and contamination risk if not handled appropriately. Useful for limited-ingredient diets. Digestibility good.

Commercial wet dog-food comes in different forms – tinned is traditional but other options such as cartons are increasingly being seen.

nutrition and feeding can help us navigate the decision-making process for our own situations.

Can I Prepare My Dog's Food at Home?

Home-preparation, cooking, fresh feeding or even DIY raw feeding, are all options to prepare your own dog's food. For many caregivers, this is an important part of caring for their dog and there is real pleasure in selecting, preparing and presenting food. Home-prepared food can reduce food-miles and support the use of locally produced and seasonal ingredients. For some, it is an important lifestyle and consumer choice and for others, it may help with dietary or other health issues that their dog has. On this basis, home-preparation is a valid option, although diets do need very careful formulation, as many are nutritionally inadequate. For this reason, supplementation is often needed to balance any nutrient shortfall. Recipes should be used that are developed to meet nutrient requirements and a number of programmes are available to aid this process and permit dynamic responses to different nutritional needs.

Home-preparation can also be done alongside more conventional dietary options and the use of 'toppers' to commercial dog-foods is an option. These toppers should make up no more than 10–20 per cent of your dog's daily calorie intake to avoid significant nutritional imbalances but can consist of fresh or cooked ingredients, such as meat, vegetables and even fruit. For many caregivers who want to balance convenience with fresh feeding, this is often a good compromise, and one that our dogs enjoy and benefit from too. On that note, it is worth saying that it's perfectly acceptable for raw, kibble and other mixed ingredients to be fed together, contrary to popular belief. Our dogs are capable of digesting mixed material with no ill effects, if they are otherwise healthy. So, if you do wish to feed a mixed-ingredient diet and get the convenience of dry with the ability to add extras (while maintaining nutritional balance), you can. This is a good option for anyone who wishes to reduce their reliance on processed dog-food.

Dogs can digest mixed ingredients. For example, raw and kibble can be mixed and fed together safely.

Every dog is unique – their nutrition should be too.

What Type of Dog Food is Best? It Depends!

Because every caregiver and dog's situation is unique, there is no one best way to feed or one best food to feed. This is in part why there is such a range of types, brands, varieties and options available. It can sometimes be confusing working out what a food actually provides, however, and some of the costs and benefits of different options.

A food labelled as a 'complete' food will provide all the required energy and nutrients to your dog if fed at the recommended feeding levels. Indeed, the term 'complete' when used on labelling or supportive material is a legal term indicating that the essential nutrient requirements will be met by that single diet. A 'complementary' food is intended to be fed in combination with other ingredients or foods, such as mixer biscuits or some treats. On its own, a complementary food will not supply all nutrients at the correct levels to support the day-to-day life and activity of your dog.

What Food Provides to the Dog (and Caregiver)

When feeding our dogs, it is important to remember that, with the exception of items they scavenge or acquire by their own means, we are responsible for their entire dietary intake. This is in contrast to keeping horses, rabbits or other species that will be fed a range of feed material, in addition to having access to grazing. These species have a significant portion of their diet that is plant-based and effectively free choice. When formulating diets for these species, their mixed dietary intake has to be considered.

For our dogs, however, rarely are they permitted to have free access to a variety of feed ingredients and even food itself. Indeed, for some dogs (and Labradors, I'm looking at you!) free access to any food would not be a sensible idea.

In the diverse world of dog food, ensuring we feed our dogs a nutritionally adequate and balanced diet is key. We have a responsibility to ensure that their needs are met nutritionally and there are a number of ways we can do this. Good decision-making and knowing the relative costs and benefits of the different approaches can help us make choices that suit our dogs and us.

Summary

- Specific dog diets have been produced by humans since our relationship with dogs began.
- Commercial production of dog food commenced in the early 1900s and has developed since.
- There are a range of types, forms and options of different dog-foods available, each with their own relative merits in terms of convenience, cost, nutritional value and acceptability to our dogs.
- Caregivers broadly have two choices to provide their dog's nutrition – commercially produced dog food or home-diet preparation, although it is possible to combine the two if desired.
- Whatever diet type is fed, it should be formulated to take account of nutritional requirements and nutrient balance because of processing, storage or bioavailability impacts.

PART TWO

How Nutrition Works: The Nutritional Needs of the Domestic Dog

CHAPTER 5 Energy

What is Energy?

Energy means different things to different people and in different contexts. For many dog-people, energy is a behavioural term and is used to identify and describe dogs as 'high energy' or 'low energy'. Food is often associated with the behavioural energy of a dog and diet is sometimes blamed or credited for the behavioural energy exhibited by a dog.

While there is a link between nutrition and behavioural energy, it is not as clearcut as many would have you believe. A frequent question is, 'What can I feed my dog to calm them down?' and the answer tends to be a complex one, considering existing diet, age, activity level, breed/type and even your dog's personality. More important, however, is the recognition that nutrition supplies energy for animals to survive and thrive. Food supplies the energy that is needed for day-to-day maintenance of the body, growth, reproduction, repair and activity. Feeding food that supplies lots of energy need not necessarily result in a dog that has 'energy to burn' – they will most likely just gain weight. But, if your dog is highly active, you must fuel that activity.

Our dog's diet must meet their energy needs before other nutritional requirements.

In nutritional terms, energy relates to the amount of 'fuel' that a diet supplies. Energy is a critical dietary component and is the first requirement that any diet must meet. While energy is itself not a nutrient, fat, protein and carbohydrate all provide a dietary source of energy. Balancing the proportions of these nutrients in a diet will supply energy in the appropriate form and amount for an individual dog's circumstances and activity levels.

All animals need a constant supply of energy for survival. Water is often noted to be 'the first limiting nutrient', but a dietary supply of energy is also critical, and energy is the first requirement that must be met by a diet. When formulating canine diets, the daily energy needed by a dog is the starting point. The first question in choosing a diet should be, 'How much energy does my dog need?'. Ensuring an adequate supply of other nutrients is then managed *after* the daily energy requirements are met. This is why focusing on ingredients rather than nutrients can be problematic in assessing diet suitability or quality. Considering the nutrients that supply energy in any diet will aid the process of working out in what form and how much energy a diet will provide and is a better way of assessing diet suitability than simply looking at ingredient lists.

Where Does Food Energy Come From?

All food energy originates from sunlight. Plants obtain energy from sunlight and convert it into stored forms of energy via photosynthesis. The main form of stored energy is carbohydrate, notably starch. Animals then eat plants and use plant sources of energy to support activity and make their own energy stores, usually in the form of fat. Animals do store some energy as carbohydrate called glycogen, which is found in muscles and the liver. However, glycogen stores are small compared to fat stores.

Dogs can obtain dietary energy from carbohydrate, protein and fat, although fat is preferentially used by the dog's metabolism. Diets consisting of animal and plant material will provide a mixed intake of various sources of energy-providing nutrients. This can be useful in managing overall dietary energy intake and altering diets for particular purposes.

What Does Energy Mean for Feeding Our Dogs?

Sometimes energy is misunderstood in the dog world. 'High-energy' dogs are often breeds and types that are naturally highly active and 'busy' creatures. These dogs may often struggle to gain or maintain weight and are often naturally lean but otherwise completely healthy. Dogs with lower energy levels are often more relaxed and sedentary types, who may be more likely to be 'couch potatoes' and might gain weight more easily. The term energy in these situations is more about the dogs' personality and biology than nutrition, although nutrition might need to be altered to suit these individual dogs. The nutritional definition of energy is about how much energy is supplied by a given amount of food.

Dog diets are formulated on an energy basis. This means the dog's energy needs are estimated and a diet is formulated to meet those needs by feeding a specific amount of that food. If less of the diet is fed than the recommended feeding levels, then other nutrients might not be supplied at the correct levels and deficiencies are possible. This is also why feeding guides on commercial dog-foods are so important – if you feed your dog much less than the amount recommended 'on pack', you may run the risk of nutritional inadequacy of other nutrients. This is why understanding both the energy needs of our dogs and the amount of energy provided by food is important.

Energy Balance

Energy balance ensures that a diet supplies the energy a dog needs to support daily life-processes and their activity output. A simplistic way of viewing energy balance is that to maintain a consistent (and healthy) bodyweight, energy intake (via food) and output (bodily processes and activity) need to be balanced. If excess energy is consumed and activity does not 'burn it off', then an animal will gain weight. Consistent dietary excess of energy will result in weight gain and the potential development of obesity, the most common form of malnutrition seen in the modern domestic dog. Obesity has a significant impact on our dogs' wellbeing and longevity.

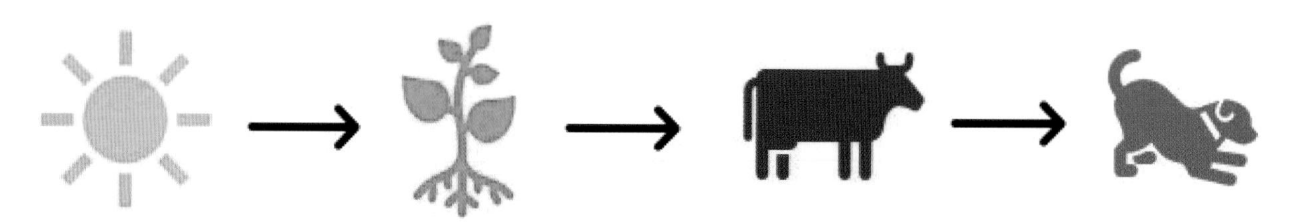

Energy comes from sunlight and is converted into stored forms in plants. This energy is transferred when plants and animals are eaten by others.

Energy balance is about balancing energy 'in' from food and the energy expended through maintenance of body processes and activity levels.

If insufficient energy is supplied in the diet to support activity output, an animal will lose bodyweight as they use stored energy sources to provide the energy needed. Long-term dietary energy deficiency will result in extreme weight loss, lethargy and other significant health and wellbeing concerns, including deficiency of other nutrients. Maintaining an appropriate energy balance is a simple way to maintain a healthy bodyweight.

Energy and Food Intake

Energy requirements must be met by diet. Animals are usually very good at balancing their food intake with their energy needs, but many factors will have an impact on this and can result in a level of dysregulation of appropriate food intake to meet energy needs. If diets high in energy are freely available, and activity output is limited (common for many companion dogs), the natural occurrence of balancing intake with output can become skewed, often towards excess energy intake and the development of overweight and obesity.

If food intake results in excess provision of energy, obesity is a significant risk, although for growing puppies it can also lead to skeletal and other developmental abnormalities, such as hip dysplasia, especially in large breeds. It is also possible that young dogs carrying excess body fat may be predisposed to be obese as adults, based on how their fat (or adipose) cells develop.

If food intake and energy consumption are restricted, this can result in reduced or impaired growth and development in young dogs. For adult dogs, impaired healing and tissue repair might result, as well as loss of bodyweight and muscle mass. Dogs that have a high-energy output, such as pregnant, lactating, highly active or extremely hard-working dogs, will often exhibit a loss of bodyweight if their food intake does not meet their dietary energy requirement.

For dogs that need to gain or lose bodyweight, a diet review and audit are essential to ensure that energy needs are met, as well as other nutrient requirements, and that an appropriate volume of food intake is provided to ensure that dogs are satisfied. A balance also needs to be struck about the volume of food fed within single meals, and the capacity of the digestive system to process and absorb the food too. In some cases, this will mean increasing the number of meals per day, in addition to feeding a diet that provides more energy in each meal.

How is the Energy in Food Determined?

The energy present in food can be measured in the laboratory. This is done by 'burning' the food in a process called 'bomb calorimetry' and collecting the released energy. Food energy is expressed in kilocalories (kcal) or kilojoules (kJ) and 1kcal is equal to 4.184kJ. One kilocalorie is the amount of energy needed to raise the temperature of 1kg of water by 1°C (from 14.5 to 15.5°C).

In canine nutrition, kilocalories (kcal) are often used to describe the energy content of a diet and/or the energy needs of a dog. While kilocalorie is the correct term, it is often shortened to 'calorie', even though, technically, a kilocalorie is a thousand calories. For clarity, kilocalorie (kcal) will be used throughout this book when referring to energy in our dog's food.

How Much Energy is there in Food?

Calorimetry allows us to know how much energy there is in a food. The total energy released during calorimetry is the gross energy (GE) of the food and is the maximum potential amount of energy the food can supply in a given amount. However, animals can't use all the energy in food because of energy loses during digestion and the processing of food. Digestible energy (DE) is the energy from food that is available after digestion but before urinary and digestive gas energy loss. After these energy losses are accounted for, the amount of energy available for the dog's body to use is called metabolisable energy (ME). ME is used to indicate the energy content of dog food, as well as the amount of energy individual dogs require. ME can be determined by feeding trials but also by calculation to obtain an estimate of the energy content of food.

The Energy-Providing Nutrients

Dietary energy is provided by carbohydrate, protein and fat. The proportion of each energy-supplying nutrient in any diet differs based on an individual dog's biology and needs. While each of these three nutrients supplies energy, they differ in how the body digests, absorbs and processes them. They also differ in the amount of energy they supply, meaning that the energy density (sometimes referred to as calorie or caloric density) of a diet can be altered by changing the amount of each nutrient. Diets that are energy-dense will have a higher inclusion of fat than diets that are energy-dilute. This is because fat supplies more than twice the kilocalories per gram than either protein or carbohydrate. Energy-dense diets are useful for dogs that need a concentrated dietary supply of energy (highly active dogs, for example), whereas energy-dilute diets are more suitable for less active dogs.

How Much Energy Do the Nutrients Provide?

Dogs are metabolically preadapted to use fat as a source of energy. Fat supplies on average 8.5kcal per gram (kcal/g), compared to protein and carbohydrate that each supply only 3.5kcal/g. These values are known as Modified Atwater Factors and consider how digestible the nutrients are and then give an estimation of how much energy each nutrient provides. For fresh or home-prepared dog-foods that are more digestible than commercial diets, Atwater Factors are often used, where fat supplies 9kcal/g and protein and carbohydrate supply 4kcal/g. These values can help calculate the amount of energy in food if you know the amount of each energy-providing nutrient within it.

Calculating the ME Content of a Dog Food

It is useful to know the ME content of a food so that you can make sure that you supply enough energy to support your dog's activity. It is also important if your dog needs a weight-management programme. The energy density of a food also affects the other nutrients in the diet, and the nutrient content of food is often described as units of nutrient per 1,000kcal ME. This is useful to allow comparisons of different foods.

Sometimes commercial food has its ME value available on the pack or from the manufacturer directly, making it easy to access this information. Occasionally you might need to calculate it yourself. To do this, you need to know the percentage of protein, fat, water, fibre and ash in the food. This information can be obtained from food labels under 'analytical constituents' or from reference tables. The 'nitrogen-free extract' (NFE) of the food also needs to be calculated and gives an idea of the non-fibre carbohydrate content.

The following steps and equation can be used to give you an estimation of the ME content of a food:

1. Calculate the NFE content by subtraction:
   %NFE = 100 — %protein — %fat — %fibre — %ash — %moisture
2. Calculate the energy supplied by each of the energy-providing nutrients using Atwater/Modified Atwater factors (depending on digestibility of food).
3. Add the energy provided by each nutrient together to get the total ME of the diet.

Worked Example

Wet dog-food: 70% moisture, 12% protein, 10% fat, 2% fibre, 3% ash.

(Using Modified Atwater Factors for a commercial food.)

1. 100 — 12 — 10 — 2 — 3 — 70 = 3%NFE
2. ME protein: 12 × 3.5 = 42kcal/100g
   ME fat: 10 × 8.5 = 85kcal/100g
   ME NFE: 3 × 3.5 = 10.5kcal/100g

3. 42 + 85 + 10.5 = 137.5kcal/100g food

The ME of this food is 137.5kcal/100g (or 1,375kcal/kg).

Calculating the Calorie Distribution of a Dog Food

The ME of food is usually expressed as kcal per kg food (kcal/kg), or kcal per 100g (kcal/100g) and is a result of the amount of energy-providing nutrients in the food. The levels of these nutrients can be shown as a percentage of total ME in the diet, or as grams of nutrient per 1,000kcal ME.

When shown as a percentage of total ME, this is known as the calorie distribution of food, and it is useful to see how much energy is provided by each nutrient type and if you are looking to choose a food that is calorie-dense (i.e. maximum energy in a small amount, typically via a high percentage of energy coming from fat) or is calorie-dilute (i.e. minimum amount of energy in a reasonable food portion – usually met by higher percentages of carbohydrate and/or protein in the diet).

Calculating calorie distribution is useful to assess diet suitability for different purposes. Diets for active and growing dogs need to have more calories coming from fat. Weight-management diets will have more calories provided by carbohydrate and protein. To calculate the calorie distribution of a diet, you first calculate the total ME of the diet using the previous method, and then calculate what proportion of that ME is provided by fat, protein and carbohydrate.

Using the earlier example of a wet dog-food where the calculated ME of the food was 137.5kcal/100g, of which 42kcal/100g came from protein, 85kcal/100g from fat and 10.5kcal/100g from NFE, the calorie distribution can be calculated as follows (note values have been rounded for ease):

1. Calculate the percentage of total calories from protein (ME protein/total ME),

   e.g. (42 ÷137.5) × 100 = 30%

2. Calculate the percentage of total calories from fat (ME fat/total ME),

   e.g. (85 ÷ 137.5) × 100 = 62%

Calorie Distribution Example

Total ME = 137.5 kcal/100g, of which 42 kcal/100g protein, 85 kcal/100g fat and 10.5 kcal NFE

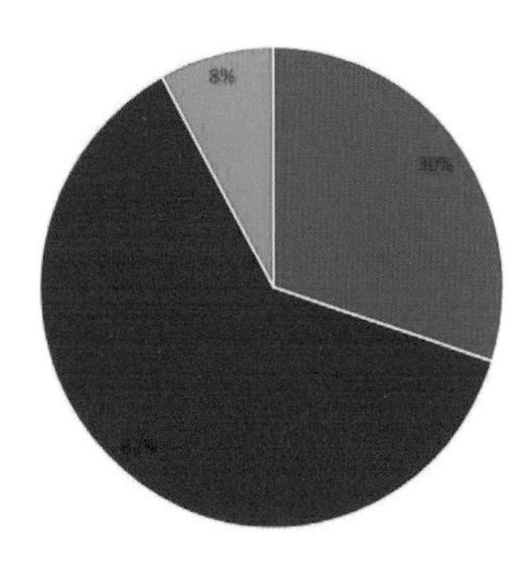

The calorie distribution of food is often best presented as a pie chart.

3. Calculate the percentage of total calories from NFE (ME NFE/total ME),

   e.g. (10.5 ÷ 137.5) × 100 = 8%

4. Check by addition that the percentages equal 100%,

   e.g. 30 + 62 + 8 = 100%

A pie chat is often used to visually represent the percentage calorie distribution of a diet.

Maintenance Energy Requirements (MER) and Daily Energy Requirements (DER) of Dogs

The minimum amount of energy that a dog needs each day from its food is represented by the maintenance energy requirement (MER). The MER differs based on the biology of individual dogs – age, spay/neuter, activity level, breed, personality and factors such as housing, all affect MER. Older, sedentary dogs have a lower MER than active, growing or pregnant/lactating dogs. Spayed and neutered dogs have an MER that can be 25 per cent less than a reproductive entire dog of the same age. Breed also has an effect with some breeds, such as Jack

Different breeds and types appear to have different energy requirements – bearded collies tend to have higher requirements than other breeds.

The West Highland white terrier is an example of a breed that typically has a lower dietary energy requirement than others.

Russell terriers, vizslas, flat coat retrievers and bearded collies having higher requirements than Airedale terriers, golden retrievers and West Highland white terriers, for example.

The daily energy requirement (DER) is an alternative way to estimate the energy needs of active adult dogs instead of MER and works with very similar calculations. Instead of using the age of the dog as a key determining factor, activity level and breed are taken into consideration.

It is possible to calculate the MER or DER of your dog, in order to gain an idea of how many calories their food needs to supply. In some cases, calculated values are either above or below an individual dog's actual needs, so flexibility and monitoring are needed to ensure activity is supported and that a healthy bodyweight and condition are maintained.

How to Calculate Your Dog's MER – Useful for Sedentary Pet Dogs

Calculating MER is based on the metabolic bodyweight of your dog. This is their bodyweight in kilograms raised to the power 0.75 ($kg^{0.75}$) and is lower than their actual bodyweight. It can be calculated using the scientific function on calculators. Once metabolic bodyweight has been calculated, this value is multiplied by a factor that accounts for the age of the dog. For an older dog, metabolic bodyweight is multiplied by 95 – for a young dog, the value used to multiply metabolic bodyweight is 130. Different multiplication values are available to account for individual dog age variations (*see* Table).

Reference table of factors for MER calculations

Age of dog in years	Multiplication factor for MER calculation
7+	95 (range of 80–120 can be used based on individual)
3–7	110 (range of 95–130 can be used based on individual)
1–2	130 (range of 125–140 can be used based on individual)

(Adapted from: *FEDIAF Nutritional Guidelines for Complete and Complementary Pet Food for Cats and Dogs*, 2021)

Worked Example of MER Calculation

This is Bertie, a 15kg, two-year-old, entire male, cocker spaniel. He is highly active and partially kennelled during the day but sleeps in the house at night. He is in a good, lean condition with a body condition score of 4 on a 9-point scale (where 9 is grossly obese).

Bertie.

- Bertie's metabolic bodyweight is: $15^{0.75} = 7.62$kg
- Using data from reference tables for MER based on age, the multiplication factor chosen is 130.
- Bertie's calculated MER (ME/day): $130 \times (15)^{0.75} = 990$kcal

Notably, Bertie actually gets fed somewhere between 200 and 500 extra calories per day based on his activity level in order to support a lean, healthy body condition, but this calculation is a starting point for assessing his dietary energy needs.

Calculating Daily Energy Requirements (DER) – Useful for Active Dogs

MER represents the baseline energy needed by your dog to support body functions and basic activity. However, MER calculations don't account for the activity level, breed or the predisposition to developing obesity in individual dogs. A useful alternative is to calculate their DER.

Daily energy requirements (DER) are calculated in an equivalent way to MER and use multiplication factors based on activity level. Activity is separated into five different categories with descriptions of intensity, frequency and duration (*see* Table). Some breed-specific differences are also known, notably for Newfoundlands and great Danes, giving rise to different multiplication factors for their DER. There is also a multiplication factor that can be used for adult dogs that are prone to obesity. This method can give an estimation of the number of kilocalories that your dog's diet needs to supply each day.

Reference table of factors for DER calculations

Activity level	Multiplication factor for DER calculation
Low (<1 hour per day, low impact e.g. lead walking)	95
Moderate (1–3h per day, low impact)	110
Moderate (1–3h per day, high impact)	125
High (3–6h per day, e.g. working dogs)	150–175
High in extreme conditions (e.g. sled dogs in the cold)	860–1240
Breed differences and obese-prone dogs	
Adult dogs prone to obesity	≤90
Great Danes	200 (200–250 range)
Newfoundlands	105 (80–132 range)

(Adapted from: *FEDIAF Nutritional Guidelines for Complete and Complementary Pet Food for Cats and Dogs*, 2021)

Worked Example of DER Calculation

This is Bobbi, a 14.5kg, seven-year-old, spayed female, cocker spaniel. She is highly active as a working gundog between two and three days per week in the winter months, typically working in cold, wet conditions for between four and six hours per day. She can lose weight very quickly and is quite an anxious personality type, but is usually in a good, lean condition with a body condition score of 3.5 on a 9-point scale (where 9 is grossly obese).

- Bobbi's metabolic bodyweight is:
  $14.5^{0.75} = 7.43$kg
- Using data from reference tables for DER based on activity level, the multiplication factor chosen is 175 (the upper value chosen because of her temperament and body condition).
- Bobbi's calculated MER (ME/day):
  $175 \times (14.5)^{0.75} = 1300$ kcal

Bobbi's diet provides 1300 kcal per day and she maintains her body condition. If her workload and frequency increases, then her DER is reviewed and diet amended accordingly.

Bobbi.

How to Use the MER and DER Calculations

Calculating either MER or DER is a useful step in working out how many kilocalories (i.e. how much energy) your dog needs to get from their food. It can help you to make decisions about what to feed and how much to feed. This is dependent upon information about the food ME being available (on the pack or perhaps from the manufacturer/formulator). Alternatively, you can calculate the approximate ME of the food.

In general, for most pet dogs, MER is a good way of estimating their daily energy needs and the outcomes are dependable in most cases. For very active dogs or those with energetic or anxious personalities, DER is a better way of estimating how many kilocalories their diet must provide. As with most things in nutrition, measuring, monitoring and then managing your dog's diet, energy intake, bodyweight, condition and performance will help you to determine the best approach for your individual situation.

If you are feeding a commercial food with clear feeding guides, they will be based on these calculations. It also explains why commercial feeding guides often suggest a wide range of possible amounts to be fed – accounting for nutritional individuality and the possible range in MER or DER requirements.

It could even be that your dog has a perfectly healthy, lean bodyweight and body condition and you don't need to use these calculations at all. Providing that their overall nutritional needs are met, then perfect. An awareness of energy-requirement calculations might be useful should your dog's circumstances ever change.

Summary

- A consistent and constant supply of energy is required to support life-processes and activity output – diet must first meet the energy requirements of an animal before other nutrient needs are considered.
- The energy content of a diet relates to the amount of 'fuel' or metabolisable energy (ME) it will supply and is commonly measured in kilocalories (kcal).
- Fat, protein and carbohydrate are all dietary energy sources, but fat provides more than twice the calories of protein or carbohydrate.
- The ME content of food and calorie distribution can be calculated to give an idea of diet suitability for individual dogs.
- A dog's energy requirements change throughout their life, based on their biology, growth, health, activity level, plus other factors, such as housing.
- MER (maintenance energy requirement) calculations can give an idea of energy needs for sedentary dogs or DER (daily energy requirement) can be calculated for more active dogs.

CHAPTER 6 Canines and Carbohydrates

Canines and Carbohydrates – a Conundrum?

A long-running and perennial debate in the dog community is the importance (or not!) of carbohydrates in the canine diet. Carbohydrates are one of the six nutrient groups and are important for dietary energy. The carbohydrate classification includes the simple sugars, such as glucose, to the more complex molecule, starch. It also includes fibrous forms of carbohydrate such as cellulose – a structural component of plants. Notably, these different forms of carbohydrate have different physical, nutritional and digestive properties.

Here, we will explore carbohydrates in the canine diet and examine whether our dogs need them, if they can digest them and review some of the current evidence around carbohydrates in our dogs' diets.

What are Carbohydrates?

Carbohydrates are a group of substances that contain the elements carbon, hydrogen and oxygen. They are diverse, ranging from simple, small molecules, such as glucose, to large, complex polymers (molecules comprising lots of individual subunits linked together) like cellulose, which is the most abundant polymer on the planet. Carbohydrates are the major energy-containing substances in plants, comprising up to 90 per cent of plant dry matter content and are also a major source of dietary energy.

Carbohydrate is how plants store energy. Grain crops are important food ingredients and sources of carbohydrate.

Sucrose is more commonly known as table sugar and milk contains the sugar lactose.

Carbohydrates are classified as monosaccharides, disaccharides and polysaccharides. The monosaccharides are the simplest form of carbohydrates and are often called the simple sugars. They are small molecules comprising a single 'unit' – 'mono' referring to one. Key monosaccharides include glucose, fructose and galactose. Disaccharides are formed when two monosaccharide units are joined together – 'di' meaning two. Lactose is a disaccharide found in milk and consists of one glucose molecule joined to a galactose molecule. Adult dogs lack the enzyme lactase that is needed to break lactose into its component monosaccharide parts, meaning that they cannot efficiently digest milk sugar and are effectively lactose-intolerant. Consequently, digestive upset can occur if adult dogs consume lactose. Other common disaccharides are maltose and sucrose – the sugar we commonly add to our tea and coffee.

Polysaccharides are large polymers of individual monosaccharides all joined together to form long chains. These carbohydrates are either energy-storage forms, such as starch, or structural forms, such as cellulose. Glycogen is the storage polysaccharide found in animal tissues. It is critical to support normal levels of energy in the body, especially when energetic demands are high. Dogs naturally have low levels of glycogen and its replacement after exercise can be supported by targeted nutrition.

The simple carbohydrates can be readily digested, absorbed and are then used as an energy source, whereas the larger, more complex carbohydrates are more difficult to digest and need specialised digestive systems and processes to be digested. Our dogs mostly lack these specific adaptations, although they can digest starch. Some fibrous forms of carbohydrate are not digestible at all but remain valuable from a digestive health perspective. This is why overly simplistic statements that dogs do not need carbohydrates are problematic, because not all carbohydrates are equal.

Do Dogs Need Carbohydrates?

A common and oft quoted statement is that 'dogs cannot digest carbohydrates'. Based on this, there is an assumption that dogs do not need carbohydrates in their diet. Indeed, some commentators would have you believe that carbohydrates in dog food are the root of all evil in terms of canine health, wellbeing and longevity. The problem is that the story is not this simple. As with most things in biology, there are many nuances that we must consider.

It is true that there is no minimum dietary requirement for carbohydrate in the dog's diet. When examined experimentally, dogs can do well on a very low carbohydrate diet. However, we know that in certain situations, carbohydrates are beneficial, often as a targeted energy source and to support gut health and digestive function. Pregnant and lactating bitches benefit from dietary carbohydrate to support the nutritional demands of reproduction. Carbohydrates are also useful in the diet of some highly active dogs, to support performance and recovery.

In order to understand the relationship between dogs and carbohydrates more fully, we need to consider carbohydrates in terms of their fundamental chemistry and their role in nutrition and digestive health. We must also consider their value in terms of ingredient supply, environmental sustainability and other factors relevant to the nutrition of our dogs.

The Simple Carbohydrates – the Sugars

Glucose is an essential simple carbohydrate and is a key nutrient to support the overall functioning and effective metabolism of the body. Glucose is also the major endpoint of all digestion and is the carbohydrate found in the bloodstream. Indeed, glucose is critical for the brain, which requires a constant supply to fuel normal neurological function.

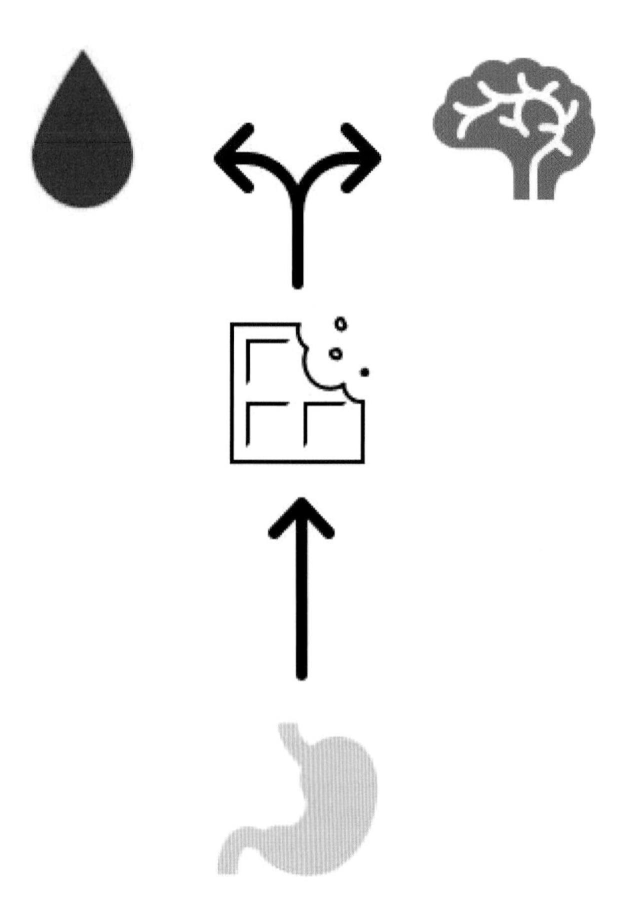

Glucose is the end point of all digestion and is critical to support blood-sugar levels and normal nervous system functioning.

A supply of simple carbohydrates is useful for highly active, sporting or working dogs that are expected to have a high-performance output on consecutive days. These dogs may deplete their liver and muscle stores of glycogen, and dietary carbohydrate can help support its replenishment. Glycogen is an important energy source when respiration and the associated biochemical and cellular pathways are challenged in their ability to generate energy for the animal to function. In these cases, glycogen is broken down into glucose molecules that can then be used as a source of 'fuel' by cells to support cellular work, which translates into the activities we ask our dogs to perform.

The problem with excess simple, soluble carbohydrates, however, is that they can be converted to fat if not metabolised by the body. They can also cause problems for normal, healthy functioning of organs, such as the pancreas. Excess and sudden intake of soluble carbohydrates can also cause digestive upset and loose stools in many dogs, so care does need to be taken with the dietary supply of them.

Complex Carbohydrates – the Polysaccharides

The complex carbohydrates are large molecules that consist of many monosaccharides joined together in long chains. The structure of these chains determines whether they can be digested by our dogs or not. Common complex carbohydrates are starch (of which there are two forms – amylose and amylopectin), glycogen and the different forms that make up dietary fibre, including cellulose.

Starch is commonly found in cereals as a major source of stored energy. Starch digestion requires enzymes to break the bonds between individual subunits and amylase is a key one that our dogs produce. Conversely, dietary fibre cannot be easily digested by our dogs directly. However, intestinal microbes can digest some fibre by a process of digestion called fermentation. Some types of fibre are more easily digested by the gut microbes and are described as highly fermentable. Fibre is also described in terms of solubility. Soluble fibres mix with fluid in the digestive system and form a gel-like mix – these fibres also tend to be highly fermentable and can increase the speed at which material moves through the digestive system. Many soluble fibres are useful prebiotics and support the health of the gut microbiome. Insoluble fibre is much less fermentable and can help slow digestive transit and increase faecal size. Cellulose, the major structure carbohydrate in plants has very low solubility and fermentability. This is why much of the plant material eaten by our dogs appears to pass through the digestive system unchanged – grass is a particular culprit.

The Dog's Dietary Requirement for Carbohydrates

Let's consider the dog's dietary need for carbohydrates and examine whether they are really needed or not. Unlike other nutrients, such as protein, fat and specific vitamins and minerals, there is no recorded minimum dietary requirement for carbohydrates for the dog. Consequently, there is truth in the common assumption that dogs do not actually need carbohydrates in their diet.

Dogs, in common with many other species, have an impressive biochemical process called gluconeogenesis that predominantly occurs in the liver. Gluconeogenesis literally translates as the new synthesis of glucose and is a biochemical pathway by which the dog can make glucose from non-carbohydrate precursor molecules, such as protein.

Obligate carnivores, such as cats, have high levels of gluconeogenesis, meaning that dietary carbohydrates are of much less importance than in other species. Our domestic dogs are more omnivorous in their feeding habits, but also have high levels of gluconeogenesis. This means that providing their diet supplies adequate levels of substances that can be used as precursors for the gluconeogenic process, typically protein, then dietary provision of carbohydrate is not strictly necessary.

But, while dietary carbohydrates are not strictly necessary in the canine diet, carbohydrates confer certain benefits for our dogs. In addition, there are specific situations when dietary carbohydrates can be extremely useful for our dogs, such as during pregnancy, when lactating or highly active, sporting dogs. Because dietary carbohydrate can be used as an energy source, it can have a 'protein-sparing' role, which is useful. This means that, instead of having to use protein to synthesise carbohydrate via gluconeogenesis, dietary carbohydrate can be used directly as an energy source and dietary protein can be used for other essential body functions, such as growth, instead. This could have metabolic benefits, as well as being positive for wider environmental sustainability. However, before considering the potential benefits of dietary carbohydrates, we need to consider the question as to whether dogs can actually digest them.

Can Dogs Digest Carbohydrates?

If there appears to be no minimum requirement in the canine diet for carbohydrates, then an obvious question is why are they often included in formulated diets and are our dogs capable of digesting them? Well, it depends! Some carbohydrates are very easily digested and absorbed – others are much trickier.

In order to answer whether dogs can digest dietary carbohydrates, we need to consider how their digestive system deals with the different forms of carbohydrates that we find in dog food, from seeds and grains, to potatoes, sugar beet and a whole host of other potential ingredients.

Digesting Simple Carbohydrates

The simple carbohydrates, such as glucose and sucrose, are small, soluble molecules that are easily digested and absorbed in the small intestine. Some require specific enzymes to aid their digestion. For example, adult dogs lose the capacity to digest milk sugars after weaning, due to lack of the enzyme lactase. This means that if they do consume foods containing milk sugar, they can suffer flatulence, digestive upset and even diarrhoea.

Simple carbohydrates are easily digested and absorbed by our dogs. Dogs also have taste receptors to detect sweet flavours. It is thought that this may account for dogs showing taste preferences for certain sweet-tasting foodstuffs. This includes the occasional accidental foray into human foods that might otherwise be toxic, such as chocolate and artificial sweeteners such as xylitol (which is extremely dangerous for dogs), and may also explain why some dogs show a preference for the consumption of young, fresh grass and other plants that are rich in sugars.

So, yes, dogs can digest and absorb many simple carbohydrates.

Digesting Fibrous Carbohydrates

Fibrous carbohydrates are those that give many plants their structure but are also found in the outer casings of seeds and grains – bran, for example, is high in fibre. When it comes to fibrous carbohydrates, dogs have extremely limited digestive capacity. For anyone who has had to deal with the aftermath of a dog devouring large amounts of grass, vegetables or other plant material, it will come as no surprise that dogs are incapable of digesting the large, complex and fibrous forms of carbohydrate, such as cellulose.

Unlike grazing species, such as cattle and horses, our dogs do not have a digestive system specialised to digest fibrous carbohydrates. Cattle have evolved a highly specialised digestive organ, the reticulorumen, which is a huge microbial fermentation chamber, characteristic of ruminants, including sheep and goats. In the reticulorumen, the extensive population of microbes that reside there can digest fibrous plant material and derive nutritional value from it. These microorganisms are described as cellulolytic, meaning they can break down cellulose into its component, molecular building-blocks.

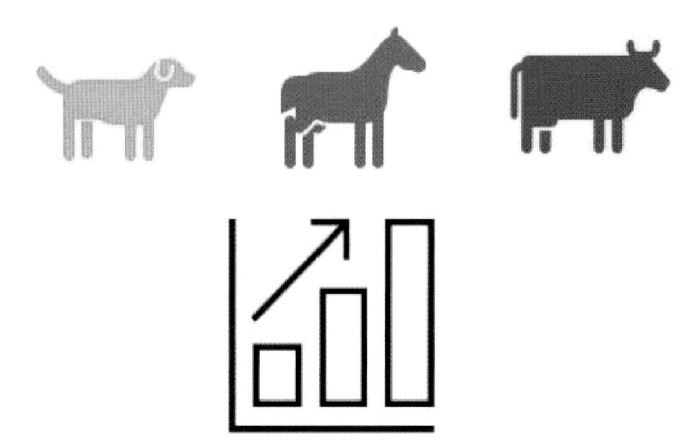

In comparison to horses and cattle, dogs have a very low ability to digest fibrous carbohydrates.

Horses also have a modified digestion system to digest plant material, with their enlarged caecum. The horse's caecum forms a microbial fermentation vat of cellulolytic microorganisms that can break down and utilise plant material as a source of energy and other nutrients. Dogs and humans do have a caecum, but it is much smaller and of much less digestive importance than observed in horses and other hind-gut fermenters. As a result, dogs have extremely limited capacity to digest fibrous plant-material and use it as a source of energy.

When structural and fibrous carbohydrate has been consumed by our dogs, it travels through the digestive tract, unchanged in shape, size or even colour, before being excreted. Sometimes, these complex forms of carbohydrates are pre-processed before being included in dog food, to reduce their size and visibility. However, they remain undigested by the dog's digestive system and will typically add to faecal shape and size on excretion.

However, while not digested, fibrous carbohydrate does have benefits for our dogs' health. Dietary fibre supports the health and functioning of the digestive system, helps to bulk out faeces and empty anal glands and can act as a prebiotic by effectively feeding the microbiome – the population of microorganisms within the digestive system increasingly recognised as important for overall health. Consequently, while dogs cannot digest fibrous carbohydrates, they are valuable in our dog's diets, to support microbiome and digestive health.

Digesting Starch

In contrast to cellulose, there are other forms of complex carbohydrates that our dogs are capable of digesting and utilising. Starch consists of two forms: starch-amylose and starch-amylopectin. These two forms of starch are long, repeating chains of individual units linked together and differ only in their molecular structure and the type

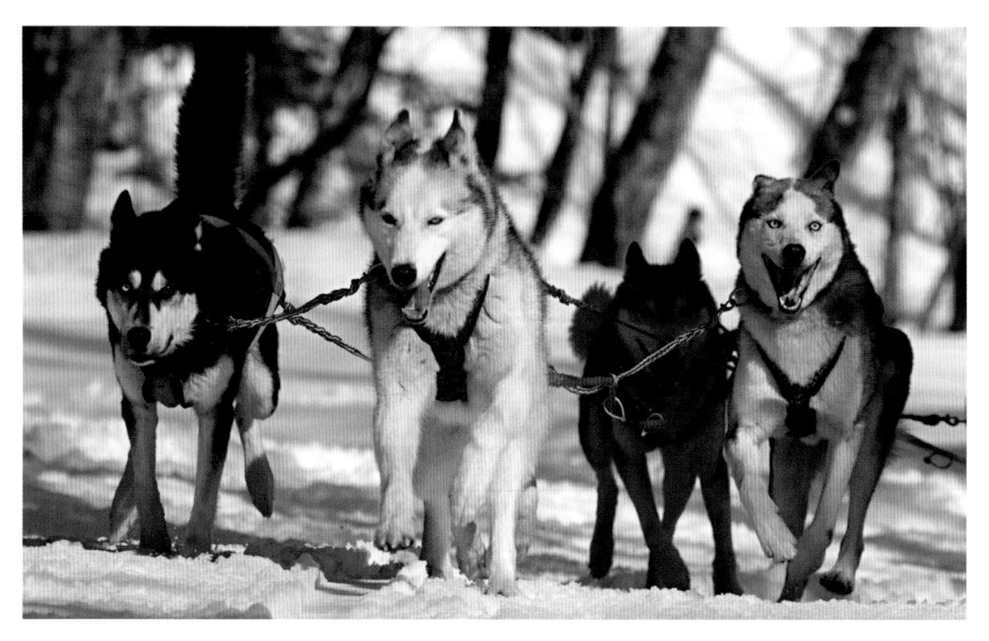

Many northern dog breeds, such as these sled dogs, appear to have a lower capacity for starch digestion compared to spaniels, for example.

of chemical bonds that hold the individual building-blocks together. To be digested, the chemical bonds between individual subunits need to be broken and specific enzymes are needed for this.

The enzyme amylase is needed to break the molecular bonds between the subunits of starch-amylose. Amylase is often found in the saliva of many species, where it initiates the digestive process of breaking down dietary starch. This is then continued in other parts of the digestive system, with amylase being produced in other organs such as the pancreas.

Dogs don't have significant levels of salivary amylase, so there is limited carbohydrate digestion in the mouth. However, research has demonstrated that dogs do produce amylase in other parts of their digestive system, notably from the pancreas. As a result, dogs do have the digestive capacity to digest the amylose form of starch and derive nutritional benefit from it. However, there is a breed difference in the capability of dogs to digest starch – huskies and northern breeds appear to have less capacity than springer spaniels, for example, a likely consequence of selective breeding.

Low-Carbohydrate Diets for Dogs

Because there has been some concern about feeding carbohydrates to dogs, and an increased desire by many caregivers to explore diets that might be more representative of what 'ancestral' dogs ate, there has been a move to feeding low-carbohydrate diets. This means that minimal grains or other plant material is included in the formulation. For some dogs, this is beneficial for a health and performance perspective – indeed, high-endurance dogs have better activity output when fed low-carbohydrate and high-fat diets. Some health conditions may also benefit from managed dietary carbohydrate levels.

The commercial dog-food world has responded to caregiver desires by formulating grain-free diets for dogs. This has been a significant growth area with sales of grain-free dog-food increasing significantly. However, these diets are not necessarily carbohydrate-free and often include potato or sweet potato as sources of carbohydrate, needed for production or formulation reasons. It is important that caregivers recognise this because some of these diets have different digestibility and nutrient bioavailability. Even faecal quality can be impacted (positively or negatively) by feeding diets that don't include more traditional dog-food ingredients. There has also been some concern about potential links of diets developed using alternative ingredients and heart problems in dogs, notably dilated cardiomyopathy (DCM). Research is continuing to explore the implications of alternative dietary ingredients in our dogs' food and to understand possible causative factors, both nutritionally and more generally.

Summary

- Carbohydrates are a major source of dietary energy and are found in different forms, from simple to very complex.
- Dogs have no minimum dietary need for carbohydrate as they can make their own, but pregnant, lactating and active dogs might benefit from additional dietary carbohydrate.
- Simple carbohydrates, such as glucose, are rapidly and easily digested and absorbed by dogs and are good sources of energy.
- Fibrous carbohydrates found in many plants cannot be digested by dogs but may be beneficial for digestive health.
- Dogs can produce the digestive enzyme amylase, meaning that they are capable of digesting starch carbohydrate.
- Grain-free dog-foods are not necessarily carbohydrate-free – they usually include alternative carbohydrate sources.

CHAPTER 7 Protein: The Building-Blocks of the Body

Protein in the Dog's Diet

Protein attracts much attention in the canine nutrition world. Protein is essential to grow, repair and reproduce, and effectively supplies the building-blocks of the body. Dietary protein can be provided from animal- or plant-derived ingredients, and there are costs and benefits to each. A wide range of proteins occur in nature. They are complex molecules that fulfil a number of key functions in biology. Dogs can use dietary protein as a source of energy but, in this chapter, we will explore the other roles that protein has, what our dogs need, as well as examining sustainability concerns about protein in canine nutrition.

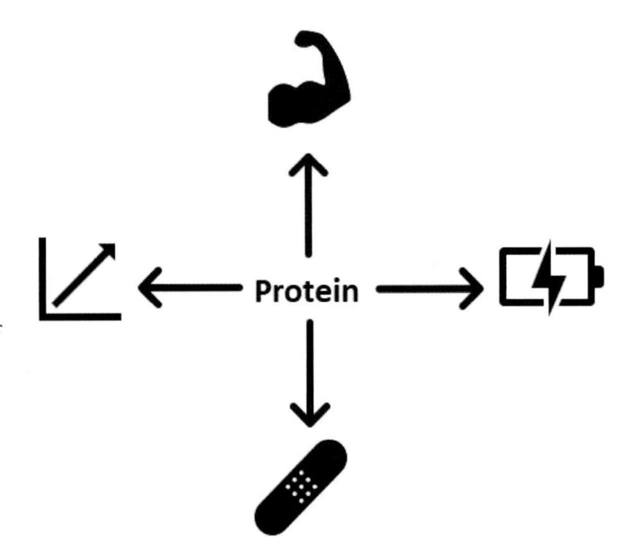

Protein is essential to support reproduction and growth, body structure and function, repair and it provides a dietary energy source.

The Importance of Protein

In our dogs, protein has many forms and functions. Collagen is a fibrous form of protein that is widely distributed within the body as a structural component of hair, nails, skin, ligaments, tendons and cartilage. Skeletal muscle is protein-rich in the form of structural and contractile proteins – notably actin and myosin that are essential for supporting muscle movement. Enzymes and hormones are proteins, and both groups of substances are critical for normal biological functioning. Various proteins help to keep the body under tight homeostatic control – that is, keeping the body's systems working safely within specific limits. Proteins also work as transporters to move substances around the body, and the immune system is heavily dependent upon protein to support normal functioning. The diversity of proteins found in the body is a consequence of differences in their fundamental structure. This also has nutritional consequences.

The Structure of Protein

Proteins are chains of molecules called amino acids, all linked together. Some proteins are small and consist of only a few amino acids, while others are long, complex chains of mixed amino acids. Differences in protein structure can affect their nutritional value. Large, complex proteins are often poorly digested and not particularly nutritionally valuable. Processing and cooking ingredients can alter the shape and structure of proteins, again affecting on their nutritional value. It is actually the amino acids that animals need in their diet rather than protein itself. Nitrogen is a key element found in protein (at approximately 16 per cent) and must be supplied in the diet. Dietary protein thus supplies amino acids and nitrogen, and this is why we refer to protein requirements in nutrition, acknowledging that it will supply both components.

Amino Acids – the Building-Blocks of Proteins

In nature, there are 22 amino acids commonly found in proteins. These are classified as 'essential', meaning that they must be supplied in the diet, or 'non-essential', which refers to the fact that these can be synthesised in the body and a dietary supply is not needed (*see* Table). Taurine is listed as a non-essential amino acid because dogs can synthesise their own. However, there is increasing interest in taurine in dog diets and its role in health, and it is likely that we will continue to learn more about the importance of taurine in dog diets.

Because proteins differ in their constituent amino acids, ingredients supply amino acids in different amounts. Some food ingredients are known to be limiting in certain amino acids, and diets need to be formulated carefully to take account of this to ensure adequate supply of key amino acids. A common way to achieve this is by mixing protein sources as ingredients – for example, using both animal and plant derived proteins in a diet. This can balance the supply of dietary amino acids.

The essential (must be supplied in the diet) and non-essential amino acids in canine nutrition

Essential amino acids	Non-essential amino acids
Arginine	Alanine
Histidine	Asparagine
Isoleucine	Aspartate
Leucine	Cysteine
Lysine	Glutamate
Methionine	Glutamine
Phenylalanine	Glycine
Tryptophan	Hydroxylysine
Threonine	Hydroxyproline
Valine	Proline
	Serine
	Tyrosine
	Taurine (?)

Protein Quality and Nutrition

Protein quality is important to consider because poor-quality protein will have low nutritional value for our dogs – it will not be digested and used effectively or efficiently in the body. You also need to feed more of diets containing low-quality protein to meet the dog's protein requirements. If the digestibility of protein is low, some of it will escape the digestive processes, overflow into the large intestine and be excreted in faeces. It may also cause digestive problems, including flatulence, if it is fermented by the intestinal microbiome. As the quality and digestibility of protein in the diet increases, the amount to be fed to meet needs can decrease, because more will be available following absorption.

Processing protein-rich ingredients (especially cooking at high temperatures) can affect the quality of the protein. However, there is a fine balance between levels of processing. Research shows that for some protein ingredients, light cooking can actually increase digestibility – lightly steamed chicken breast meat has a slightly higher digestibility than raw chicken breast, and both have higher digestibility than processed chicken meat. Some commercial dog-foods will have high levels of poor-quality protein with low digestibility – sometimes as low as 70 per cent. Diets formulated with high-quality protein can reach 90 per cent digestibility. This is significant, because where a dog needs a good source of dietary protein, you want to provide highly digestible forms. Equally, where a dog might benefit from weight management, reducing the digestibility of the diet might be beneficial, albeit with the caveat that their requirement for essential amino acids must be met. Notably, it is rare for digestibility values to be available for commercial dog-foods. This is because feeding trials are needed to determine digestibility, and they are time-consuming and expensive. As a result, digestibility values are often based on reference table data and estimated values from prior research. Information on the pack, including ingredient lists, rarely gives you any indication as to the quality or digestibility of protein ingredients.

The Biological Value (BV) of Proteins

Some protein sources are poor quality, based on their structure. This can affect the quality of the protein and its 'biological value (BV)'. High-quality dietary protein is highly digestible and has an amino acid profile that is similar to the body – this means that the protein has a high biological value also. Biological value is often expressed as a percentage – 100 per cent BV shows that the protein can be easily digested and that it supplies amino acids in the ideal amounts. Egg, milk and other animal-derived proteins have some of the highest BV at 75 per cent and above. Plant proteins tend to have lower BV – rice has a BV of about 65 per cent – because they tend to be more limited in their amino acid profile.

The Practical Impact of Protein Structure in the Dog's Diet

To feed your dog a high-quality, highly digestible diet that supplies protein that can be used by the body, look for protein ingredients that supply all the required amino acids. This might mean formulating a diet with mixed protein sources. Animal-derived protein sources that are high quality include egg, dairy and skeletal muscle (meat), although note that egg and dairy ingredients can cause problems for some dogs. Plant proteins can also be valuable – soya, rice and corn all have reasonable BV but are limited in some essential amino acids, so cannot be used in isolation. Ensure that the protein included has a good BV and has not been extensively or over-processed, as this will negatively affect its quality and nutritional value and increase the amount you need to feed to meet requirements.

The Protein Requirements of Our Dogs

Our dogs have a constant turnover of protein in the body. The body is constantly being repaired and parts replaced. Growing dogs need extra protein to supply the building-blocks for growth and development. Pregnant and lactating bitches need protein to support the development of puppies and the production of nutritious milk. Active, working and sporting dogs often need elevated levels of dietary protein in comparison to adult dogs at maintenance, to support the added demands on their bodies and the development of increased muscle mass. Notably, dogs recovering from injury or illness will often benefit from increased dietary protein, as will older dogs, whose ability to efficiently digest and absorb protein can diminish with age. It is clear that protein is important to support the health, structure and function of our dogs' bodies.

Protein is essential to support the overall health of our dogs, including growth, development and activity.

How Much Dietary Protein Does a Dog Need?

Our dogs need protein to be digestible and to supply the required amino acids to support their biology. The minimum amount of protein recommended for healthy adult dogs at maintenance is 18 per cent (18g/100g food DMB). This increases to 25 per cent (25g/100g food DMB) for young puppies (14 weeks old and younger) and pregnant/lactating bitches. If the diet of a pregnant/lactating bitch has no, or very little carbohydrate, then up to double this amount is needed to support the health of dam and puppies. Young, growing dogs older than 14 weeks need 20 per cent protein. These values are minimum recommended amounts and assume that the dietary protein has a minimum digestibility of 80 per cent and has sufficient levels of essential amino acids.

Protein Deficiency

Protein deficiency is rare, except in cases of extreme starvation or neglect. Protein-deficient dogs are underweight with poor body, skin and coat condition, and increased susceptibility to infections. Even for diets that otherwise provide sufficient protein, if dietary protein is not provided in a form that is digestible, then that can be problematic for our dogs and limit their ability to utilise it. Equally, in cases where a dog's physiological needs, pregnancy or performance, for example, exceed amounts supplied in the diet, then the success and survival of the offspring and performance output could be affected. There are also situations where individual amino acids might be limited – restricted ingredient use, for example, and this will lead to deficiency symptoms for specific amino acids, particularly the essential ones. In reality, most well-formulated diets supply more protein than is needed, but awareness of the risks of protein and amino acid deficiency is important.

Protein Excess

When excess dietary protein is provided to our dogs, they are very efficient at metabolising it and excreting it. Occasionally, excess protein not used as an energy supply will be converted to glycogen or fat – something to be aware of when managing a dog's weight. Unlike excess dietary fat or carbohydrate, excess protein (in the form of amino acids) is not usually stored in the body and is excreted in the form of urea in urine. When urine is

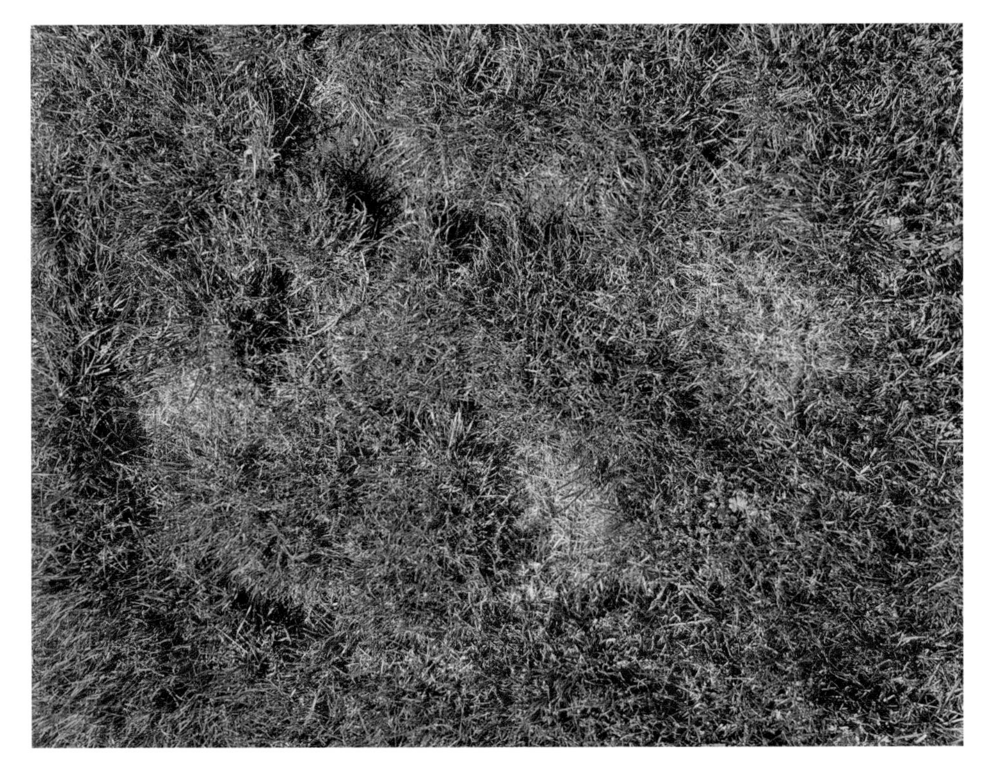

A characteristic of dog urine is that it 'burns' grass – a result of excreted waste products.

excessively smelly and even 'burns' lawns and plants, this is generally because of the compounds that are excreted as a result of protein processing in the body. Evidence has even shown that in areas frequented by dog walkers, the plant life at the side of paths is negatively affected by the amount of dog urine excreted.

Healthy dogs have no problem with managing the removal of excess protein and its breakdown products. Some health conditions will limit this process, however, and dietary protein levels might need managing to support normal function. Dogs in kidney (renal) failure often fall into this category – it was considered that high-protein diets caused kidney disease in dogs, but we now know this is not the case. Indeed, dogs with kidney issues often benefit from diets that supply quality, digestible protein to support the functioning of kidneys that are impaired. Levels of dietary protein are only restricted when dogs have significantly impaired kidney function and should be done under professional guidance. While excess dietary protein might not be a particular concern for the health and wellbeing of our dogs, it is something we need to consider in wider environmental sustainability concerns, both in terms of protein production and supply, as well as the environmental impacts of urea and other nitrogenous waste products that are environmentally damaging. It is also interesting to note that the bulk of feed and food costs are linked to their protein content – animal-derived protein being particularly expensive. Consequently, feeding excess protein is environmentally and financially costly.

Protein and Sustainability

Environmental sustainability is a key concern, and what we feed our dogs can have substantial environmental impacts. Production of animals to supply dietary protein as meat, eggs and dairy is an industry that can have significant negative environmental impacts. There is increasing pressure to reduce the demand for animal-derived products and to limit some of the environmental challenges that result. This also applies to what and how we feed our dogs.

Protein from animal-derived sources requires substantial amounts of energy, water, land and other resources to produce it. While animal-derived protein is often high quality and highly digestible from a nutritional perspective, increased demand for this protein source for feeding humans and animals is creating a serious environmental challenge. Put simply, the environment cannot continue to support the production of this type of protein long-term. The increased use of 'human or food grade' material as dog food is also creating direct competition for protein entering the human food-chain. Commercial dog and cat food originally used by-products from human food production, such as offal and meat and bonemeal. This in itself is a form of sustainability, as otherwise these by-products would be waste. In many cases, these by-products are still valuable for feeding our dogs because they are often not desirable for human consumption – sometimes because of choice, custom or culture.

The sustainability issue is not restricted to our dogs' diets. Globally, there is interest in exploring alternative sources of dietary protein for all species. Dog food is also seeing a shift in the use of certain ingredients and options are becoming available that are considered to be favourable steps towards improving sustainability.

Protein Alternatives for Dog Diets

Plant-Based Diets for Dogs

Plant-derived protein is one possibility that is already used in many dog diets. Plant protein is high quality and highly digestible, and more sustainable to produce than animal protein. However, the original plant source is important to consider. Many protein-producing plants are grown abroad and need to be flown around the world. Others are grown in areas that have been reclaimed from rain forest or other protected habitats. Nutritionally, not all plant proteins supply all the required amino acids, so formulations need to account for this. Plant products also need varying degrees of processing in order to make their nutrients available, as well as limit the effects of compounds within plants known as anti-nutritional factors. These can affect digestion and the bioavailability of certain nutrients. This is, however, countered by the fact that many plant ingredients supply a host of other beneficial nutrients, from antioxidants to fibre, and there do appear to be health benefits from including fruit, vegetables and other plant-derived ingredients

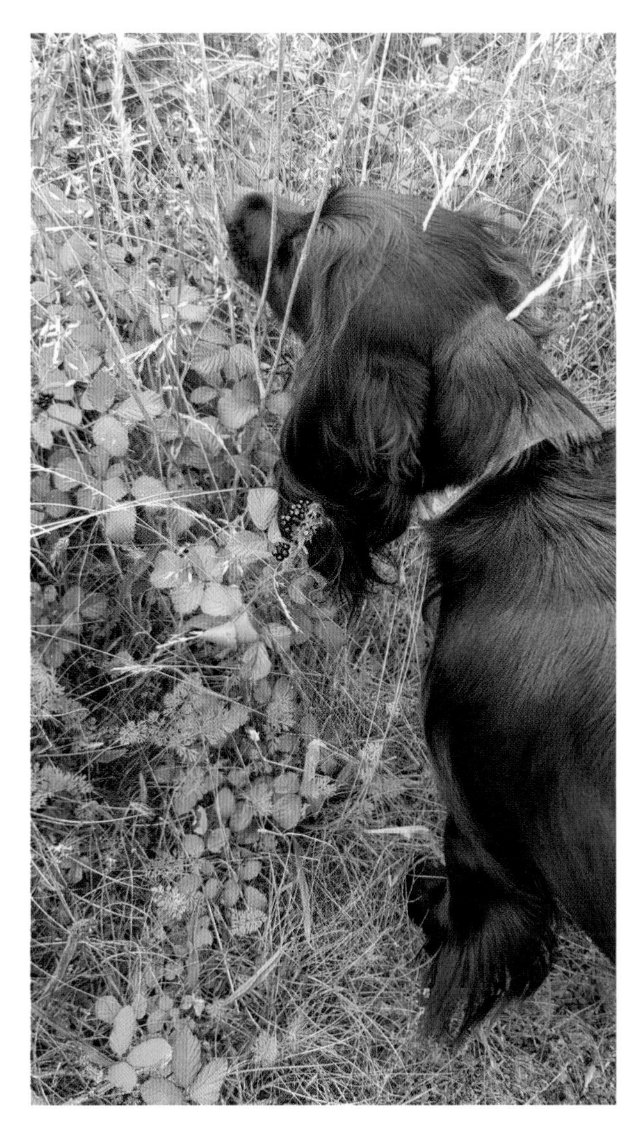

Dogs often self-select plant material, including fruit and vegetables.

in our dogs' diets. Many dogs will also actively choose to consume plants, despite having a taste preference for animal-derived ingredients. Plant proteins are also cheaper to produce, meaning that they are often a cost-effective way of supplying nutrients in a diet. So, adding plant-derived ingredients and protein sources into our dogs' diets can have a range of environmental, financial, nutritional and, potentially, health benefits for our dogs.

Can Dogs be Vegetarian or Vegan?

Some caregivers are choosing to explore flexitarian, vegetarian or vegan diets for their dogs. This might be a caregiver lifestyle choice, an environmental choice or sometimes to support dogs that have dietary intolerances. It is possible to formulate a vegan or vegetarian diet for dogs that supplies all the required nutrients in the right amounts and forms, but this is not necessarily easy and does need professional input, as well as supplementation in most cases. A number of diets are now commercially available that meet this evolving need in canine nutrition – some are better formulated than others, so care should be taken. Unlike the domestic cat that absolutely needs a number of nutrients that can only be obtained from animal-derived tissue, dogs can thrive on diets with no or minimal animal ingredients. The debate about whether dogs themselves would choose vegetarianism or veganism is beyond the scope of this book.

Insect-Based Dog Food

Insects are another alterative and sustainable source of protein for animal diets. Wild canids will often eat insects as part of their usual diet, and their nutritional profile is favourable. The production of insects on a commercial scale for animal diets is also linked to sustainability gains over animal-production systems. Insects are a good source of high-quality and highly digestive protein, with a good profile of constituent amino acids.

Insects as a protein source are gaining interest in the animal nutrition world, including as dog-food ingredients.

Providing the insects have been processed appropriately, their tough external 'skeletons' and other components that would limit their usefulness as ingredients is minimised. Research suggests that insect meals and flours are highly acceptable to dogs, and make useful and sustainable ingredients in dog food and treats. Insect ingredients might also be useful for dogs with allergies and intolerances to more conventional ingredients. It is likely that insects, such as the black soldier fly, will increasingly become mainstream ingredient options, for both commercially produced and home-prepared dog-food.

Summary

- Protein supplies the building-blocks for our dogs' body structure and function.
- Dogs can use protein as an energy source, but excess protein will be excreted and not stored.
- The nutritional value of protein depends on its quality, digestibility and comprising amino acids.
- Active, reproducing and growing dogs will benefit from digestible diets high in quality protein.
- Alternative sources of dietary protein are attracting increased interest to meet sustainability, financial and health needs.

CHAPTER 8 Fat: Is it Your Dog's Friend?

Fat is often a dietary component that we view with fear. Anyone who has had to be aware of their waistline, or that of their dog, will know that the level of dietary fat is something to be aware of. Excess fat in the diet is linked with an increased risk of developing overweight and obesity, both of which predispose animals to a range of health and wellbeing problems. However, while knowing the levels of fat in the food we eat and feed to our dogs is important, we also need to appreciate the key roles that dietary fat has – indeed, dietary fat actually consists of many distinct types.

Not all fats are bad and not all fats are equal either. Indeed, many fats (in the right amount) are essential for normal health and function. Other fats can be useful to support overall health and wellbeing. Sometimes reducing the amount of fat in a diet is critical to support a healthy waistline or manage health conditions. In other situations, fat is essential to support the activity of working or sporting dogs, and levels might need to be substantially increased in a diet.

This chapter will explore the chemistry of dietary fat and its nutritional importance for our dogs. A key characteristic of dietary fat is that one gram of fat provides more than twice the kilocalories of protein or carbohydrate. This is significant when considering the amount of fat that a diet supplies for particular situations – managing weight loss versus supporting performance output, for example.

The Terminology

Dietary Fat

Fat is one of the energy-providing macronutrients found in food. Fat is also one of the components included in the information on the label of commercially available food. Dietary fat is a term that encompasses a range of chemically related substances that have certain characteristics – a key one being that they are insoluble in water.

Fats or Lipids?

All fats belong to a group of compounds called lipids – a class of molecules that includes the fats and oils. Fats are traditionally viewed as being solid at room temperature, e.g. lard or butter. Oils, such as olive or vegetable oil, are liquid at room temperature. These different properties are a result of differences in their chemical structure. In nutrition, the terms 'fat' and 'lipid' are often used interchangeably, but lipid is more scientifically correct to describe the whole class of compounds.

Fats and Fatty Acids

Triglycerides (TGs; also known as triacylglycerols, TAGs, or triacylglycerides) are the most common form of fat found in dog diets. The basic structure of a TG is one molecule of glycerol linked to three fatty acids.

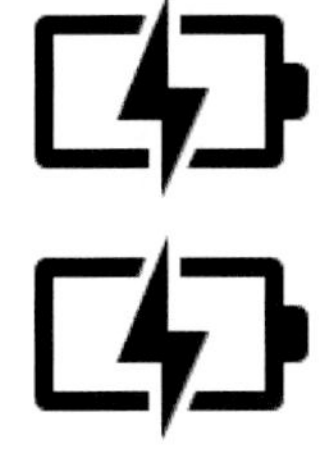

Dietary fat supplies more than twice the energy per gram than either protein or carbohydrate.

The fatty acids consist of carbon atoms in a chain, with 'branches' of hydrogen atoms – this is where the term 'hydrocarbon' comes from. The chain of carbon atoms differs in length and the names of fatty acids reflect the number of carbons. These fatty acids are significant chemical stores of energy and are why dietary fat is a significant source of kilocalories in the diet. Most fatty acids are long chains of between sixteen and twenty-six carbon atoms, but some are called short-chain fatty acids (SCFAs) and medium-chain triglycerides (MCTs). SCFAs have fewer than six carbon atoms and are produced by microbial digestion of fibre in the digestive system. SCFAs can be used as a source of energy and are also beneficial for digestive health. MCTs are typically between eight and ten carbon atoms long. Coconut oil is a useful source of MCTs and there may be some health benefits to MCTs' inclusion in the diet of older dogs and epileptic dogs. Elevated levels of MCTs in a diet can reduce palatability and cause digestive upset, however, so care should be taken. They are also a rich source of extra kilocalories, so potentially problematic for weight management.

Saturated and Unsaturated fats

Fats are often described as being saturated or unsaturated. You might also have heard of polyunsaturated and monounsaturated fats. These terms refer to the bonding between carbon atoms in their constituent fatty acids. Saturated fatty acids only have single bonds between carbon atoms. Unsaturated fatty acids have double bonds between carbon atoms – the presence of one double bond in a fatty acid means it is called monounsaturated and if there are multiple double bonds, then the fatty acid is a polyunsaturated fatty acid (PUFA).

The level of saturation of dietary fats is important. Saturated fats tend to be solid with a higher melting temperature than unsaturated fats. They tend to come from animal-derived ingredients, such as beef, pork, lamb and dairy. Saturated fats are chemically unreactive but can be problematic for health in terms of how the body digests, absorbs and uses them. Unsaturated fats are often found as oils and include many vegetable and plant oils, as well as oils derived from whole fish or particular parts, such as cod liver oil. Unsaturated fats are often considered to be more 'healthy' than saturated fats and there appear to be some particular health benefits to including them in the diet.

What Does Fatty Acid Saturation Mean for My Dog and How I Feed It?

Unsaturated fats are more reactive than saturated fats and can go rancid more rapidly, especially if exposed to heat, light and metals. This is of practical importance because rancid fats are less palatable and can be dangerous for health. Rancidity (effectively the fat goes 'off') creates other chemical compounds, which often have a distinct smell, but these affect the taste of the food and cause oxidative damage in the body. For this reason, unsaturated fats that are to be added to a diet (either during manufacturing or at home) should be carefully stored – ideally in a cool, dark place such as the fridge. Antioxidants, such as vitamin E, should also be added to a diet high in unsaturated fats to counterbalance the potential for oxidative damage. Equally, prepared dog food of all types should be stored carefully, especially if high in fat. Dry kibble is often surface-coated with fat. If that fat is unsaturated (sunflower oil and other plant oils are commonly used)

Fat from dry dog-food can coat food containers and go rancid. It is good practice to wash containers well with warm, soapy water between different batches of food.

then rancidity is a concern if the food is poorly stored. Cleaning food containers well is also important to remove residual fat that can become rancid.

The Function of Fats

Fats are essential in the body and fulfil a wide range of important roles. While we don't want our dogs to carry excess fat stores, fat deposits (in the form of adipose tissue) in the body are important for protection against physical injury and insulation against cold. Our dogs' paw-pads, for example, have protective fat layers within. The cells that make up our dogs' tissues and organs depend on fats to support their overall structure and integrity, and various fatty acids are important for development and the functioning of the nervous system. More generally, dietary fat is a key source of energy to support activity, as well as being the source of fat-soluble vitamins and essential fatty acids (EFAs).

Fat is useful for active dogs.

Fat is Our Active Dog's Friend

In contrast to many other species, dogs have an impressive ability to use dietary fat as a source of energy. Indeed, dogs have a metabolism that preferentially uses fat over either carbohydrate or protein as an energy source. This means that dogs do not usually suffer some of the unfortunate consequences of a high-fat diet that humans do, such as high cholesterol or heart disease. Some breeds and types, however, do have genetic issues related to how well they deal with dietary fat, so sometimes care does needs to be taken. Additionally, any excess dietary fat is a problem for our dogs' waistlines. Active, working and sporting dogs benefit from diets high in fat, as do active, growing dogs and pregnant/lactating bitches – all of whom have high energetic demands. Dietary fat also enhances the palatability, texture and digestibility of our dogs' food. Diets formulated for weight management are often not as tasty for our dogs as a result. The other important aspect of dietary fat is that it increases the energy density of that diet. This might be important for dogs that need high dietary provision of energy, and/or have reduced appetites. This often occurs with very fit, very active dogs and those who undertake prolonged, endurance activities – sled dogs, for example.

Oily fish is a good source of omega-3 fatty acids. Tinned sardines can be a useful addition to our dog's diets.

Essential Fatty Acids (EFAs)

The EFAs are an important class of fats that are important in the body for supporting normal hormone function, circulatory health, blood-clotting, immune and inflammatory processes, and a host of other essential roles in the body. EFAs are so called because they cannot be synthesised by the body and must be supplied in the diet. Deficiencies in EFAs typically result in poor skin and coat condition and increased susceptibility to infections. There are several types of EFAs, but the omega fatty acids are increasingly interesting from a nutrition and wellbeing perspective for our dogs.

The Omega Fatty Acids

The omega fatty acids form distinct families of EFAs, with omega-3 and omega-6 fatty acids attracting particular attention, although omega-9 fatty acids also of interest. The omega fatty acids are polyunsaturated fats and the classes are so called because of the relative location of the first carbon–carbon double-bond in the fatty acid chain. This confers a very particular chemical structure that gives the omega fatty acids certain properties that are important for health. The levels of different omega fatty acids need to be carefully balanced for good health. Modern food production methods often mean that both human and dog diets have much higher omega-6 levels than omega-3 fatty acids. This can have some health and nutritional consequences. This is because omega-6 fatty acids tend to be linked to pro-inflammatory processes in the body, while omega-3 fatty acids appear to manage and potentially reduce inflammation. Consequently, (re) balancing the dietary levels of omega-3s and omega-6s is becoming increasingly important. The ratio of omega-6 to omega-3 fatty acids in the diet is important and should ideally be around 5:1, not exceeding 10:1, although some ingredients and forms of processing can skew the ratio in favour of omega-6 fatty acids. Research suggests that increasing dietary omega-3 fatty acid levels can be a straightforward way to support overall nutrition and health.

Omega-6 Fatty Acids

Dogs need three key fatty acids for normal biological function – linoleic acid, gamma-linolenic acid (GLA) and arachidonic acid (AA). All three are omega-6 fatty acids. Linoleic acid is an important omega-6 fatty acid because it acts as a 'parent' molecule from which gamma-linolenic acid (GLA) and arachidonic acid (AA) can be synthesised by dogs. This means that providing there is an adequate dietary supply of linoleic acid, then there is no requirement for GLA or AA to be provided in the dogs' diet. Common sources of linoleic acid include vegetable oils. Animal-derived fats tend to have low levels, although they are a good source of arachidonic acid. Omega-6 fatty acids are important to support the normal functioning of the immune system, but excess levels can become problematic and pro-inflammatory.

Omega-3 Fatty Acids

Oily fish, such as herring, salmon and sardines, are well known to be a good source of omega-3 fatty acids, although they are also found in some plants, seeds and nuts. Linseed (sometimes called flaxseed) and some other plant-derived oils are good sources of alpha-linolenic acid (ALA), which is not to be confused with the omega-6 fatty acid GLA. ALA can function as a 'parent' molecule from which other omega-3 fatty acids can be synthesised. The important omega-3 fatty acids for health are EPA (eicosapentaenoic acid) and DHA (docosahexaenoic acid). EPA and DHA have been shown to confer benefits for growing puppies in terms of eye, brain and behavioural development, as well as supporting the management of inflammatory conditions in adult dogs. Dogs are capable of synthesising EPA and DHA in the body from ALA, but the process is not very efficient. Consequently, to supply effective omega-3 fatty acids for health support, then directly supplying EPA and DHA is the best way.

EPA and DHA

Research has shown that both EPA and DHA confer significant health benefits in a range of species, including humans and dogs. EPA and DHA have anti-inflammatory effects. This means that for dogs with conditions linked to inflammation, such joint and skin conditions, a dietary supply of these fatty acids in the diet can be useful. EPA and DHA are also important for the health of the eye, heart, reproductive system and nervous system, including cognition. Diets rich in EPA and DHA can also support the activity of working and sporting dogs, and are important to support the development and learning of puppies. Puppy diets often have enhanced levels of EPA and DHA as a result.

Because the synthesis of EPA and DHA from ALA is not very efficient in the body, plant sources of dietary omega-3 are not ideal. Plant sources of omega-3 fatty acids will provide some nutritional benefits in the form of ALA but adding pre-formed EPA and DHA directly to your dog's diet is the most effective way of providing your dog with these key fatty acids. Marine algae are highly efficient at converting ALA to EPA and DHA. The fish and shellfish that eat marine algae become good sources of EPA and DHA, meaning that you can feed oily fish, such as sardines, direct to your dog. Equally, the marine algae itself is a reliable source of EPA and DHA. Supplements of fish oil can be used, although there are increasing concerns about contamination, rancidity and sustainability of fish oils. Alternative sources include shellfish, such as green-lipped mussels or marine algae powder. Marine algae are more environmentally sustainable than fish and are also useful for dogs that dislike or cannot have fish in their diet. Always look for declared levels of ALA, EPA and DHA on any supplements, so that you can make informed choices about how much to add – this might be important if you need to add certain amounts as recommended by your vet or nutritionist to support certain conditions. If you are feeding a well-formulated diet, it might already have a suitable ratio of omega-6 to omega-3 fatty acids. Indeed, care should be taken, as it is possible to feed too much omega-3 in the diet, which can affect blood-clotting and other systems, so checking the overall levels for your individual dog's situation is essential.

Fat Requirements

The amount of fat that our dogs need in their diet will differ based on individual circumstances. Highly active dogs, underweight dogs, pregnant/lactating dogs and growing dogs will all benefit from diets that are higher in fat – these diets will be energy-dense, palatable, digestible and provide the calories needed. However, because dietary fat is also a source of vitamins and EFAs, all dogs do need some fat in their diet – even those who are on weight-management plans.

How Much Fat is Needed?

When a diet is correctly formulated, it will supply the required amount of energy in a suitable amount. Dogs need fat to supply calories for energy, fat-soluble vitamins and EFAs. Different requirements for individual dogs will mean that ingredients that add fat to the diet will differ in the amounts added to diets. Recommendations suggest a minimum of 5.5g fat per 100g of food (DMB) for adult dogs. This is increased to a minimum of 8.5g for reproducing and growing dogs. Many adult maintenance diets will have fat levels of between 12 and 16 per cent (DMB), although some will be much lower. Diets for weight management or specific health conditions will often be less than 10 per cent fat (DMB) and diets for dogs needing more energy will have higher fat levels, sometimes 20 per cent plus (DMB). Consequently, most dog food supplies more than the minimum fat requirement. It is important to be aware of this when considering feeding for weight management. Remember, if you are looking at high-moisture foods, such as raw or tinned, the value on the pack will need converting to DMB for correct comparison to low moisture/dry foods and will be much lower than the actual dry matter fat content of the food. If you are home-preparing meals, their nutritional profile should also be formulated and assessed on a DMB.

Summary

- Fat supplies more than twice the calories per gram than carbohydrate and protein.
- Dogs will preferentially use dietary fat for energy instead of carbohydrate or protein, so active, reproducing and growing dogs will benefit from diets higher in fat than standard maintenance diets, and it is our dogs' friend.
- Diets or supplements that are high in fat can rancid quickly, so correct storage in a cool, dark and air-tight environment is good practice.
- Antioxidants, such as vitamin E, are often added to diets high in fat and should be supplemented if dogs are consuming high-fat diets.
- Omega-3 fatty acids are important for your dog's immune, heart, eye, brain health and to support puppy learning and development.
- Oily fish, such as herring or sardines, can be a tasty, omega-3-rich treat for your dog.

CHAPTER 9 Vitamins and Minerals

Vitamins and minerals are micronutrients. This means that while essential for health, the amounts required in the dog's diet are small in comparison to the macronutrients of fat, carbohydrate and protein. Vitamins and minerals have essential roles in supporting the body's metabolic processes and must be supplied in the diet to meet those needs, although dogs do have the capacity to synthesise some vitamins themselves.

A well-formulated and balanced diet will supply adequate levels of essential vitamins and minerals. This is achieved by using a variety of ingredients that are sources of these micronutrients. However, sometimes there can be issues with the appropriate supply or bioavailability of some vitamins and minerals. This results in deficiency or potentially toxic excess, and diet formulation needs to account for this. Because deficiencies in many vitamins and minerals tend to be cumulative in their effects, it can actually take time for the signs of deficiency to appear. This is especially relevant for home-prepared diets where appropriate micronutrient levels are sometimes poorly managed and care needs to be taken to ensure that appropriate levels are supplied. This is also a risk with any diet that has not been formulated, stored or even processed appropriately.

It is also important to know that vitamins and minerals have the potential to cause significant harm if fed in excess of safe levels. Indeed, each micronutrient has a specific deficient–optimal–toxic response curve. Some micronutrients, such as vitamin E, have a broad 'safe' level of intake, whereas others, such as selenium, have a much smaller 'safe' intake amount.

An awareness of the roles, importance, signs of excess and signs of deficiency of the key vitamins and minerals

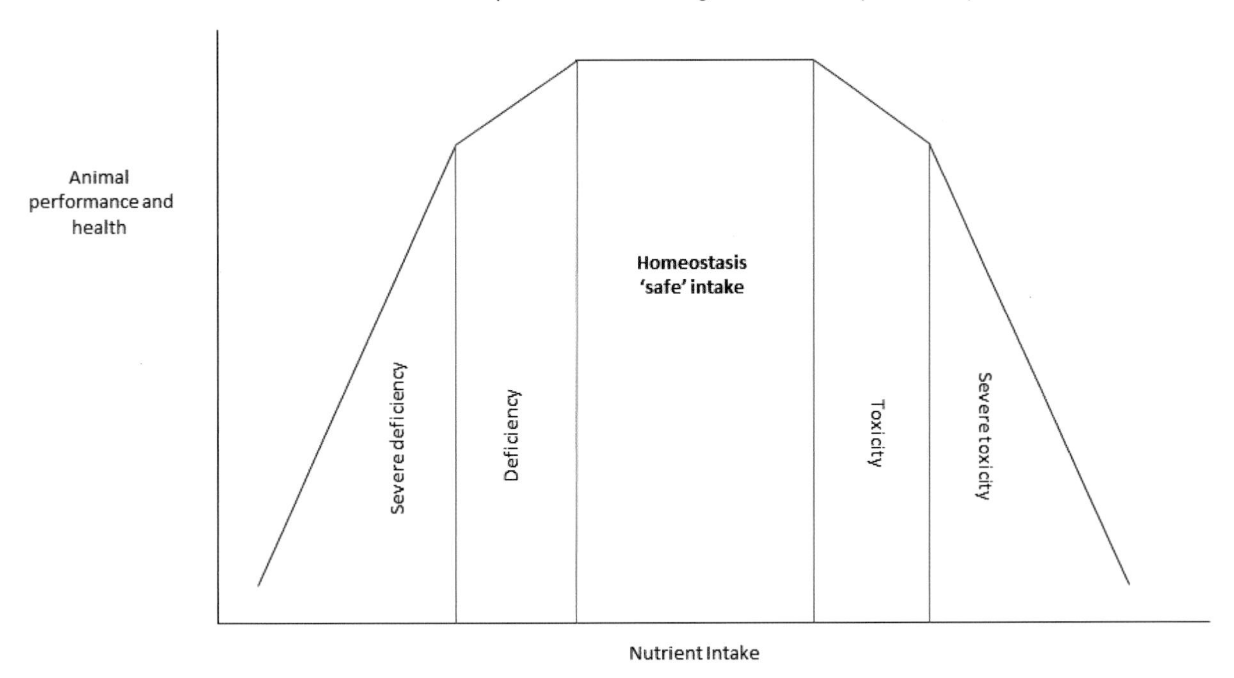

A typical response-curve for micronutrients in the diet. Each micronutrient has its own specific response curve, and some will have much wider 'safe' intake zones than others.

in our dogs' diets can help us to make sure that we provide a safe and suitable dietary supply of them. This will be achieved either in the food fed, the ingredients incorporated or supplements used. Commercial diets typically use vitamin and mineral 'premixes' to fortify their diets, supplementing nutrients lost or damaged during processing or storage. Home-prepared diets often need to use mixed ingredients to provide key micronutrients, and supplements might be needed if there is a shortfall or bioavailability issues. Sometimes we will use specific micronutrient supplements to support specific health conditions in our dogs, even where dietary supply appears adequate.

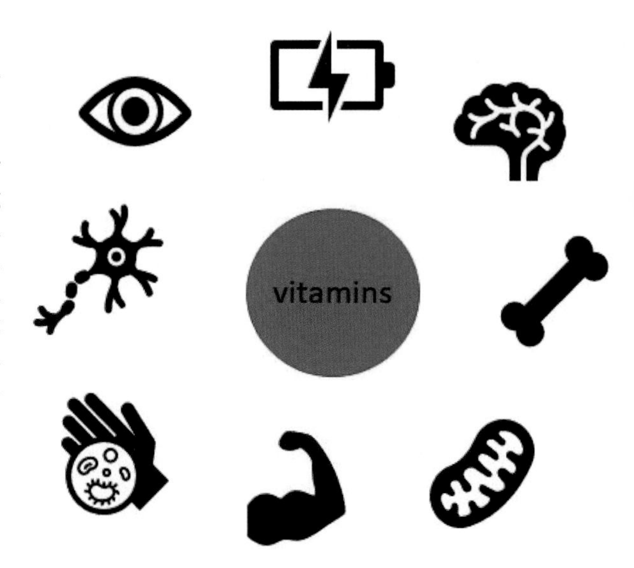

Vitamins are essential to support many body functions, including energy release from food and bone health.

Vitamins

Long before the chemistry of vitamins was understood, it was known that some diseases were related to diet. Scurvy was a particular issue for sailors spending long periods at sea, without access to fresh fruit and vegetables. We now understand that they were suffering from a lack of vitamin C, a situation that was reversed when it became standard for sailors to be given fresh limes to eat whilst at sea.

Unlike humans, dogs can make their own vitamin C. Even so, there are certain situations when additional vitamin C is beneficial for our dogs. Indeed, while each vitamin has a recommended minimum dietary level, sometimes those levels need to be altered or managed. This might be as a result of genetic traits in certain breeds, health conditions or even simply because the dog's activity level or physiological state needs more support.

The term 'vitamin' was first described by the Polish biochemist Casimir Funk before vitamin chemistry was fully understood. The original naming system for vitamins involved simply naming them after letters of the alphabet and nine vitamins, from A to I, were originally described. While some of this naming system remains, there have been additions and amends, with some compounds later discovered not to be true vitamins, such as vitamin F (now known to be essential fatty acids), and others were mixtures of several different vitamins – the vitamin B complex.

Vitamins are organic substances that are critical for normal body function but are not used as energy sources or for body structures. They are classified as either water-soluble, which includes the vitamin B complex and vitamin C, or fat-soluble, which includes vitamins A, D, E and K.

Water-Soluble Vitamins

The water-soluble vitamins include vitamin C and vitamin B complex, which comprise compounds known by their number or specific name. Water-soluble vitamins have a wide safety margin, as any excess is usually excreted, meaning that toxicity, or hypervitaminosis, is unlikely. However, these vitamins are not stored in the body, so a regular dietary supply is required. In most cases, dogs synthesise adequate levels of their own vitamin C and their diet provides adequate B vitamins.

Vitamin C

Dogs are able to synthesise their own vitamin C, meaning that a dietary supply is not needed. Vitamin C is a powerful antioxidant, however, and supplementation might be useful for highly active dogs or those recovering from severe illness. Because vitamin C is synthesised in the liver, dogs with liver problems may also benefit from supplementation. Vitamin C is also important for supporting the health of the skin – in some cases, additional dietary vitamin C might be useful.

B Vitamins

There are eight B vitamins and choline, a vitamin-like substance, originally designated as vitamin B4 (*see* Table).

The water-soluble vitamins of importance in the dog's diet

Vitamin	Function	Common dietary sources	Signs of deficiency	Signs of excess
Vitamin B1 (Thiamine)	• Supports nervous system health	• Yeast • Wheat • Grains • Meat	• Nervous system issues • Weakness • Lack of energy	• Rare
Vitamin B2 (Riboflavin)	• Skin and coat health • Eye and visual health	• Synthesised in the intestine • Liver • Eggs • Yeast	• Lack of energy • Skin issues • Eye problems • Growth issues • Nervous system issues	• Rare
Vitamin B3 (Niacin)	• Energy production in cells • Skin and coat health	• Meat • Fish • Cereals • Mushrooms	• Lack of energy • Skin issues • Digestive issues	• Liver damage • Gastric ulcers
Vitamin B4 (Choline)	• Metabolic reactions • Cell membrane structure • Nerve impulses	• Eggs • Liver	• Fatty liver	• Poor red blood cell formation
Vitamin B5 (pantothenic acid)	• Co-factor for energy production in cells	• Meat • Eggs • Dairy	• Growth issues • Rare	• Rare
Vitamin B6 (Pyridoxine)	• Skin health • Nervous system function	• Meat • Wheatgerm • Yeast	• Lack of energy • Anaemia • Growth issues	• Rare
Vitamin B7 (Biotin)	• Skin health • Nervous system function	• Liver • Eggs • Yeast	• Poor skin, coat and nail condition	• Rare
Vitamin B9 (Folic acid)	• Red blood cell function • Development • Protein synthesis	• Liver • Green vegetables • Yeast	• Developmental problems • Anaemia	• Rare
Vitamin B12 (Cobalamin)	• Red blood cell function	• Liver • Meat/fish	• Anaemia • Lack of energy	• Rare
Vitamin C (Ascorbic acid)	• Antioxidant • Supports skin health	• Synthesised in the liver • Fruit and vegetables	• Scurvy – poor skin condition • Anaemia	• Rare

The B vitamins are primarily involved in critical metabolic reactions and the release of energy from food. B vitamins tend to co-exist in the same food. Meat, eggs, nutritional yeast and dairy are rich sources, although some plants are also. Well-formulated dog-foods will supply sufficient levels of B vitamins but, occasionally, supplementation is needed. Some genetic conditions can affect the absorption of B vitamins in the small intestine, as can digestive illness. The intestinal microbiome synthesizes some B vitamins. Digestive upset and disruption to the microbiome can affect levels of synthesis. In these situations, supplementation with vitamin B12 is often useful. Vitamin B6 requirements increase as the amount of protein in the diet increases and for active dogs, the B vitamins are important to support their metabolism and energy generation. Folic acid is important for normal foetal development. Supplementation of pregnant bitches with folic acid before mating and during early pregnancy, may reduce the incidence of some developmental disorders. Dogs with skin and nail problems might benefit from supplementation with biotin and other B vitamins. The bioavailability of B vitamins can also be affected by other dietary ingredients. Biotin deficiency can be caused by feeding high levels of raw egg white, which contains a substance that binds to biotin, making it unavailable. Similarly, thiamine (vitamin B1) deficiency can occur when high levels of raw, white fish are fed – this is due to an enzyme, thiaminase, that destroys the thiamine. Thiaminase is destroyed by cooking, a useful way to process food ingredients and minimise this risk.

The Fat-Soluble Vitamins

The fat-soluble vitamins, A, D, E and K, are absorbed in the small intestine and are mostly stored in the liver and fatty tissues of the body (*see* Table). These stores can be useful during periods of nutritional deficiency but also means that excess levels of these vitamins can lead to toxic consequences. Some fat-soluble vitamins are found in plant tissues as provitamins, which are converted to functional vitamins after ingestion. A good example is beta-carotene, or pro-vitamin A, commonly found in carrots.

Vitamin A

The dog has a high tolerance for excess dietary vitamin A, meaning that toxicity is rare. Vitamin A is important for normal vision, immune and reproductive function. Deficiency in vitamin A affects these systems, as well as impacting on skin condition, and skeletal structure and development, if the deficiency occurs during growth. Vitamin A deficiency is rare in dogs as they can convert beta-carotene to the active form of vitamin A, and commercial diets contain adequate amounts.

Vitamin D

Unlike humans, dogs have a limited capacity to synthesise the active form of vitamin D in their skin from sunlight. This means that dogs need a dietary supply of vitamin D to support their skeletal structure and to maintain normal body levels of the minerals calcium and phosphorous. Vitamin D is closely linked with the regulation of calcium and phosphorus levels in the body – deficiencies or excess of any of these nutrients can result in severe skeletal abnormalities, especially in growing puppies.

Vitamin E

Vitamin E is a powerful antioxidant and is useful for highly active dogs and should be supplemented in dog diets that are high in polyunsaturated fatty acids, such as when fish oils are added. Older dogs can benefit from vitamin E supplementation to help to reduce the impact of age-related changes. Vitamin E is often added to commercial dog-food as an antioxidant to reduce rancidity. Vitamin E works synergistically with selenium and levels of the two nutrients need to be balanced for optimum function.

Vitamin K

Vitamin K is a group of compounds, critical for normal blood-clotting mechanisms. Deficiency is rare, although dogs that have accidentally eaten some forms of rodent poison are treated by administration of vitamin K. The dog's intestinal microbiome synthesises vitamin K as a by-product, which can then be absorbed and utilised, although commercial diets will provide adequate levels also.

Minerals

Minerals are only required in small amounts in your dog's diet but are essential for normal body structure and function. Minerals are known by their common name, as well as their characteristic chemical symbol. Common minerals are recognisable elements such as iron (Fe) and copper (Cu). Other minerals are less well-known, but are also important for metabolic function, such as manganese (Mn) and selenium (Se). Minerals are split into macrominerals, which are required in larger quantities (g/day) in the diet than the microminerals (mg/day), also known as trace elements. Examples of macrominerals include calcium and phosphorus. The microminerals are more numerous and include examples such as cobalt (Co) and molybdenum (Mo).

All minerals are termed inorganic because they are single chemical elements that do not include carbon.

The fat-soluble vitamins of importance in the dog's diet

Vitamin	Function	Common dietary sources	Signs of deficiency	Signs of excess
Vitamin A	• Growth and development • Eye and visual health • Supports immune health	• Fish oils • Liver • Eggs • Fruit and vegetables • Premixes	• Poor growth • Skeletal abnormalities • Poor reproduction • Skin issues • Eye problems	• Skeletal issues • Joint disorders • Skin disorders
Vitamin D	• Maintenance of skeletal structures • Regulation of calcium and phosphorus levels	• Fish oils • Fish meal • Egg yolk • Premixes	• Skeletal abnormalities – rickets • Incorrect levels of calcium and phosphorus	• Calcium in soft tissue • Excess calcium in the blood • Renal issues
Vitamin E	• Antioxidant • Works with selenium • Supports immune health	• Cereal grains • Liver • Eggs	• Skin disorders • Skeletal muscle changes • Immune system dysfunction	• Rare
Vitamin K	• Blood-clotting • Calcium uptake in bones	• Synthesised in the intestine • Liver • Green, leafy vegetables	• Blood-clotting disorders • Growth disorders	• Skin disorders

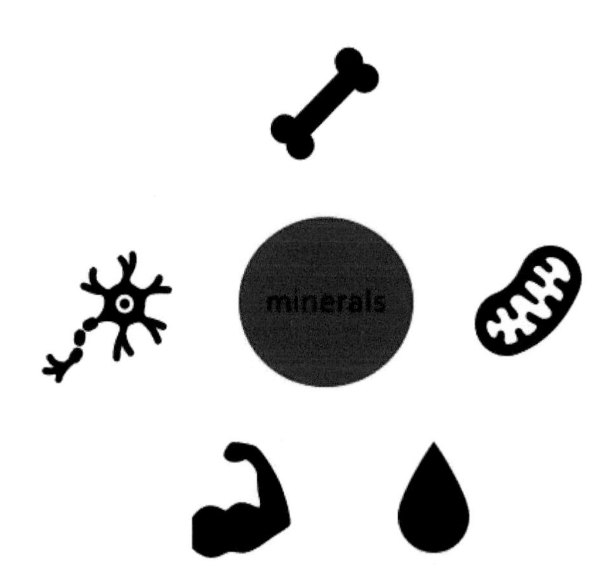

Minerals are involved in a number of key body processes, including skeletal structure, fluid balance, energy generation and functioning of the nervous system.

However, minerals are often found in specific chemical forms within foods, often as salts, meaning the mineral element forms a compound with another element. Table salt, also known as sodium chloride, is a good example of this, consisting of both sodium and chlorine, two minerals, each with important roles in the body. The mineral forms that exist in different foods can affect their bioavailability and this must be considered when formulating diets.

Approximately 4 per cent of an animal's bodyweight consists of minerals, most being found in the skeleton, which is rich in calcium (Ca) and phosphorous (P). Other minerals are also important, but are found in much smaller amounts, such as iodine (I), which is critical for the functioning of the thyroid gland and the production of hormones involved in the regulation of metabolism.

Electrolytes

The electrolytes are a classification of minerals that carry electric charge in the body and are critical for normal cell function. Electrolytes are required for the transmission of nerve impulses and a whole range of other essential body functions, including maintaining the water balance and pH of the body. Minerals that typically function as electrolytes include calcium (Ca), potassium (K), sodium (Na), phosphorus (P) and chloride ions. Electrolytes are lost when animals sweat and need to be replaced in highly active animals and those living in warm climates. However, because sweating is limited in dogs, electrolyte loss via this route is minimal and a balanced diet will normally supply sufficient levels of electrolytes.

Mineral Requirements

The exact dietary requirements for minerals are difficult to determine. There are reference ranges available that indicate minimum to maximum levels. However, the wide variation in the biology of the domestic dog means that a single 'recommended daily amount' to cover all individual dogs and their situations is unlikely to be appropriate. There is also the complication that minerals interact with each other (as well as with other nutrients) and simply adding one mineral to a diet because of a suspected deficiency, can cause additional issues. This is because some minerals have antagonistic interactions with others, meaning that increasing the level of one, also necessitates increasing dietary levels of another in order to avoid dietary deficiencies. Similarly, some minerals work with each other, or with other nutrients, and levels need carefully balanced. There is a close relationship between selenium and vitamin E, for example, and the levels of each need careful consideration. It is also possible for some minerals to work in an agonistic way with others, which can mean they become more bioavailable to the animal. Care should be taken when supplementing, because some minerals have a narrow safely margin and toxicity is a concern.

There are more than sixty minerals found in the dog's body, although not all of these are considered essential. Many are present in the body because they exist in the food and water consumed. Minerals considered important for our dogs are considered individually.

Macrominerals of Importance in the Dog's Diet

Calcium (Ca) and Phosphorous (P)

Ca and P are critical for skeletal development and health. They also have a number of other functions in the body, but their bioavailability can vary, and requirements change throughout a dog's life. A dietary ratio of Ca:P of 1.2:1 is generally considered ideal, and a minimum of 1 per cent Ca and 0.8 per cent P for growth and reproduction. Large-breed puppies are more sensitive to Ca and P levels while growing than smaller breeds and careful formulation for balanced Ca and P levels is recommended. For adult maintenance, minimums of 0.6 per cent Ca and 0.5 per cent P are suggested. Ca and P from plant sources are less bioavailable than from animal sources, but fresh meat, meat meals and organ tissue all tend to be low in Ca, whereas P is widely distributed in foods. This means that poorly formulated diets rich in meat can cause unbalanced levels of Ca and P, typically resulting in skeletal disorders, especially in growing puppies. Excess Ca can also be problematic, also resulting in problems with bone growth and development. Avoiding excess Ca supplementation is important if an otherwise balanced diet is fed to avoid these issues. If you are home-preparing a diet, ensuring that the levels of Ca and P are appropriate is also essential. For dogs with renal (kidney) problems, levels of phosphorus (as phosphate) in the diet might need to be reduced as part of dietary management.

Potassium (K)

K is an important electrolyte for normal nervous system function and, in combination with Na, regulates the body's fluid balance. Deficiency can affect heart function and cause weakness, growth issues and diarrhoea.

Sodium (Na)

Dogs appear to manage high dietary Na levels well in comparison to humans. Hypertension and high blood pressure as a result of high Na diets is rare, although increased water intake is common and can be useful in certain situations. Na is an important electrolyte, and a constant supply is needed due to constant excretory losses. Na deficiency can result in dehydration, an important consideration for active dogs.

Sulphur (S)

This is a mineral with an important structural function as a key component of amino acids and proteins in the body, such as skin and hair.

Magnesium (Mg)

Mg is important as an electrolyte and for skeletal structure. It is also important in the generation of energy in

Common macrominerals of importance in the dog's diet

Mineral	Function	Common dietary sources	Signs of deficiency	Signs of excess
Calcium (Ca)	• Skeletal structure • Electrolyte	• Dairy items • Bone/bonemeal • Meat and meat meal	• Skeletal issues (rickets, osteomalacia)	• Skeletal issues • Growth issues
Phosphorus (P)	• Skeletal structure • Electrolyte	• Meats (including poultry and fish)	• Skeletal issues (rickets, osteomalacia)	• Skeletal issues • Growth issues • Ca deficiency
Potassium (K)	• Electrolyte • Fluid balance	• Mineral salts	• Nervous system issues • Weakness • Diarrhoea	• Rare
Sodium (Na)	• Electrolyte • Fluid balance	• Mineral salts	• Nervous system issues • Dehydration	• Increased drinking • Rare
Sulphur (S)	• Involved in protein synthesis and structure	• Meats (including poultry and fish)	• Skin and coat issues	• None recorded
Magnesium (Mg)	• Electrolyte • Skeletal structure and integrity	• Cereal/grains • Bonemeal	• Skeletal issues • Nervous function issues	• Rare – excess is typically excreted
Chlorine (Cl)	• Stomach acid • pH of body	• Mineral salts	• Poor growth	• Rare

cells and can be important for highly active dogs. Mg is found in the form of mineral salts in bones and some plant material, especially cereals and grains. Deficiency in Mg is rare but results in weakness and uncoordinated movement. Excess Mg can have a laxative effect.

Chlorine (Cl)

Cl is generally present as chloride ions and is an important electrolyte to maintain the body within normal pH limits. It is also important as a component of hydrochloric acid (HCl) in the stomach – essential for digestion.

Microminerals of Importance in the Dog's Diet

Iron (Fe)

Normal carriage of oxygen in red blood cells and muscle is dependent on Fe, a key component of the pigments haemoglobin (in blood) and myoglobin (in muscle). Fe deficiency can lead to anaemia, lack of energy and occasionally pica, which is the consumption of non-food items, such as soil. Fe toxicity is rare because absorption is well regulated, but high levels can result in constipation.

Copper (Cu)

Copper is an important mineral with several essential roles. Deficiency affects the pigmentation and condition of skin, hair and nails. Cu is also involved in the formation and functioning of red blood cells and is critical as an enzyme co-factor for metabolic reactions. As with many minerals, copper can be toxic at high levels. The liver is the main site of copper storage in the body and toxicity can lead to liver disease. Bedlington terriers have a genetic propensity to problems with Cu storage. Other breeds that are sensitive to potential copper toxicity, include the Labrador retriever, Doberman pinscher, West Highland white terrier, and American cocker spaniel. Where there is a breed predisposition to potential copper toxicity, dietary monitoring and management of copper levels is recommended, alongside veterinary support and guidance. There has been a recent a trend of liver disease associated with copper toxicity in dogs, possibly linked to commercial diets,

Bedlington terriers can suffer from an inherited condition where there is excess storage of copper in the liver which can lead to toxic consequences.

but not all dogs are necessarily at risk. Further advice about a diet's complete nutritional analysis can be sought from the manufacturer if you are concerned.

Iodine (I)

Functioning of the thyroid gland and hormone production is dependent upon I. Deficiency can result in significant problems with hormonal functioning, growth and overall metabolism. Prolonged deficiency results in goitre, an increase in size of the thyroid gland in the neck. Fish and seaweed are good sources of dietary iodine.

Cobalt (Co)

Co is critical as a component of vitamin B12 and is involved in supporting normal body function and preventing anaemia.

Zinc (Zn)

Zn is an important mineral to support health and wellbeing, with many essential roles, including reproduction, skin health and immune system function. Storage of Zn is limited, meaning that a dietary supply is essential. Zinc is predominantly absorbed in the small intestine and excess is excreted in the faeces. Some breeds, such as huskies, are genetically predisposed to having issues with Zn absorption and metabolism and may benefit from supplementation.

Manganese (Mn)

In common with many minerals, Mn is a cofactor to support enzymes involved in metabolic processes. It is also important for bone and cartilage health and supplementation may benefit dogs suffering from joint issues.

Selenium (Se)

Vitamin E and Se work together and have critical antioxidant roles in the body. Levels of vitamin E and Se in the diet need to be carefully balanced. Se is important for active dogs and situations where there is increased oxidative stress, such as older dogs or those suffering from inflammatory conditions. Se is a highly toxic mineral and care must be taken when supplementing.

Common microminerals (trace elements) of importance in the dog's diet

Mineral	Function	Common dietary sources	Signs of deficiency	Signs of excess
Iron (Fe)	• Oxygen transport in the blood	• Meat and organ meat	Anaemia	• Rare
Copper (Cu)	• Co-factor for enzymes • Skin, coat and nail health • Skeletal growth	• Organ meat • Sweet potato • Legumes • Some fish	• Poor pigmentation • Skin and coat issues	• Liver disease
Iodine (I)	• Thyroid function • Hormone synthesis	• Fish • Seaweed	• Thyroid problems • Growth problems	• Rare
Cobalt (Co)	• Component of vitamin B12	• Fish • Offal • Cereals	• Anaemia • Pica	• Nervous system issues
Zinc (Zn)	• Co-factor to support enzyme function • Skin, coat and nail health • Reproduction • Immune health	• Cereals • Mineral salts • Animal products	• Skin issues • Immune problems • Poor reproduction	• Vomiting
Manganese (Mn)	• Co-factor to support enzyme function • Bone and cartilage health	• Meat • Mineral salts • Cereals • Seeds	• Poor joint health • Lack of energy	• Anaemia • Poor growth
Selenium (Se)	• Antioxidant • Supports vitamin E	• Mineral salts • Meat	• Poor growth	• Very toxic • Skin and nail issues

Summary

- Vitamins and minerals are micronutrients and an adequate dietary supply is essential to support life.
- Some vitamins can be synthesised from dietary precursors and by intestinal microbes.
- Fat-soluble vitamins include vitamins A, D, E and K.
- Water-soluble vitamins include the B complex and vitamin C – dogs are capable of manufacturing vitamin C.
- Minerals are needed in small quantities relative to other nutrients but are critical for normal biological processes, e.g. correct dietary levels of calcium and phosphorus are essential for skeletal health.

PART THREE

Feeding for Function: Applying Canine Nutrition Knowledge in the Real World

CHAPTER 10 How to Feed

Nutrition is Not Just About Food

Nutrition is as much about how you feed, as it is about what you feed. How you deliver your dog's food, how often and what other approaches you can take to feeding your dog, can all affect their digestion, health, wellbeing and behaviour. While it might sound obvious, in this chapter we are going to explore the feeding behaviour of the dog, examine what this means for how we then feed our dogs and consider some of the food-related behaviours we might see.

Feeding Behaviour of the Domestic Dog

The dog has evolved as a gorge feeder, eating substantial amounts of food quickly. This mimics the natural feeding behaviour of many wild canid species that scavenge, hunt and eat on an opportunistic basis, including with other individuals. Our own domestic dogs are more than capable of consuming their entire daily calorie needs in a rapidly eaten, single meal. This often appears as a 'gorge–fast' cycle, with dogs often resting and relaxing after eating to support prolonged digestion. But what does this mean for how we feed our dogs? Should we mimic what wild canids do?

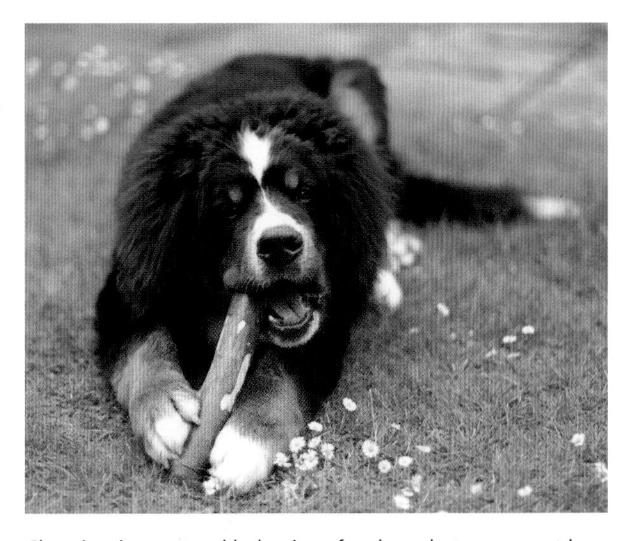

Chewing is a natural behaviour for dogs, but care must be taken to ensure chew items are safe and suitable, such as this coffee wood chew.

Social Facilitation and Transmission of Feeding Behaviour in Dogs

The evolution of dogs from species that had cooperative hunting strategies, helps to explain the typical, rapid ingestion of food seen – many caregivers will describe their dogs as 'inhaling' their food and mealtimes can be over in minutes, if not seconds. Eating quickly would have been important where there was competition for key resources, including food. This also accounts for the social facilitation of eating commonly seen in domestic dogs, where the presence of other dogs increases the speed of eating and the amount eaten, as well as occasional resource-guarding of food.

Food preference also has a social aspect to it in dogs. The social transmission of food preference has been suggested from research where dogs were more likely to consume foods previously consumed by other dogs. This was shown by dogs detecting odours of food on the breath of other dogs. While these data have not been fully replicated, including in a later study where dogs were assessed for their ability to learn food preference through odour from their caregivers and other dogs (they didn't), there is good evidence that dogs can learn through visual and other behavioural cues. Indeed, many an apparently 'fussy' dog has been encouraged to eat when in the presence of one or more 'food-motivated' dogs. Further research is likely to expand our knowledge on how social interactions between both dogs and people may drive food preferences.

Experience and Feeding Behaviour

An important and sometimes overlooked aspect of feeding behaviour is experience and familiarity of food during growth and development, and adulthood. This has been observed in many species and can have a profound influence on later feeding and diet choices. When puppies have a limited and restricted diet, they

Weaning is a time when puppies start to experience solid food and can help develop their future feeding behaviours.

It is not unusual for puppies to explore the world via their mouths, although care should be taken to ensure that inappropriate items are not ingested.

can become reluctant to eat new flavours or foods. This is termed neophobia and is characterised by the avoidance of new or novel experiences, including of food flavours and ingredients. Conversely, puppies and adult dogs fed diets that are varied will often be neophilic – happy to consume a range of flavours and ingredients, sometimes to the extreme of actively seeking out new and novel dietary experiences. Puppies also spend a lot of time exploring their world through touch and taste – this is why many will eat and chew items that we would often prefer they didn't. Plants, soil and other materials are commonly eaten, or at least tasted, by puppies and is part of their normal development. We do need to be careful to limit potential access to toxic or otherwise dangerous items during this stage – for example, many garden plants and bulbs can be toxic.

Palatability

Factors that will affect the intensity of neophobic or neophilic feeding behaviours include the acceptability, palatability (or tastiness) of the food, its novelty for the dog and also how hungry the dog is. From a practical feeding perspective, if dietary changes are needed for dogs, it is recommended to gradually introduce new foods or ingredients over one to two weeks. Start with a small level of inclusion of the new food or ingredient and gradually increase the amount of the new material. This allows behavioural feeding adaption. It also allows the digestive system and microbiome to adapt to dietary change, which will aid our dogs' health and wellbeing, and minimise potential digestive upset.

The term palatability is sometimes difficult to apply to animal nutrition. This is because palatability refers to the 'tastiness' and enjoyability of a food, which is very much a human perspective and one difficult to assess in animals. We can only presume to know what our dogs actually taste when they eat food.

While we know what taste receptors dogs have, and what chemicals in foods they can detect, we cannot know how they perceive them, nor can we presume to know what will and will not be preferred. A simple definition of palatability as 'tastiness' also doesn't consider the potential for acceptance of a food or flavour, followed by a digestive response that might limit future acceptance of the food. This has been found in animals where food has initially been consumed and 'enjoyed' but later events, e.g. illness, become linked to that food. This is a 'conditioned' response and when it occurs, certain associated foods or flavours are likely to be avoided in future – many people have experience of this after bouts of food poisoning or other illness after eating or drinking particular items! However, in the dog-food world, palatability typically means how acceptable a food (or flavour) is and how keen animals are to eat it. Food palatability relates to characteristics (chemical and physical) that increase or decrease the amount eaten, without considering any longer-term conditioned behavioural responses to that food. Indeed, plenty of dogs will eat items that have previously made them ill.

The palatability of a food for our dogs will affect its acceptability and amount eaten. A highly palatable food will be eaten in preference over a less palatable food. The amount eaten will be greater for a more palatable food. The practical application is that awareness of the palatability of food or individual ingredients can have a significant impact on the food intake of our dogs. If our dogs need supported or enhanced food-intake, in the case of illness, recovery, old age, feeding of weight-management diets, high-performance output or other situations where food intake might be reduced, highly palatable foods are suggested. This will include ingredients that increase palatability, such as animal-derived protein and high fat levels. The aroma and texture of food is important, and this includes chemical compounds that can develop during the storage and deterioration of food. Where a dog has previously accepted a particular food and suddenly refuses it, investigations should focus on the health of the dog, but also consider the potential for spoilage and the production of unpalatable compounds within the food. Sometimes simply soaking food, adding a little warm water or even serving food warmed can increase the palatability and acceptability of food for some dogs.

The Daily Feeding Behaviour of the Dog

All animals are exposed to the natural light–dark cycle as a result of the earth's rotation. This gives rise to circadian rhythms that regulate aspects of animals' biology, including sleeping and awake periods, as well as eating. Dogs have irregular sleep–wake cycles and domestic dogs will spend a sizeable proportion of each day resting, sometimes up to twenty hours. Dogs are less affected by circadian rhythms and light–dark cycles than cats are, for example, and can adapt well to human routines and lifestyles.

The Feeding Behaviour of Wild Canids

Wild canids show diverse feeding behaviour, strongly supporting a dietary move towards a mixed intake of plant and animal material. Wild canids and free-living or feral dogs are often limited in what they can eat because of availability, either seasonally or geographically. Being able to survive on a variety of foods is helpful. Hunting and scavenging are heavily energy-dependent. Failed hunting or scavenging expeditions are energetically costly and means that more energy has been used in looking for food than has been replaced by the consumption of food. For wild species, this is a significant factor in diet composition. Many wild canids eat infrequently, based on food availability, rather than having regular and consistent mealtimes.

What Does Wild Canid Behaviour Mean for Feeding the Domestic Dog?

Unlike wild and free-living dogs, our domestic dogs tend to have a much more consistent dietary intake, in terms of ingredients and amount consumed. This is because they depend on us to supply what, when and how they eat. As a result, we tend to view the feeding behaviour of our dogs from a very domesticated perspective, often in terms of regular mealtimes that typically fit within human schedules; food is fed in a bowl, and opportunities for scavenging and hunting are rare.

For many dogs, scavenging is still a common behaviour, but hunting is more limited. This is because for many dogs, while behavioural aspects of predatory and hunting have been retained and selected for (e.g. working gundogs, herding dogs and terriers involved in rodent control), the drive to consume prey as part of those behaviours has mostly been eliminated – a consequence of selective breeding, training and dietary provision to reduce the biological urge to consume. However, our dogs will still show ancestral feeding behaviours, some of which are not particularly attractive or acceptable to human sensibilities.

Coprophagy (or the Eating of Faeces)

Dogs routinely seek out and eat faeces (poop), often much to our disgust and dismay. Coprophagy is the term used to describe the eating of faeces. Dogs may eat their own faeces, those of other dogs and the faecal matter of other animals, both carnivores and herbivores. My own dogs have a particular penchant for cat faeces and can seek it out with alarming and quite disgusting accuracy.

Many parasites are transmitted in the faecal matter of dogs and other animals. Measures to control internal parasites may be needed and minimizing consumption of faecal matter is important.

Our dogs eating faeces is clearly distasteful from a human perspective and is associated with health concerns, both human and canine. Many diseases are transmitted by the faecal–oral route, with lots of parasites relying on this route of transmission. However, coprophagy is a natural behaviour for dogs and one that may have had evolutionary benefits. Coprophagy may be associated with the evolution of the dog as a species that would have needed to keep clean their 'den' and immediate living environment. Indeed, contrary to much dog-training advice, dogs that do eat their own or other dog's faeces rarely have any specific veterinary, nutritional or behavioural concerns, and it is not clearly linked to sex, breed or other characteristics. Research suggests that dogs are most likely to consume fresh poop, and this is consistent with the idea that removing faecal matter may reduce the transmission of parasites. This is because many parasite species that are spread by eggs excreted in faeces, need time to hatch and mature before they are infective. If they are eaten before they have matured, then infection of new hosts might be limited. Similarly, bitches suckling litters of puppies will routinely clean up and consume their puppies' wastes to keep their living area clean. In fact, until puppies are developed enough to move freely, they need their dam to lick and stimulate their urogenital area for both urination and defecation. Some bitches will continue this beyond weaning, and this behaviour is kept into adulthood for some dogs.

How Can I Stop My Dog Eating Poop?

If coprophagy is a concern, strategies that include changing diets or adding ingredients or supplements are rarely effective. In studies examining canine coprophagy, there are very few consistent factors making it more or less likely, although where dogs do see other dogs indulging in the behaviour, it can become a learned behaviour that has its own rewards. Equally, where young puppies, or even older dogs, have been raised or live in poorly managed environments, coprophagy may be seen as a cleaning behaviour. Dogs that have been punished for defecating in the house may also learn to consume any faeces as a way of reducing future punishment. Where coprophagy is a concern or a specific problem, either because of health concerns or simply due to human sensitivities (and let's be honest, eating poop is not the most attractive thing our dogs can do), the evidence suggests that simply preventing access to faecal matter is the most consistent and robust way of managing the behaviour. Other strategies are less effective and may not consistently or fairly result in behavioural change. Coprophagy is a natural behaviour shown by our dogs and is not necessarily one that is associated with ill-health or other problems.

Eating Grass and Other Plants

Dogs often choose to eat grass and other plants. While it is important to be aware of plants that are potentially toxic, eating plants is a widely reported behaviour of domestic dogs. Eating plants is often linked to illness, digestive discomfort or nutrient deficiencies, but in reality, plant-eating is a natural behaviour, based on the dog's exploratory and scavenging behaviour. Young dogs are more likely to be seen to eat grass, as part of natural exploration and learning about the world. Research exploring grass-eating in dogs has shown no definite link to diet, breed, sex or the spay/neuter status of dogs.

It is worth remembering that dogs can detect sweet tastes and young grass and other plants will be rich in sweet carbohydrates, so there may be a simple taste preference for sweet plant material. Similarly, dogs often eat sweet fruit and vegetables – this behaviour is also seen in wild canids. The faeces of foxes, wolves and others often include the pips and stones from eaten fruit when it is in season. Dogs are more likely to consume young, growing grass – especially before their normal meal – perhaps because of taste and hunger, especially as grass consumption appears to decrease as the day progresses. There may also be a health benefit to self-selecting some plant material for consumption. Many animals are known to 'self-medicate' and select certain plants for consumption. This is related to compounds naturally occurring within these plants that have potent effects to support health and wellbeing. Dogs may also indulge in this behaviour when access to such plants is possible. It is also thought that dogs will eat grass when they need to be sick, and vomiting is common after the ingestion of substantial amounts of indigestible plant material. However, vomiting after eating grass is not consistently seen. When vomiting is seen, it may simply be a result of ingesting indigestible material. However, there is the potential that dogs learn that the consumption of plant material can induce vomiting and they may indulge in this behaviour in cases where there is gastric discomfort. It seems that for most dogs, eating plants is part of their natural feeding behaviour. It is not always or necessarily associated with digestive, nutritional or other health problems, and is more probably linked to their feeding and taste preferences.

How Many Meals Should My Dog Have Each Day?

How many meals each day does a dog need? It depends. Dog and caregiver factors will decide. Many dogs do well on one meal a day, but most dogs are conventionally fed twice a day, to fit with human eating patterns and convenience. Dogs can be flexible in their feeding schedule. Some dogs have individual preferences in the amount eaten, the time and frequency of meals – some dogs

Dogs often eat grass and young, fresh plant material through choice. Eating grass is not always a sign of digestive discomfort, nutritional inadequacy or ill-health. Dogs have the ability to detect sweet tastes and young plants are often rich in sweet-tasting compounds that dogs will seek for.

actively choose to eat only once a day. Some dogs prefer multiple small meals throughout the day, especially toy breeds or those on weight-management programmes. Providing multiple meals allows targeted supply of food in relation to exercise or performance output. For dogs that require significant quantities of food to support their energetic demands, multiple smaller meals throughout the day allow the delivery of nutrients more effectively than a single, large meal.

Indeed, the capacity of the stomach and digestive system may limit intake, digestion and absorption. This is also seen in pregnant bitches, where large litters can significantly affect their digestive ability. This is also important for dogs predisposed to gastric dilation, gastric torsion or bloat, where single, large meals are often contraindicated. Feeding once a day has been suggested to be beneficial for health and longevity, but the individuality of each situation (dog and human) always needs to be considered.

When Should I Feed My Dog?

Most dogs are fed in line with the mealtimes of their caregivers or at other lifestyle-convenient times. Regular feeding times can be good for dogs with sensitive digestive systems or for those who predict mealtimes and get digestive upsets – so-called 'hunger pukes' are common when a dog's digestive system is empty and they expect or anticipate food. This can often be managed by feeding small, regular meals. Other dogs get behaviourally anxious near mealtimes. If you are feeding two meals a day, morning and evening are most common. Added meals (if fed) can be fitted around the daily schedule.

Timing of feeding around exercise and activity is important. Make sure that there is at least an hour (and ideally longer) between eating and activity. This minimises exercise-induced digestive upset and promotes better digestion. It is also useful to feed larger meals before a prolonged period of rest, to help the digestive system process the food fully. For many active dogs, feeding a third of their daily intake in the morning and then two-thirds before their night rest period can support performance and digestive health – this strategy is useful for those dogs who suffer from loose stools or diarrhoea when they exercise. Interestingly, one study demonstrated that thirty minutes after having breakfast, dogs were more accurate on a search task than when assessed ninety minutes later, suggesting that less hungry dogs may have transiently improved memory. This further indicates that timing of feeding can be tailored to the individual dog and to the task required.

Should I 'Fast' My Dog?

It used to be common for dogs to be fasted (food withheld) one day per week. This was based on wild canid diets and was intended to mimic the gorge–fast cycle of feeding. Some caregivers continue this approach, and they feel it helps their dogs' health and digestion. Feeding once a day is a simple method to incorporate periods of fasting in your dog's routine but will depend on individual circumstances. Fasting and calorie restriction is known to support longevity and to reduce the incidence of some health problems in many species including dogs, so there is some justification of applying it for health.

Most dogs expect their regular meals, which can be broken-up by short 'fasting' periods to potentially get some benefits. If you train using food rewards or use food as environmental enrichment, fasting becomes problematic. For working, highly active, pregnant or lactating dogs, fast days could significantly limit their performance and affect their wellbeing. Behaviourally, withholding food may cause frustration and anxiety for some dogs, and for those with health conditions, it could be dangerous. Indeed, based on the 'five domains' model of animal welfare, freedom from hunger and thirst is one of the foundations of welfare. We all have a legal responsibility to ensure that animals in our care have access to fresh water and a diet to support health. If done, fasting needs to be carefully managed.

Should I Make Food Freely Available for My Dog?

Occasionally, dogs are fed free-choice or *ad libitum* – they are given free access to food without regular mealtimes. This is common for puppies, especially after weaning, to support the development of independent feeding behaviour and nutrition provision for growth and development. However, for adult dogs, consideration might be needed. For some dogs, free access to food works very effectively and they regulate food intake and bodyweight well. For other dogs, however, this is a potentially dangerous, expensive and inappropriate choice. For some food-types such as raw, fresh, moist or cooked foods, there is a risk of contamination and growth of bacteria and other potentially dangerous microorganisms, if these foods are left exposed to ambient temperatures and environmental conditions for extended periods of time. *Ad libitum* feeding is also problematic for dogs that require weight-management and calorie restriction to support either weight loss or the ongoing maintenance of a healthy, lean body condition after weight loss. Regular, managed meals supply a controlled intake of nutrients, while making sure that the dog is also allowed to express a level of feeding behaviour and experience feelings of satiety. We do not want these dogs to experience prolonged feelings of hunger or frustration around food, as these can cause added, unwanted problems – behavioural and, sometimes, metabolic. Consequently, *ad libitum* feeding does need careful consideration and is not for all dogs.

What About 'Foodie' Dogs?

We all know dogs who are absolute 'foodies' – those who cannot be trusted to control themselves! Dogs that are behaviourally more food-orientated, such as the Labrador retriever, are unlikely to adopt a regulated food-intake strategy. Indeed, a loss-of-function gene mutation in a gene that encodes a protein involved in appetite regulation (POMC – proopiomelanocortin) has been found in Labradors and flat coat retrievers, with dogs carrying the mutation being more 'foodie' and more trainable as a result. The ancestral behaviour of gorge-feeding is also possible for any dog that has free access to food. It is common for dogs to present at veterinary surgeries after consuming copious quantities of food in a single go. Such dietary indiscretions can be serious, especially if dry food has been consumed – speak to your vet for advice if this occurs. Preventing access to food is an important management strategy for dogs that might be more likely to over-indulge. The use of bins and sealed containers to store dog food is useful for hygiene and to prevent inappropriate access.

What About Food Hoarding?

Occasionally, dogs show hoarding behaviour. This is where food resources may be hidden, buried or simply placed elsewhere and revisited at a later time for partial or complete consumption. Doméstic dogs will often do this with bones or other items that might not be eaten in a single meal. Sometimes dogs will choose to move their food to another location and consume it at once or at a later time. Hoarding can also be linked to the intermittent, meal-based feeding seen in many canids, and might be linked to situations where excess food is provided, and dogs effectively choose to hoard it for eating later. This is common in small dogs that tend to be less food-orientated than larger dogs and more likely to eat only to appetite and no more.

'Fussy' Dogs

Many caregivers say they have 'fussy' dogs that are choosy about what they eat. These dogs will sometimes go to the extreme and refuse to eat anything. These dogs are sometimes experts in 'encouraging' their person(s) to add extra 'treats' to their food, or to present more palatable and exciting options. 'Fussy' dogs are often small and commonly live in single-dog households where they have no social pressure from other dogs to eat at all. They are also very effective at 'training' their people to respond to behaviours that might suggest a lack of interest in the food offered, so as to get something different provided. While palatability is important and we should want our dogs to enjoy what they eat, many fussy dogs are suddenly 'cured' when fed in the presence of other dogs or other animals such as cats. The appearance of potential competition, in addition to the social facilitation of eating, is an important consideration when managing feeding behaviour of apparently fussy dogs, in addition to palatability and choice of food fed. It is important to assess if fussiness is behavioural, individual preference or even due to a health condition.

How Should I Feed My Dog?

Traditionally, dogs are fed from bowls – they are an effective way to deliver food. If you feed a raw or carcass-based diet, your dog might be offered the animal part and allowed to settle where they wish and eat at their leisure, without the use of bowls at all. Some caregivers offer their dogs meals that are split into individual ingredients on a tray, allowing their dog to self-select items and consume them in an order of preference. How you deliver food to your dog is as dependent on your choices as your dog's. As long as your dog can eat safely and without fear of their food being 'stolen' by another dog, then there are a number of ways you can feed.

Dog Bowls

Any bowl used for food or water should be large enough to allow your dog's muzzle to fit easily inside. They should be made of a material that is easily cleaned – plastic, metal and ceramic are all options and have pros and cons. Ceramic bowls can be easily broken and chipped, but are often very attractive and heavy, making them useful for large dogs as they tend to be less likely to move around when the dog is eating. Plastic bowls can degrade in light over time and can become scratched and harbour bacteria but are cheap and easily replaced. Sometimes plastic bowls can 'taint' food by odour or taste. There is some concern about our dogs being exposed to chemicals from plastics that can affect their hormones, meaning many caregivers avoid plastic bowls for water and food. Metal bowls tend to be robust and inert – they are also easy to clean by 'scalding' with boiling water. This makes them an excellent choice for multiple-dog households and where infection is a potential risk, although they can be light and noisy if your dog has the habit of moving their bowl around while eating.

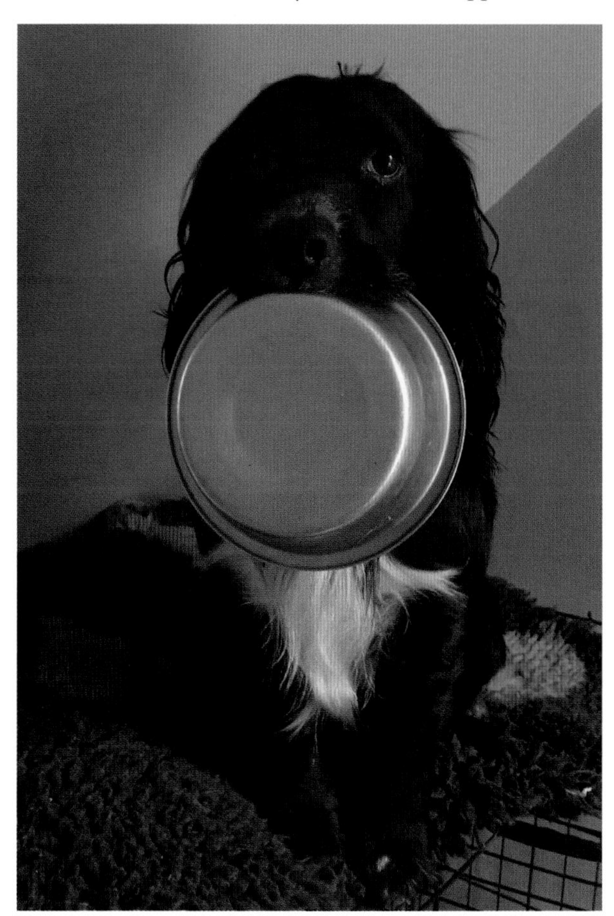

Metal bowls are easily cleaned and robust.

Specialised Dog Bowls

Slow-feeding bowls have inserts that can make it more difficult for our dogs to eat. This is useful for dogs that gulp or gorge their food, or where the amount fed is so small (e.g. for weight-management) that you wish to prolong your dog's mealtime. Raised bowls are another possibility and often used for feeding larger, deep-chested breeds. They are often described as useful for dogs prone to 'bloat', although the evidence is inconclusive. Some dogs do, however, appear to prefer to eat from raised bowls, including older dogs with mobility issues.

Alternative Food Delivery Methods

Bowls are not the only way we can feed our dogs. Scatter-feeding is a way to increase activity around mealtimes or promote sniffing behaviour. This works best using dry food and a 'clean' surface, such as a patio, indoor floor or lawn. You throw (scatter) food widely and encourage your dog to 'forage' for their food – something many dogs find relaxing and intensely enjoyable. Similarly, using your dog's daily food allowance, either fully or partially, as training rewards can be effective for some dogs and can become a form of trickle-feeding. Food-activity toys, chews and treats can also be useful ways to prolong mealtimes, add activity around eating and add some behavioural enrichment. There is a vast range of these on the market – some can be filled with, or smeared with, food and used for mealtimes or throughout the day. Some are difficult to extract food from and create a challenge for our dogs. It is also possible to freeze some

A number of alternative ways to deliver food to our dogs are available, including many different food-activity toys.

Chews are useful to provide environmental enrichment but should be included in your dog's daily food intake as they often supply additional calories.

food-activity toys, complete with food, and give to your dog on hot days or to further increase eating time. If using chews, look for items that are not excessively hard, as these can be linked to dental damage if your dog is a confirmed chewer. Edible chews should be included in your dog's daily food intake too – remember that some will be potentially calorific and not ideal for your dog's waistline.

Summary

- How and when you feed your dog is as important as what you feed your dog.
- Palatability and acceptability of food are important to support food intake, especially for dogs that might be fussy or otherwise reluctant to eat because of inexperience or novelty.
- The dog evolved as a scavenger and gorge-feeder – dogs will still occasionally demonstrate these 'ancestral' behaviours, e.g. coprophagy.
- Individual dogs and their situations will determine if a single meal per day or more are needed – one size does not fit all.
- There are a variety of ways in which food can be presented to dogs, from bowls to food-activity toys.

CHAPTER 11 Critical Canine Nutrition

Being a Critical Canine Nutrition Consumer

Being a critical consumer when deciding what and how to feed your dog is important. It can help you to make the right choice for you and your dog, and if you support or advise others too. Emotion is as important as nutrition knowledge when deciding what and how to feed our dogs. Critical thinking can help you to determine what advice is good, evidence-based advice and what might be more anecdotal and biased. A common refrain in the dog world is 'it works for me and my dog' but that doesn't mean 'it' will work for everyone else. Asking questions and being alert to some of the strategies and techniques that individuals, or even businesses, might use in an effort to change your mind and, in this case, your dog's diet, is an important step in being a critical canine nutrition consumer.

'I Feed You X Because I Love You'

Our relationship with our dogs is often one with deep emotional bonds. Food is often directly associated with love and care, so it is only natural that many canine caregivers take a huge amount of pleasure in providing nutritious, healthy and tasty meals for their dogs – I love preparing a special meal for my dogs and seeing them enjoy it… in the thirty seconds or so it takes them to eat it!

Choosing what and how to feed our dogs is as much about emotion as it is about nutritional knowledge.

Images on commercial dog-food can appeal to our emotions and desires to feed specific ingredients to our dogs, while also representing ingredients included.

Companies can exploit our emotional bonds with our dogs quite cleverly. Think about the images you see on packs of food, treats and supplements. They are often specific dog breeds or types, include hearts and sometimes images of ingredients suggesting a wholesome, loving and natural approach to feeding your dog. The use of natural images, or even wording, is also something to note – the term 'natural' has no clear definition beyond being used to describe components in pet food that have only been processed to make it suitable for pet food and to which nothing has been added. It does not necessarily mean a product is healthier or safer than one that is not labelled as 'natural.'

Rather, wording and imagery that is reminiscent of 'natural' can be a clever way of tapping into our emotional bond with our dogs, and potentially modify our purchasing choices. 'Superfoods' is a common term also often seen on products containing blueberries and other ingredients that are acknowledged to have some nutritional benefits, but the term itself is essentially meaningless. In addition, the inclusion level of many of these 'superfoods' is actually minimal and may be unlikely to confer any real nutritional value. A similar phrase to be alert to is 'chemical-free' – because, by definition, nutrients are chemicals. I would be especially worried of buying something to feed my dogs that was chemical-free. Clarity of terms and definitions is better (e.g. no added artificial preservatives/additives) but is much less attractive from a marketing perspective.

Who is Providing Your Information?

Assessing the source of your canine nutrition information is a good starting point. Is it coming from an independent source or a source with potential bias (while recognising that we are all biased to a greater or lesser extent)? Are you being advised by a company or salesperson and is that advice general advice, or specific advice suggesting that their product is the only one that can meet your needs? What experience and qualifications support the source of that information? The term 'nutritionist' is not a protected term in the same way that other professional titles are. This means that almost anyone can label themselves as a nutritionist, even with the most basic training. Equally, don't rule out speaking to your vet or veterinary nurse for nutrition advice.

Too often, our veterinary profession is labelled as not being nutrition experts, when in fact they are more than capable of looking at the overall health and wellbeing of our dogs and recognising the value of nutrition and nutritional interventions. I know many vets whose biochemical and pharmacological knowledge, understanding and training surpasses even the best applied animal nutritionist – this is why cohesive and united advice and guidance can be so powerful. Yes, some vets will be more experienced in aspects of nutrition than others, but where there are health concerns, your vet should always be an integral part of your dog's overall management strategy, even where food and feeding is concerned.

Try not to be impressed by heady testimonials or stories of 'miracle cures'. Nutrition is important and can be a huge asset in supporting health and wellbeing, but it is not everything. You might be feeding the most brilliantly formulated diet, consisting of the best organically grown, sustainability sourced and freshest ingredients, but if other aspects of your dog's care are lacking, then nutrition alone will not be a magic bullet. It is a common human trait to look for the instant, quick fix – sadly, nutritional amends usually take time, and sometimes experimentation, to find the best fit for each individual dog and person.

Be Alert to Slick Marketing

Because the pet-food industry is so lucrative, it can be a rather 'dog eat dog world' and companies are in constant competition to retain and acquire customers. This means that their products need to be 'fit for purpose' and create either loyalty for existing customers or generate a desire that new customers want to meet. Marketing is an important way that manufacturers inform and educate about their products and it takes many forms, from the product packaging to supplementary information, adverts, ambassadors and, increasingly, via social media 'influencers'.

Many advertisements use celebrities to promote their products and we know that the psychology of celebrity endorsement can be extremely powerful in changing consumer behaviour. The influence that celebrities exert, even on the choice of dog breeds and types, is clear, with 'fashionable' dogs massively increasing in popularity when they accompany their famous caregiver on the red carpet or on social media. Remembering that often these celebrities endorsing or promoting dog food are paid or are share-holders in associated businesses, highlights the potential economic bias at work. Similarly, marketing can appeal to our desire for authority figures by suggesting that their products are recommended, used or approved by breeders, high-profile canine competitors, vets and para-veterinary professionals. While this might be a sign of a quality product that an individual is happy to be associated with, it can also be a clever way of manipulating the purchasing power of the canine consumer.

Be alert to clever marketing and cute images that can impact on your rational decision making when it comes to feeding your dog.

Marketing is a great way to help spread the word about products and their USPs (unique selling points). Many dog foods are well supported by advertising campaigns, especially when new products or updates to existing products are launched. But sometimes marketing can confuse and even create a level of fear and uncertainty for caregivers. A critical awareness of marketing that tries to highlight why one product is superior to another, without robust evidence, can help you to avoid potentially costly purchases that don't live up to expectations. If something sounds too good to be true, it probably is.

Buyer Beware

Claims and information found on our dog food, treat supplements and on any additional product or marketing material, are subject to specific regulations limiting the scope of what can and cannot be claimed. This can go some way to protecting consumers from unsubstantiated claims. Anything that suggests it can cure, prevent or treat a specific condition is in potential breach, unless the product has robust supporting evidence and has met with the requirements to make such claims. This is why much language around nutritional products includes wording such as 'may support joint health' or similar – no specific guarantee is offered, and the potential benefit is broad and vague. If you are not sure about the veracity of a specific product or even claim, ask the manufacturer or supplier for more information. They should be more than willing and able to assist you, and even to provide additional evidence and guidance where it exists.

How to Read Labels and What the Information Actually Means

A useful way that can support you as a critical consumer is reading the labelling and supporting information for any product. The analytical constituents must be declared on commercially available dog-food and will give percentage values for crude protein (or protein), crude fat (or fat content), crude fibre and ash (sometimes called incinerated residue or inorganic matter). The wording is very limited for this section of information but does provide basic nutritional information. It doesn't, however, provide any idea as to the quality or bioavailability of those nutrients. It is also worth noting that the term 'crude' has no bearing on quality and is simply the terminology used a as result of the laboratory analytical techniques used to identify the composition of the food. Ash represents the mineral fraction of the food – no manufacturer adds ash to their food, contrary to some common nutrition myths. The ash fraction will be higher in foods rich in bonemeal and other mineral-rich ingredients – it is not necessarily an indicator of quality. The moisture content will be detailed on dog food if it exceeds 14 per cent, so will be seen on wet, raw and semi-moist food labels.

'It's All in the Name'

Product names are also limited by regulations and guidelines. This is where the amount of a given ingredient in a food can restrict or limit what the food can be called. If a product is named as 'flavoured with chicken' (for example), then it will contain more than 0 per cent chicken but less than 4 per cent. A product named 'with' or 'contains' will include at least 4 per cent of the named material and a food described as 'rich in', 'high in' or 'with extra' will include at least 14 per cent of the named material. If a food contains at least 26 per cent of a named material, then it can be called that (e.g. lamb, beef or chicken) or 'chicken menu' or 'chicken dinner'. Where a product is named 'all', then that indicates there are no other feed materials, except for water and any other required additives to make the food nutritionally complete. Having a critical eye for labelling and naming can help your diet-decision-making for your dog.

What About Ingredient Lists?

The value of ingredient lists has already been noted as potentially of less value that might first appear. An ingredient list will include all major ingredients in descending order of weight inclusion – the first ingredient on a list is present in the greatest weight and this then decreases, to the bottom of the list where the inclusion level could be tiny. If fresh meat is the first ingredient, remember that will include the moisture component as well as the dry matter component, so although it appears high up on the ingredient list, its actual contribution to the whole diet could be less than first impressions suggest. Similarly, look for inclusion levels that differ only by a percentage or so (if the percentages are declared) because an ingredient can be included in a high (or low) placement on an ingredient list, but the amount is only subtly different from another more (or less) 'attractive' ingredient.

The naming of ingredients is also relevant. Some manufacturers will name exact ingredients and feed materials. This adds real clarity and specificity to the ingredient list and is useful to get a complete idea of what is actually in a given food, treat or supplement (e.g. chicken meat-meal or fresh chicken). Alternatively, category labelling terms for feed materials can be used and a common category term that creates much discussion is 'meat and animal derivatives'. This is a category labelling term defined as:

> All the fleshy parts of slaughtered warm-blooded land animals, fresh or preserved by appropriate treatment, and all products and derivatives of the processing of the carcass or parts of the carcass of warm-blooded land animals.
>
> (From the *FEDIAF Code of Good Labelling Practice for Pet Food)*

Sometimes it is thought that the term 'derivatives' means that parts of animals, diseased or otherwise undesirable parts of slaughtered animals are used in the dog food. This is not the case and all other category labelling terms have specific definitions. Category definitions are sometimes used where ingredients might vary slightly between batches, for example, and minimises the needs for manufacturers to constantly update packaging. In other cases, they are an easy way to present ingredients in a consistent and compliant fashion. If you have any queries about ingredients or the terms used, speak to the manufacturer/supplier for more information, or access some of the freely available guidance from organisations such as FEDIAF, the trade body representing the European Pet Food Industry.

What About Additives?

A number of additives are added to dog foods of all types to support nutritional adequacy, as well as adding additional safety, preservative, flavour and texture benefits. The use of additives and what can be included in our dogs' food (and supplements) is limited to substances identified as feed materials or feed additives, and are authorised and registered as such. Many vitamins and minerals added for nutritional benefit are classed as additives and are subject to specific labelling and inclusion-level guidance. Other additives include substances that help to preserve foods and add to the stability of nutritional content over time. These do support the integrity of foods, but some caregivers have concerns about their use in diets and especially long-term exposure. Indeed, the artificial antioxidant ethoxyquin, for example, has been prohibited as an animal feed additive in the European Union (EU) since 2020. Tinned and other wet forms of food often contain gelling agents, some of which can impact on digestion and faecal output. While many additives are useful and have critical nutritional, functional and processing roles, there is increasing interest in more 'natural' alternatives, such as vitamin C as an antioxidant. The ongoing compilation of safety data and other information permits continual review of additive suitability in our dogs' food.

Should I Use Nutritional Supplements for My Dog?

While the dog-food industry is huge, the supplement industry is also growing, but in many cases it is not as well-regulated as is the animal-feed industry. A supplement is classed as a complementary feed and thus does not supply all the required daily nutrient intake. In theory, if a dog is otherwise healthy and is fed a nutritionally complete and balanced diet, then additional supplementation is not required. In some cases, supplementing specific nutrients can even be associated with potentially harmful or toxic outcomes, so professional advice is often suggested before using any supplements. This is especially important if your dog is on treatment or medication for certain conditions, as supplements may interfere with these.

Where a specific condition or nutritional inadequacy is identified, however, supplementation may be beneficial, but as with food, be alert to the ingredient list, inclusion levels and even supporting information about the bioavailability and suitability of the product. For some nutritional supplements, such as omega-3 fatty acids, there is supporting evidence about efficacy and value, but for many, the evidence of their value is lacking.

If you are using a supplement, it is always worth monitoring your dog's health and wellbeing carefully for four to six weeks after first using it. This can give your dog time to adapt and potentially benefit from it. If no

A range of nutritional supplements and options are available for our dogs, offering different potential benefits. Always consider what you are trying to achieve in using supplements and be critical about their value.

NUTRITION FACTS:

	Per pump (1 ml)	Per 100 g
Energy	34 kJ/8 cal	3766 kJ/900 cal
Total Fat	0.9 g	100 g
- Saturated Fat	0.1 g	14 g
Total Carbohydrate	0 g	0 g
- Sugars	0 g	0 g
Protein	0 g	0 g
Sodium	0 g	0 g
Omega-3 Fatty Acids	126 mg	14000 mg
EPA (Eicosapentaenoic Acid)	18 mg	2000 mg
DHA (Docosahexaenoic Acid)	27 mg	3000 mg
DPA (Docosapentaenoic Acid)	9 mg	1000 mg
Omega-6 Fatty Acids	99 mg	11000 mg
Omega-9 Fatty Acids	270 mg	30000 mg

Nutritional information on supplements can give a clear indication about value and the amount of nutrients supplied.

specific changes are observed, then the supplement may not be as useful as you hoped, and an alternative strategy should be adopted. One word of caution is – never try to use supplementation as an alternative to good veterinary care or advice for your dog – this is especially critical if your dog suffers from painful conditions Always seek veterinary advice in the first instance.

How to Choose Well

When deciding what to feed and how to feed, always look at the big picture – that is, consider everything about your dog, your living situation, lifestyle and expectations. Ask yourself lots of questions, including the really important one, 'Can I afford to feed this?'. It might sound brutal, but budget is a key deciding factor and will decide what is 'doable' and sustainable. This will benefit your dog by ensuring a level of nutritional consistency. Choosing well means finding a diet for your dog that fits both of your needs.

Never feel pressured to change your dog's food if what you are currently feeding works. If your dog looks, feels and performs well, then something is clearly going right. If you are happy feeding it, can afford it, supply and storage isn't a concern, and it fits with your wider views as a consumer, then feel confident in sticking with what works. Nutrition is very much a controllable variable and can be effectively used to support health, performance and wellbeing. However, nutrition is not a 'silver bullet' and while nutritional changes can have positive impacts, sometimes the effects are neutral and, occasionally, there can even be negative impacts of change. Always feed according to facts rather than fads or fashions.

How to Advise Well

If you are a canine professional or even just a dog enthusiast, it is likely that nutrition will come up in discussions, either with clients or with friends and family. Advising well and offering empathetic, respectful and compassionate advice is important. Be aware of the potential for 'food shaming', a uniquely modern concept, often seen on social media platforms, where individuals are criticised and occasionally ridiculed for their dog-food choices, even those made with the best of intentions, however ill-advised. Being aware of the nuances of human behaviour, the complexity of individual caregiver–dog relationships and nutritional science, are all essential to being able to advise and support well.

Because every dog and caregiver situation is unique, appreciating the diversity of needs (and wants) is key. Supporting the caregiver through asking questions and coaching them, can help identify what the critical factors of importance are. One size rarely fits all – challenge your own biases and expectations. You might even really dislike a particular food, ingredient or even brand or manufacturer, but that is not necessarily applicable to all situations.

It is also critical that you recognise your professional or knowledge limitations – for example, clinical nutrition advice is best done in consultation with a veterinary surgeon. Indeed, where there is a health concern, the first advice should be that a full health-check is undertaken.

Good advice recognises the individual situation. Good nutritional advice does so too.

Summary

- Be alert to marketing language and how it can affect purchasing behaviour, especially appealing to our emotional bonds with our dogs.
- Understanding the information on the pack and any supplementary material and what it means are important for effective decision-making – this information is subject to regulation and specific guidance.
- Analytical constituents and ingredient lists provide a level of information about the nutritional value of food, but you might need more detail in order to fully assess the quality of a given diet.
- Choosing a diet for your dog well means looking at the bigger picture and assessing all the variables.
- If you are advising, be empathetic, respectful and compassionate, and remember that one size rarely fits all in canine nutrition.

CHAPTER 12 Feeding for Life Stage

Our dogs go through various changes throughout their lives, from puppyhood to senior status. Tailoring their nutrition and how we feed them in those life stages is an important way to support their overall health. Age and life stage do alter the nutritional requirements of our dogs in the same way that there are individual differences between dogs of different breeds/types, shapes and sizes, as well as how active (or not) they are.

Many commercial diets have ranges formulated and marketed for specific life-stages – puppy, junior, adult and senior are the most common. Commentators sometimes describe these as a marketing gimmick. However, scientific research increasingly demonstrates that feeding well for specific life-stages does vary, no matter what dietary choice you make for your dog.

But what are the crucial differences and distinctions to be aware of during our dogs' lives? Let's explore the key nutritional requirements our dogs have, from before birth, to their senior years and everything in between. Practical application of this knowledge will also be examined.

Nutrition for Reproduction

Our dogs' nutrition starts long before they are even born. The nutrition of previous generations, good or bad, can impact on the health and longevity of subsequent generations. For this reason, the diet of dogs and bitches intended for breeding should be carefully considered, in terms of nutrient provision and the quality of nutrients provided. This is obviously in addition to ensuring that the prospective mating partners are suitable matches from a more general health, genetic and breed/type perspective.

Nutrition Before Breeding

Animals intended for breeding benefit from good overall health and being maintained in a fit, lean body condition. A good mantra for any breeding dog is 'fit not fat.' Dogs with obesity can have significant reproductive problems, including difficulty mating, reduced litter size and, potentially, even dystocia (problems giving birth). Obesity can also affect the longer-term health of offspring. Studies from a range of species indicate that the offspring of overweight parents may have long-term impacts on gene expression and overall wellbeing. It is equally important to ensure that animals are not underweight either. Underweight bitches are likely to have delayed reproductive cycles and may have problems conceiving, carrying a litter to full-term or whelping.

An area that is gaining more interest is also the effect of environmental chemicals and how they can affect fertility in a range of species. Canine and human studies have shown that a range of chemicals and toxins found in the environment (and thus also in food) can negatively affect reproduction and development. Because dogs often share the same environment and even dietary components as us, their health and reproduction are an important indicator of what might be problematic for us also.

A number of different chemicals have been identified as having negative effects on reproductive health and development – some are found in food ingredients naturally, some as contaminants, some as a consequence of processing, storage or even packaging. Others are found in the wider environment, including in water. Many are known to be 'endocrine disrupting' – that is, they affect the normal functioning of the body's hormonal system. These environmental chemicals induce adverse effects on sperm health, although they are typically found at higher levels in the dog ovary than in the testes. Indeed, it seems that, in common with a decline in the quality of human sperm, dogs also have declining sperm quality. This suggests a common mechanism is at play.

Early development (prenatal and postnatal) is also sensitive to exposure to chemicals that may disrupt normal processes. Exposure to certain environmental chemicals can affect the number of male and female offspring

Breeding dogs should be 'fit not fat' and have a good lean, body condition.

produced, with a skew towards female offspring. Consequently, an awareness of diet (and the wider environment) for reproducing animals is important. A simple measure is to minimise the use of plastics for bowls, using stainless steel or other inert materials instead. Take care in using any medications, especially in pregnant bitches, and seek veterinary advice if you are unsure. It is also sensible to limit exposure to other potentially toxic or damaging chemicals, such as weedkillers or even cleaning agents. This can reduce exposure to at least some potentially problematic chemicals.

Nutrition of Stud Dogs

The bitch attracts most attention during breeding, although the health and nutrition of the stud dog is also important. He needs to be fit and capable of mating, especially if his services are in demand. Ensuring adequate dietary supply of energy is important, while also making sure there is good provision of protein and key micronutrients, such as zinc, to support sperm health, viability and motility. A stud dog that is active, in a good fit, lean condition and fed a nutritionally balanced diet should not need specific dietary amends. However, awareness of diet quality is important, because of the potential long-term impact of potentially damaging environmental chemicals, in addition to ensuring that the diet supplies all nutrients in the correct amounts and forms.

What About Nutrition of the Brood Bitch?

Before mating, a bitch should be in a fit, lean, but not thin, body condition. This supports her fertility, ability to conceive and to carry a pregnancy to full term. Whelping and lactation are energetically demanding for a bitch, so ensuring that she is on a good 'nutritional plane' before breeding, will help her successfully raise a healthy litter.

Nutrition Before Breeding

In advance of breeding, it is sensible to ensure that the bitch is fed a diet that meets her activity needs and is nutritionally balanced. Reproduction is demanding and can deplete body stores of certain nutrients. Providing those nutrients in advance of breeding and afterwards can help your bitch to recover faster after whelping. Folic acid is important for normal embryonic development. Minerals such as zinc, copper and manganese are also important to support litter size and development. Provision of the omega-3 fatty acids, DHA and EPA, are also important to support fertility, as well as the normal eye and brain development of puppies. Well-formulated diets will provide these nutrients in the correct forms and amounts.

Nutrition After Mating

For the first five weeks of the typical canine nine-week-long pregnancy, there should be no need for any specific change to the bitch's diet, or an increase in amount fed. During this time, the developing foetuses do not substantially increase in size, but they are developmentally sensitive, especially in the first two weeks, so care should be taken to minimise exposure of the pregnant bitch to anything that could impact on normal development. Around weeks three to five after mating, many bitches lose their appetite and may vomit or have digestive upset. This is usually limited and transient, although veterinary advice should be sought if it is prolonged or you are concerned. During the last four weeks of gestation, the developing puppies place significant demands on their dam. It is at this point that nutrition should be increased, both in amount and nutrient supply, although careful monitoring of the bitch and estimation of litter size is useful to ensure that she does not gain bodyweight from over-feeding instead of growing puppies.

Typically, bitches are transitioned on to a diet formulated to support performance or puppy growth and development. These are higher in energy, protein and fat than standard maintenance diets, as well as often providing elevated, or managed, levels of other key nutrients. The bitch's daily intake could be 50 per cent greater than her maintenance intake and regular bodyweight monitoring is useful – ideally, her bodyweight should increase by 15–20 per cent by the time of birth, depending on the size of litter carried.

As pregnancy proceeds, the developing puppies can start to impinge on the bitch's digestive capacity, meaning that more frequent, smaller meals are needed. Immediately before giving birth, many bitches will stop eating, which can be a sign of impending labour, or indeed that early labour has started.

A heavily pregnant bitch resting in her whelping box, ready for the arrival of puppies.

Nutrition and Feeding During and Immediately After Birth

When a litter of puppies is delivered rapidly and consistently, the bitch will often not have time or desire to eat. If labour is prolonged, or after a caesarean section, small meals can be offered regularly, but do not be surprised if she refuses them. Offering palatable and easy-to-digest food is recommended after whelping. If using dry food, soaking it in some warm water is useful to increase palatability and to provide additional fluid intake. Fresh, clean drinking water should be available at all times. It is often worth having alternative foods to hand to tempt bitches who might have lost their appetite.

During the birth process, bitches will typically eat the placenta and other membranes expelled with the puppies. This is entirely normal but can result in short-lived digestive upset and diarrhoea. Providing food and water in her whelping area is often important in the first few days after giving birth – many bitches dislike leaving their puppies to eat, drink or go to the toilet.

Nutrition Post-Whelping and During Lactation

Food should be freely available for the bitch to feed as and when she is hungry (which might be constantly if she has a large litter), certainly for the first two to three weeks after giving birth, and often up to week five nursing puppies too. The bitch will clean her puppies and ingest their waste products. This can sometimes also cause digestive upset, especially as the puppies' transition on to solid food, although after that point, the bitch is less inclined to clean them herself.

A supply of energy and water is critical for supporting the demands of lactation, which reach a peak around three to four weeks after whelping. This is when the bitch has maximum energetic demands on her and needs suitable nutritional support. Ideally feed a diet providing a minimum of 4,000kcal/kg – most performance- or puppy-formulated diets will meet this requirement, but it is useful to check.

In the event that puppies need hand-rearing or additional nutritional support, as can happen with very large litters, commercial puppy milk can be purchased and fed via bottle-feeding. Home-prepared alternatives are possible but may be deficient in energy and other key nutrients, unless they are carefully formulated.

Occasionally puppies need additional nutritional help or hand-rearing.

Nutrition for Weaning

From about three weeks of age, puppies become mobile, and their sight and hearing develop. If a bitch has access to her food around her puppies, often she will allow puppies to taste and try some of hers. Occasionally bitches will eat and then regurgitate partially digested food for their puppies to eat – this is a natural and normal evolutionary process and can be stimulated by puppies licking at their dam's mouth. As the puppies grow and reach weaning age, gradually reducing the amount fed to the bitch and moving her on to her usual diet can help to reduce her milk production, as well as transitioning the puppies on to their new diet. Most bitches will also gradually reduce the frequency with which they make themselves available for nursing. These actions can make weaning as stress-free and relaxed as possible for all concerned.

Weaning can be a messy process but is an important developmental stage for all puppies.

Do Brood Bitches Need Supplements?

Be careful in nutritionally supplementing pregnant bitches, especially early in their pregnancy. Some nutrients can have negative effects on the developing puppies if they are fed in excess. Vitamin A is a good example, where excess supply during pregnancy can seriously affect normal eye development in puppies. For this reason, supplements such as cod liver oil should only be used under advice and with caution. Minerals such as calcium and phosphorous must be provided in the correct amounts for the health of both bitch and puppies, so again care should be taken. If a diet is nutritionally balanced or individually tailored, then no specific supplementation should be needed.

Puppy Nutrition – Up to Eight Weeks Old

Immediately after whelping, and within the first 24hours, it is important that puppies suckle and obtain colostrum from their dam. Colostrum is the first milk produced and contains essential substances that provide immunity and support immune system development. The puppy's digestive system can only absorb the protective substances in colostrum for about 24–48 hours after whelping, after which normal digestive processes commence and these substances would be destroyed. Puppies will nurse regularly for the first two weeks of life and their bodyweight and condition should be monitored and recorded daily to check that they are growing well.

After the initial colostrum-rich milk, the composition of milk alters, and this is what puppies will exclusively consume for the first three to four weeks. After this point, they will often start to explore different solid foods and the weaning process can be started. Puppies will start by tasting their dam's food and this can be made easier by soaking a small amount of the chosen food in some warm water to make a paste or mash. Avoid the temptation to use cows' milk to soak puppy food as the lactose content can cause digestive upset. Raw or home-prepared food can also be offered as minced, finely ground or pureed meals. Beware – puppy weaning is a messy job – puppies often end up covered in as much food as they consume.

The amount of food offered daily to puppies is gradually increased as they reach eight weeks of age. By eight weeks, most puppies are fully weaned on to solid food and rarely

Puppies should be weighed regularly to ensure they are gaining weight consistently.

nurse, although some dams will try to continue feeding for longer. It is important to support a managed and high-welfare weaning process, as this is behaviourally and nutritionally important for both. It is also beneficial to expose puppies to a range of different foods and flavours during their early development. This can support the development of a healthy and robust digestive microbiome, as well as reducing the likelihood of fussy or neophobic feeding in later life. It is also important to ensure puppies have been exposed to several types of food to support an easy transition to their new homes and potentially new diets.

Puppyhood and Growth

Puppies are ready to leave their littermates and dam from eight weeks of age, transition to a new home and sometimes a new diet. Any dietary changes should be done carefully and gradually for young puppies – leaving their litter can be a stressful time, combined with exposure to new environments, dogs, people and a host of challenges, including vaccinations. Digestive upset is common and should be self-limiting, but puppies can be prone to infections and sometimes accidentally eating things they should not while exploring, so care and awareness is important.

Nutrition of the Growing Puppy

As puppies grow, they need a ready supply of energy in the form of calories, quality, digestible protein to support the growth of tissues and organs, and other nutrients to support growth and development. Young puppies (up to approximately six months old) will benefit from three to four meals per day. After this age, the number of meals can gradually be decreased until the desired number of adult meals is reached, while ensuring that the puppy is developing appropriately and maintaining a healthy bodyweight and condition.

A typical puppy diet is higher in fat and protein than an adult maintenance diet. Growth is rapid during the first six months of puppyhood, and this is when nutrition is critical to supply the energy and 'building-blocks' for growth. Small and medium breeds and types will often reach an adult bodyweight between six and twelve months of age, so will often benefit from a growth-supporting diet until this point, after which they can transition to a suitable adult diet. Large and giant breeds will often continue maturing until about two years of age and typically need their slower physical growth supported through more managed nutrition before moving to an adult diet.

Supporting growth is important, but young dogs should not be allowed to carry excess bodyweight. This is especially important for larger breeds and types, where a moderate level of energy supply will support steady growth rates. As puppies reach physical maturity, their dietary energy requirement decreases. During periods of rapid, early growth, at least twice the number of kilocalories need to be supplied as for adult maintenance. This requirement decreases as the puppy reaches maturity and adulthood. It is important to recognise this point and to modify the diet and amount fed accordingly. This ensures that growing dogs are kept in a fit, lean condition, rather than encouraging the development of 'puppy fat'. Growth should be gradual, and nutrition should not be used to try and accelerate growth and development. Indeed, rapid growth can predispose the animal to skeletal problems. Fat deposition as a puppy may increase the likelihood of adult obesity.

Diets formulated for puppy and junior growth will have managed levels of calcium and phosphorus to support steady skeletal growth and development. This is especially important for large breeds. Young dogs also have limited ability to excrete mineral excess, meaning many adult diets are unsuitable.

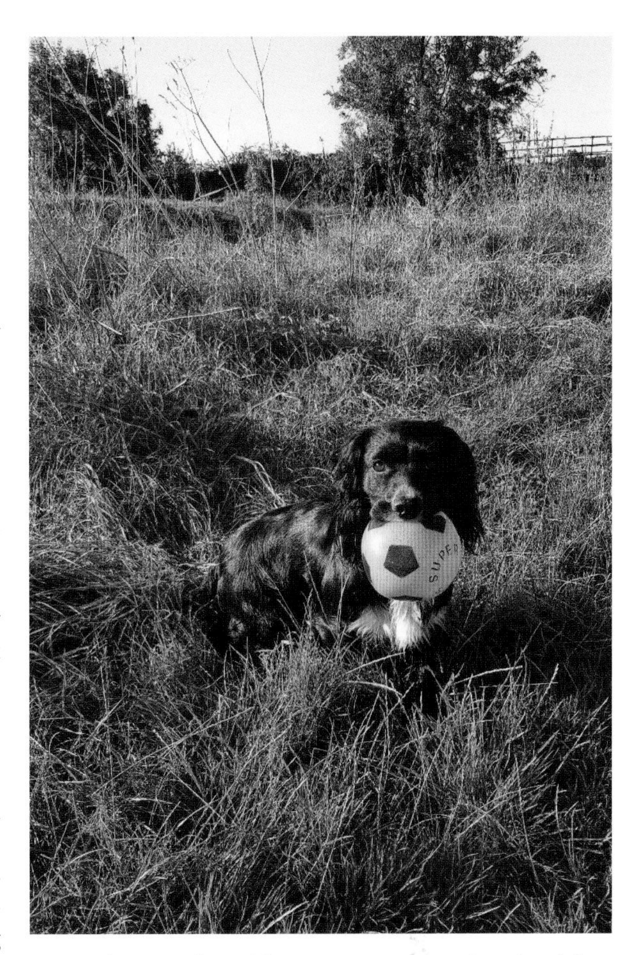

Young dogs need nutrition to support growth and activity before being transitioned to an adult diet.

When Should I Move My Puppy On to an Adult Diet?

The point at which a dog is classed as an adult differs based on their breed/type and size. Small and medium breeds tend to reach physical maturity earlier than large or giant breeds and types. A dog is an adult when they have stopped physical growth in size and shape. Dogs will continue to develop their musculature into early adulthood, but this is also dependant on exercise and activity.

For small and medium dogs, the transition from a diet to support growth and development to an adult one, often starts around eight months old. These dogs typically reach adult height and maturity by one year of age. Large and giant breeds mature much more slowly, and often don't reach physical maturity until nearly two years of age. For these dogs, early nutrition that supports slow, steady growth is important. Large- and giant-breed puppies often benefit from specialised nutrition in the first two years of life, which has carefully managed nutrient levels in contrast to standard puppy or junior diets, before transitioning to an adult diet.

The Adult Dog

Adult dogs have reached physical maturity and don't need nutritional support for growth and development. However, their diet must fuel their activity level and provide the essential nutrients for repair, regeneration and to support their overall health.

Most adult pet dogs have a relaxed and sedentary lifestyle meaning that their diet needs to supply energy to support maintenance activity levels. Where their living situation, exercise and health are all consistent, the majority of pet dogs do absolutely fine on a standard adult dog diet, of whatever type preferred by their caregiver.

Does Spay and Neuter Have an Effect on My Adult Dog's Diet?

Spaying and neutering are useful to help limit unwanted reproductive behaviours and puppies. Spaying is when a bitch has her ovaries and/or uterus surgically removed to prevent pregnancy. Neutering is when a male dog has his testicles surgically removed, although vasectomies are occasionally performed. Hormonal implants are increasingly used as an alternative way to control reproduction.

Many spayed and neutered dogs show physical changes afterwards, with coat changes often reported. However, another impact that spay/neuter has is that it decreases the amount of energy the dog needs from their diet. In some cases, spayed/neutered dogs may need 25 per cent fewer kilocalories each day. If a dog's diet is not changed to account for this reduced need for calories after surgery, then they are likely to gain weight. A good strategy is to decrease your dog's calorie intake by 10 per cent after spay/neuter and monitor their bodyweight and body condition carefully. This then means you can increase or decrease the amount fed to maintain a healthy body condition – a far safer approach than waiting to see if they gain weight, as losing it is much more difficult.

What About Dogs that Need Help with Weight Management?

As dogs reach adulthood, they often become less excitable and active than they were as a puppy. They may expend much less energy when exercising. This, combined with other factors, such as breed predisposition and spay/neuter, can mean that they gain weight. Because overweight and obesity are linked with many health problems and reduced longevity, weight management is important. Good habits to support weight management include weighing and body condition scoring your dog regularly, ideally weekly. This allows you to see even small changes quickly, so that you can modify their diet. You might change their exercise to increase the amount of energy they expend and look at changing what, how and when they are fed to decrease the calories eaten. Weight management is something that usually continues for your dog's life.

The Older Dog

The point at which a dog is classed as 'senior', depends on the individual dog. Traditionally, a senior diet was recommended from seven years old onwards. However, many dogs are still in their prime at this age and continue to do well on a standard adult diet. Do not feel the need to swap your dog on to a specific 'senior' diet purely because of their age. If they look well, remain active and have no specific health conditions, then a diet formulated for adult maintenance, or activity if your dog is highly active (and plenty of older dogs remain very active), should be suitable. A decision to change the diet of an older dog might be the result of changes in their health, bodyweight or body condition score.

What Diet Changes Might an Older Dog Need?

Diets formulated for older dogs are generally lower in calories, fat and protein than standard adult diets. This is because of their reduced energy needs and the weight gain often seen in older dogs. In some cases, health conditions that become more common with increased age, such as osteoarthritis, can lead to reduced activity and increased bodyweight. A vicious cycle then ensues where the dog becomes less active as a result of the osteoarthritis, they gain weight and this then exacerbates the discomfort from their joints which, in turn, makes them less likely to be active. Maintaining a healthy bodyweight through diet and exercise is important, as is seeking advice and possible supportive care from your vet if your older dog is showing signs of slowing down, stiffness, discomfort or pain. Nutrition alone cannot support some of the conditions that our older dogs develop and while some nutritional interventions such as omega-3 fatty acid supplementation might be useful, sometimes veterinary support is also required. Sometimes older dogs have dental issues and dietary changes need to be made to account for this – perhaps offering wet or soaked food.

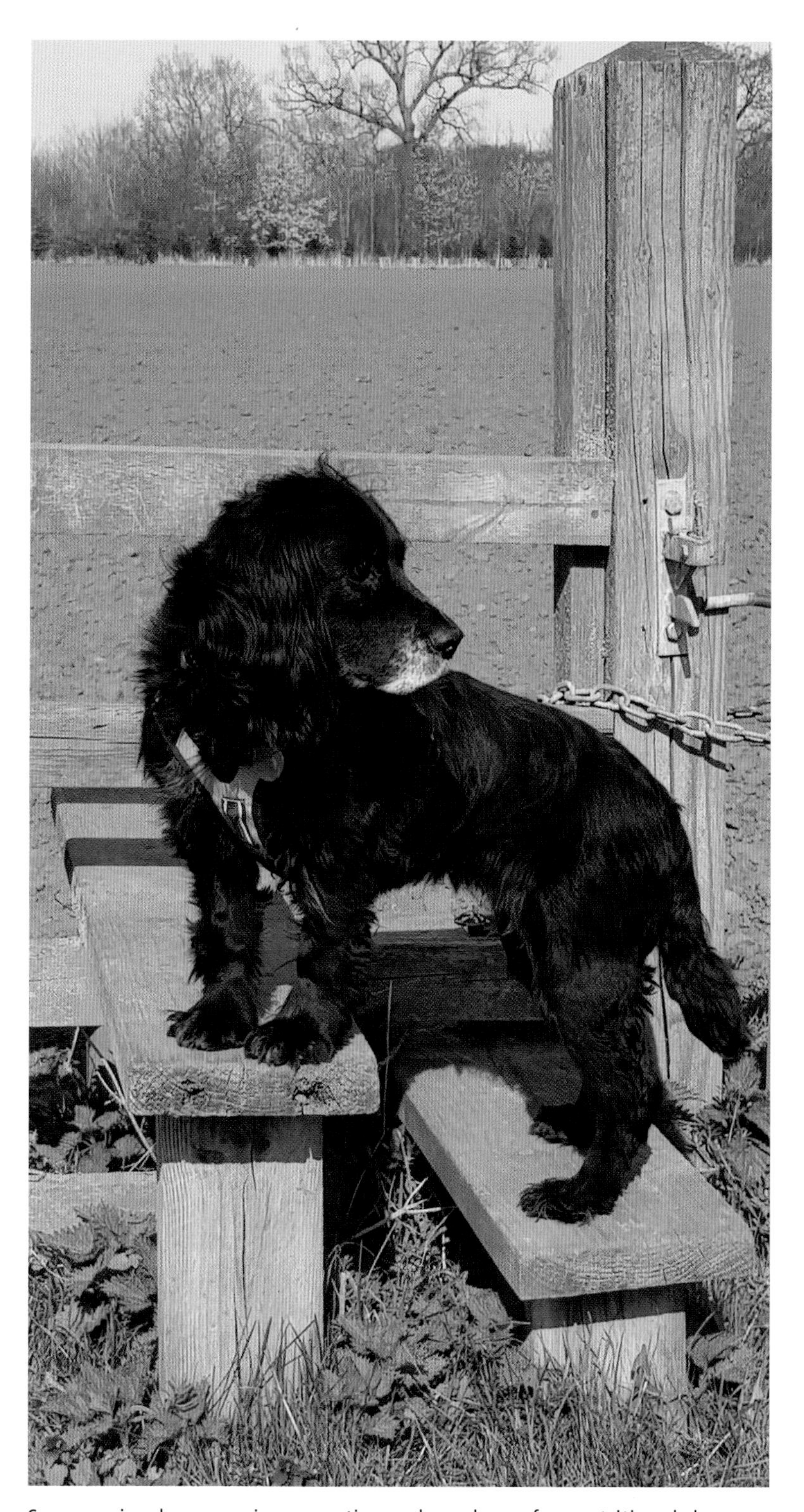

Some senior dogs remain very active and need very few nutritional changes. Molly still runs with her person several kilometres each week aged eleven.

Does My Older Dog Need Food with Reduced Protein Levels?

Traditionally, it was considered that high-protein diets were linked with kidney disease, and many diets for older dogs had lowered levels of protein as a result – many still do. We now know that high-protein diets do not cause kidney disease and that, in fact, older dogs may actually need higher levels of quality, digestible protein than adult dogs at maintenance, to support the additional demands on their body because of the ageing process. Protein requirements can increase by about 50 per cent in older dogs because their ability to effectively digest, absorb and use dietary protein can decrease. Sometimes, health changes mean that the turnover of protein in the body is increased and will benefit from enhanced dietary supply. At the same time, the energy requirements of older dogs tend to decrease, so a reduction in dietary fat levels can be useful. In addition, older dogs can start to lose lean muscle mass, a condition called sarcopenia. Diets too low in digestible protein can accelerate this muscle loss and lead to other health and wellbeing issues. Consequently, older dogs will often benefit from diets that have elevated levels of quality, digestible protein compared to some maintenance adult diets or more traditional 'senior diets', and where at least 25 per cent of their energy intake comes from protein.

Should I Give My Older Dog Supplements to Support Joint and/or Cognitive Health?

The supplement market is large, and a number of ingredients are described as supporting a range of health conditions, such as joint, movement and cognitive conditions. Joint-support supplements constitute one of the biggest markets, and while there is extensive use of these and an enormous diversity of ingredients used, evidence about efficacy remains inconclusive. There are many anecdotes of value, but we remain unsure as to truly effective ingredients, inclusion levels and how best to provide these. There is much more robust evidence supporting the use of marine-derived omega-3 fatty acids in our dogs' diets to support overall wellbeing, as well as targeting specific aspects of joint and cognitive health.

If you are considering a supplement for your dog, first assess what you are trying to achieve and then review the supplement, its formulation and what it might support. It is good to keep a diary or record of your dog's condition and health if you start to use a supplement (or make any dietary change) to determine if there are any positive or even negative consequences. Do not be afraid to stop using a supplement if no discernible benefits are seen.

Summary

- Our dogs experience different life stages that can benefit from tailored nutrition.
- Nutrition for reproduction includes ensuring stud dogs and brood bitches are in good physical condition and have an appropriate supply of nutrients to support the demands of reproduction – this is especially important for bitches during pregnancy, whelping and lactation.
- Growing puppies and young dogs benefit from diets with increased energy levels, good-quality, digestible protein and other key nutrients, such as calcium and phosphorous, at appropriate levels.
- Adult dogs typically need a diet to support maintenance energy requirements but lifestyle factors, including spay/neuter status and bodyweight, will impact on their required nutrient provision.
- Older dogs typically need energy-reduced diets but will often benefit from maintained or enhanced levels of quality, digestible dietary protein, and provision of omega-3 supplementation.

CHAPTER 13 Feeding for Health

What our dogs eat can have profound effects on their health and wellbeing. When our dogs experience changes in their lives – illness, injury, increased activity, pregnancy, ageing and so on – we typically look to amend their diet. Nutrition is controllable and, sometimes, very simple changes can have significant impacts on our dogs' health, wellbeing, performance and behaviour. Alterations to our dogs' nutrition can have positive effects, but sometimes has no discernible impact at all. In other situations, dietary changes, such as over-feeding and excess supplementation, have negative effects and worsen some conditions or cause other problems.

Feeding for health is important, and understanding the link between diet and health can help in making good choices for our dogs. Supplying optimal nutrition might even help them live longer, healthier and happier lives. Indeed, our dogs' 'health span' is as important as their lifespan. Health span is a recent concept that acknowledges a long life doesn't always mean high welfare, especially if a large part of that lifespan is taken up by ill health – a shorter, healthier life might be better in some cases. Nutrition is one way we can support lifespan and health span.

The Science of Longevity

How can we support our dogs in living as long and as healthy lives as possible? Well, while some aspects of health and lifespan have a genetic basis and we cannot alter our dogs' fundamental genetic 'blueprint', lifestyle is an important factor. Nutrition, exercise, healthcare and many other aspects of how our dogs live and how we live with them are directly linked to their lifespan and health span. Longevity is sometimes simply considered as living as long a life as possible. However, if a large proportion of that life is associated with poor health, pain or other conditions that affect our dogs' quality of life, longevity might not necessarily be a good thing, for them or us.

The average dog has a lifespan of somewhere between twelve and fifteen years of age, although individual dogs have lived much longer. Based on these individuals, the maximum lifespan of the domestic dog is often quoted as twenty-seven years old. As veterinary medicine, preventative healthcare, nutrition and lifestyle management have improved for our dogs, many live longer, healthier lives than their predecessors.

However, a number of factors affect lifespan. Larger breeds tend to have shorter lifespans than smaller breeds. Unfortunately, many pedigree dog breeds are predisposed to developing certain life-limiting conditions that significantly reduce their average longevity. Neutered dogs often live longer than reproductively entire dogs. In common with humans, research shows that one of the leading causes of death for our dogs is cancer. This may be connected with the increased lifespan of the domestic dog. The risk of developing certain forms of cancer is acknowledged to be linked to increasing age in a range of species, including our dogs, but other factors, including nutrition, do contribute also.

Understanding longevity and what controls it is often described as the holy grail of science. Decades of research exploring why some live longer than others across a range of species, from tiny nematode worms to dogs and humans, has consistently shown one universal 'protective' mechanism, directly linked to nutrition – caloric restriction. An evidence-based way of promoting increased lifespan appears to be reducing energy intake – although not to extremes – the body still needs to survive. Fundamentally, our dogs don't live as long as we would like them to, and ensuring that our dogs are around for as long as possible is a key desire. Well, the good news is that science clearly shows there is one, easy thing that we can all do to maximise our dogs' lifespan – keep them fit and lean.

Caloric Restriction and Longevity

Caloric restriction means limiting the number of calories consumed and keeping a lean bodyweight with minimal body stores of adipose tissue (fat). From a practical point of view, this means feeding our dogs enough calories to support their biology and activity levels without allowing them to gain excess bodyweight and certainly limiting the potential of developing overweight or obesity. It is important to support weight management and weight monitoring throughout life too. As dogs get older, it is protective for them to have a higher percentage of lean body tissue than fat, because the risk of dying is increased for each extra kilogram of bodyweight. Evidence suggests that dogs can live on average two years longer when their bodyweight is kept at a healthy level. In addition, their likelihood of developing other conditions affecting health and quality of life, such as osteoarthritis and some forms of cancer, is reduced. By keeping our dogs fit and lean, we can potentially add years to their life, and increase their health span too. It could be argued that being more concerned about *how* much our dogs eat rather than *what* they eat is key to a long life, although clearly, the quality of nutrition supplied will have some bearing too.

The take-home messages are that if you want your dog to be as healthy as possible, for as long as possible, then keep your dog at a lean, healthy bodyweight – keep them lean; weigh/measure out their food consistently; weigh and body-condition score them regularly; and amend the amount fed.

Regular weighing is a good way to measure and monitor body condition to maintain a lean, healthy condition.

Nutritionally Responsive Disorders – How Can Nutrition Support Health?

Feeding for health involves using nutrition to support good health and manage certain conditions. Sometimes diet can be used as an integral treatment strategy to help dogs suffering from some health problems. In other situations, diseases and disorders are not necessarily related to diet, but nutrition can be used as a supportive therapy. Where a condition can be supported through nutrition, it is referred to as nutritionally responsive and dietary changes form part of ongoing management.

But, first, a disclaimer: if you are at all concerned about your dog's health, veterinary advice should always be sought in the first instance. Nutrition alone should never be used in the absence of veterinary investigation, a correct diagnosis or as an alternative to seeking veterinary treatment. Occasionally, after a specific diagnosis, nutrition can be reviewed and amended. For specific clinical conditions, this should be done with the collaboration of the veterinary surgeon or by referral to a veterinary nutritionist. In the UK, it is an offence for anyone who is not a registered veterinary surgeon to diagnose, treat or perform surgery on an animal. This is an important consideration when considering, looking for and accessing nutritional advice, especially to support the management of health conditions.

Overweight and Obesity

Our dogs' waistlines are steadily increasing. Obesity is now recognised as the most common nutritionally related condition in companion animals. Some vets estimate that at least 50 per cent of their canine clients present with overweight or obesity. At its most simple, overweight and obesity are the consequences of energy excess, where more kilocalories are consumed than are 'burned off'. When a dog is 5 per cent above their ideal bodyweight, they are considered as overweight; when they reach 15–20 per cent above ideal, then they are viewed as having obesity. Unfortunately, excess bodyweight comes with significant health risks and obesity is a significant form of malnutrition. While there are many risk factors associated with a predisposition towards having obesity, weight management is one aspect of our dogs' health that is very responsive to dietary (and lifestyle) amends.

Nutritional Management of Overweight and Obesity

Reducing the amount of energy consumed is typically the first approach to managing dogs that are overweight or have obesity. Combining energy reduction with increased levels of physical activity increases the success of weight-management programmes. Standard advice is often to simply feed less of the existing diet, and while this initially appears to make sense, there are some problems associated with this approach. Diets are formulated on the basis of supplying energy (i.e. kilocalories). If you feed less than the recommended amount suggested, it is possible that other nutrient requirements will not be met. This is why feeding guidelines are so important.

In order to achieve weight loss, it is often necessary to significantly restrict the number of kilocalories consumed, and this can mean reducing the amount fed substantially. While this may result in the potential of nutritional inadequacy for micronutrients, it can also mean that the dog consuming the food feels unsatisfied and unfulfilled by their meals – a sure-fire way to encourage begging, scavenging and other behaviours that might otherwise limit weight-loss strategies. Consequently, dietary changes to support weight loss and weight management are often needed. This might involve reformulation of home-prepared diets or selecting a commercially available diet designed for weight management.

Bodyweight, Body Condition Scoring and Food Intake

Bodyweight, body condition and food intake are all linked. Overweight and obesity will cause an increase in bodyweight and changes to body condition, characterised by an increase in fat tissue. By measuring our dogs' bodyweight and checking their body condition through body condition scoring (BCS), we can manage their diet and exercise levels accordingly, to keep them at an ideal bodyweight.

A Healthy Bodyweight

Bodyweight is one of the easiest ways to check our dogs' health and it is good to get into a regular routine of weighing your dog and keeping records. Weekly or fortnightly weigh-ins mean that you can quickly make any changes to their diet or exercise before weight changes become a significant issue. Indeed, weight can easily creep on (or be lost) before we visibly notice, so exact measuring of bodyweight means rapid changes to diet can be made, if necessary. In cases of significant weight gain (or loss) in a short space of time, seek veterinary advice.

If you have bathroom scales and can pick up your dog (or train them to sit on the scales if they fit), then weighing them is easy. Simply lift your dog, stand on the scales and take the measurement. Then pop your dog down, get back on the scales, weigh yourself (also an effective way to watch your own health) and subtract this number from the first reading to get your dog's bodyweight. Keeping a diary or spreadsheet is a fantastic way to record bodyweight changes, and is especially useful for fitness programmes, weight-management strategies, pregnant bitches or any situation where knowing exactly what is happening over time is useful.

If your dog is too large for bathroom scales, many pet shops and veterinary surgeries have pet weigh-scales available and are happy for you to use them. It is a great exercise for your dog to visit the vets only for weighing – this can rapidly build positive associations with the vets, rather than the more common negative experiences of treatment. For some breeds, average bodyweights are available and give a rough sign of what to expect at maturity. For mixed breeds, this is less easy, so alternative methods such as BCS become useful.

Body Condition Scoring (BCS)

BCS is an effective and straightforward way to check your dog's physical condition, using visual charts (many dog food manufacturers produce these), as well as physically feeling your dog's condition. A dog in healthy condition will be lean. Their last ribs should be just visible when moving and you should be able to feel their ribs easily without applying too much pressure. If you cannot see their ribs and have to press through a layer of fat before feeling them, your dog is carrying excess weight. Looking at your dog from the side, there should be a clear 'abdominal tuck' where their abdomen curves upwards.

In assessing your dog's body condition, look at their side profile and you should see a clear abdominal 'tuck'. This is a young, healthy, very active, entire dog with a lean, athletic body condition.

Some dog breeds have distinct body shapes and conformations, making body condition scoring problematic. Pugs now have a devoted BCS chart to help caregivers monitor their body condition more easily.

If their lower profile creates a straight line from front to back, again they have excess fat accumulation in their abdomen. Looking at your dog from above, if they are lean and have an 'ideal' BCS, they should have an 'hourglass' shape, where their body shape curves inwards after their rib cage. If this is not seen or, indeed, if there is an outward bulge, they are carrying excess weight. If you are not sure exactly how to carry out BCS, it is worth speaking to your vet, vet nurse or nutritionist for advice and guidance. Research shows that knowing what healthy BCS looks and feels like, makes achieving it much easier. There are also specific BCS charts for individual breeds – the pug is one breed for which there is a dedicated BCS chart that considers their characteristic shape.

Food Intake

The more your dog eats, the more likely it is that they will gain weight. Managing food intake is an important way of supporting any weight-management programme. For dogs that need to lose weight, either reducing the amount fed in each meal or swapping them to a diet specially formulated for weight management will help. Remember that a diet formulated to support weight loss will be energy-dilute, meaning that the amount of food fed will be the same or more than a standard adult dog diet, but have fewer kilocalories. This can be beneficial for those dogs on significant calorie restriction or those who are not satisfied by the amount fed.

Feeding multiple, small meals per day is useful to help dogs feel satisfied and to reduce the chances of behavioural issues arising from feeling hungry or in extreme anticipation of being fed. Alternative ways of feeding are also useful to consider when implementing a weight-management programme – sometimes stopping using a bowl and encouraging your dog to be more active when feeding can increase their activity level slightly, as well as slowing their eating down. Scatter-feeding is one possibility but is more ideal for feeding dry food than raw or moist food. Soaking your dog's food can also increase their eating activity, slow down their eating and provide hydration and digestive benefits.

There are lots of food-activity toys available that can be filled or packed with food and given as environmental enrichment. These can also be frozen (if feeding wet food) and then offered to your dog as a treat or to prolong mealtimes. You can also get special 'slow-feeding' bowls or mats that make eating the food a little more difficult. These extend mealtimes and add activity to eating. Slow-feeder bowls have inserts that make accessing the food a bit trickier. They are useful for any dogs that tend to gulp their food and get either reflux or wind as a result. Slowing down the rate of eating can also help to improve overall digestion.

Weighing out your dog's food for every meal is also critical to support weight management. Evidence shows that the use of scoops or cups is wildly inaccurate and can significantly over- or under-supply food in comparison to weighing out the food on scales. If multiple people prepare a dog's meals, then there will also be differences in how they measure food using scoops. A set of basic kitchen scales is a key addition to any doggy household and only takes a few seconds more in each meal preparation to weight out the food. If you are on a tight budget, then weighing your dog's food makes economic and health sense.

Weighing your dog's food is good practice to ensure daily consistency. Scoops and cups are notoriously inaccurate.

Weight-Loss Programmes

Many dogs that need to lose weight do well with managed and supported weight-loss programmes, often with support from their veterinary surgeon or veterinary nurse. These programmes combine advice and guidance about diet, exercise and other lifestyle factors that are risks for overweight and obesity. Supporting caregivers in compliance and towards results are also important. Sadly, many weight-loss programmes fail, or dogs regain lost weight, because of poor compliance or reverting back to earlier habits, even after successful weight loss. One important aspect is ensuring that the entire household is in support of a weight-loss programme. It is common for some household members to completely derail weight-management programmes through poor compliance.

For a programme of weight loss to succeed, it needs to be sustainable and to fit with caregiver and dog lifestyle. Food choices, intensity, duration and frequency of exercise, and ongoing monitoring of bodyweight and BCS, all need to be considered and managed after the target bodyweight is reached. Encouraging dog and caregiver to have a shared exercise programme is also mutually beneficial and enhances success rates. Calculating the dog's daily ME needs (for weight loss) and then ensuring that their diet supplies this and no excess, is helpful. Minimising treat use or converting to 'healthier' treats, such as carrot and cucumber, is useful – even using some of the dog's daily food as treats and rewards and avoiding table scraps is recommended to limit the accidental inclusion of extra calories.

Exercise is an important aspect of weight management, as it helps to promote energy expenditure and maintain lean muscle mass. However, the amount and form of exercise should be increased slowly to minimise the risk of injury and to ensure sustainability.

Healthy treats, such as cucumber, make great options for weight management.

Monitoring the rate of weight loss is critical. Weight loss needs to be enough that changes and health benefits are seen quickly, but not so fast that other issues arise, including excess hunger or loss of lean body mass rather than adipose tissue. This is important because adipose tissue has a lower metabolic rate than other body tissues and might be 'spared' in cases of extreme and rapid weight loss. A target bodyweight loss of between 1 and 2.5 per cent of the dog's starting bodyweight per week is recommended.

Characteristics of Diets for Weight Management

Diets formulated for weight management are energy-dilute with fewer kilocalories per 100g, often somewhere between 300 and 340kcal/100g, than equivalent diets for 'normal' adult maintenance or working/sporting dogs; these typically range from approximately 350kcal/100g to more than 400kcal/100g. This is achieved by altering the proportions of the macronutrients that supply energy – reducing the amount of fat and increasing the amount of carbohydrate and protein. Reducing the amount of fat in a given amount of food is a simple way to reduce the energy density of a diet because per gram, fat supplies more than twice the calories of either protein or carbohydrate. As a result, the calorie distribution of diets for weight management will be balanced more to a higher percentage of energy coming from carbohydrate and protein than fat. On a dry matter basis, diets formulated for weight management will typically have a maximum of 12 per cent fat, although some will be much lower, especially if also designed to support the management of other concomitant health conditions. If fat inclusion is too low, then a diet can become unpalatable. Dietary fat is also important to support the provision of the fat-soluble vitamins and essential fatty acids.

Macronutrients for Weight Management

Diets for weight management may have increased amounts of indigestible fibre, but the evidence that this supports weight loss is limited. Instead, increased faecal bulk often results and sometimes increased defecation rate. Instead, supplying dietary energy in the form of digestible protein and/or complex carbohydrate, such as starch, might be preferable for weight loss and management, without the negative consequences of an excessively high-fibre diet. The source of starch in a weight-loss diet is important – this can have a significant impact on blood-sugar levels after eating, which in turn affects how the dog's system responds to insulin, the hormone involved in managing blood-sugar levels and fat deposition. Starch from barley (and other grains, such as sorghum) provokes a less significant spike in blood-sugar and insulin levels than starch in diets made with rice or wheat.

Supplements for Weight Management

Occasionally, some supplemental nutrients are suggested to support weight management. Antioxidants, such as vitamins C and E, can be beneficial where there is increased utilisation of body fat stores, to minimise the effect of released free radicals that can cause cell damage. L-carnitine is a non-essential amino acid, commonly found at high levels in meat. It is involved in the transport of fats across cell membranes to be oxidised or 'burned off' as a source of energy. Many diets for weight management have L-carnitine included to support the movement of fats from the bloodstream into cells as a source of fuel. When fat is released during weight loss, L-carnitine can also help protect the liver from accumulating that fat and supplementation may support weight loss and appetite control in dogs.

What About the Underweight Dog?

Sometimes gaining and 'holding' weight is an issue for some dogs. Young, reproductively entire and highly active dogs often fall into this category. Sometimes dogs have lost weight and condition after injury or illness and need to gain weight as part of their recovery. Bitches that have whelped and nursed large or demanding litters of puppies may have poor condition after weaning and will benefit from weight gain.

Caregivers of underweight or very lean dogs will often report ongoing anxiety about how their dog physically looks and will be concerned about their overall health and what to feed them. In these cases, ongoing monitoring of bodyweight and BCS is critical. Presuming that a veterinary check has ruled out any reasons that could otherwise explain the dog being underweight, and there is no evidence of ongoing internal parasite infestation or other digestive issues, then it is often simply that these dogs have an extremely high daily calorie requirement. Sometimes their existing diet and feeding routine cannot fulfil their energy needs.

For dogs in multiple-dog households, it is also important to check that they are being allowed to consume their food and are not being bullied or having their meals 'stolen' by other dogs. Indeed, sometimes stress and anxiety of situations and circumstances can affect a dog's ability to keep a good body condition, so this should be considered also.

Feeding for Weight Gain

A standard approach for supporting weight gain and an improvement in body condition is to feed more food. This can be done in several ways. One is simply to increase the amount fed per meal, although this often exceeds the dog's digestive ability, meaning there is digestive overflow and excess production of faecal matter without weight gain. Increasing the number of meals per day and splitting the increased daily ration over multiple small meals is often more effective – this doesn't put extra strain on the digestive system of the dog and might mean that they can digest, absorb and utilise their food more effectively.

Some dogs have limited appetites and are not 'foodie'. For these dogs, feeding an energy-dense diet means that smaller volumes are fed. Ensure that the diet is also highly digestible and highly palatable to promote intake – diets high in fat will be energy-dense, digestible and highly palatable in most cases. This is often important for dogs recovering from injury or illness.

Allergies and Intolerances

Caregivers often report that their dog is allergic to certain substances (allergens), including food ingredients. The incidence of allergies does appear to have increased in many species and can cause serious health problems. Allergies in dogs typically appear as skin irritation, itching, scratching, digestive upsets and other localised signs of reactions to allergens. Where reactions to food are seen, this is usually the result of an adverse reaction rather than an allergy. Severe allergic reactions have not been widely reported in the scientific literature relating to dog food.

Allergy, Intolerance, Adverse Reaction – What is The Difference?

We often talk about our dogs as being 'allergic' when they show signs of irritation or upset after exposure to something that their body reacts to. However, not all signs of irritation are the result of an allergy and might be more of an intolerance.

Allergies result when the immune system mounts a response to a particular substance. Intolerances and adverse reactions occur where there is a reaction to a substance, but it is not a result of the immune system reacting. Allergies can be life-threatening in extreme cases. Intolerances tend to be milder and sometimes fluctuate in their occurrence and impact.

When caregivers describe their dog as having dietary allergies, they are often describing intolerances or adverse reactions to foods or specific ingredients. Allergies to food ingredients are much less common than often thought and are most common to whole proteins, such as beef, soya and dairy, rather than to grains. Interestingly, many allergies are to substances found in the environment rather than to dietary ingredients.

If your dog does show signs of scratching, itching, redness of skin, hair loss, chewing of paws or digestive upsets and disturbances, first seek a veterinary diagnosis. Tests are available that claim to identify the substances to which your dog is allergic, but they are not as robust as we might like to think they are. This means these tests are not especially helpful in supporting a proactive approach to the management of allergies and intolerances. In many cases, identifying the exact cause of a reaction can be tricky and might need careful exclusion or monitoring of all substances that your dog is exposed to. This is often best done in collaboration with your vet.

Adverse Reactions to Food

When dogs have an adverse reaction to a food, it is usually seen as itching and/or digestive upsets. Occasionally adverse reactions are the result of contamination of food and signs will be seen in all dogs that eat it. If the signs only occur in some individual animals, then this is the result of sensitivity to the food, specific ingredients or even some of the metabolic products of digestion. Most adverse reactions are to intact (i.e. complete) proteins in food. In such cases, the use of novel dietary proteins can be beneficial – a protein that the dog has not already been exposed to. Venison, rabbit, kangaroo, horse, insect and others are all worth considering in such cases. Alternatively, hydrolysed diets can be considered. This is where the protein in the diet has effectively been broken down already, meaning that the dog will be less likely to react to it.

Nutritional Support for Allergies, Intolerances and Adverse Reactions

If a dog reacts to a particular substance, the best approach is minimising future exposure to it. If this is difficult or problematic, there are veterinary treatments that can be useful. In some cases, changes to nutrition might also be helpful. If the problem is food-related, then a food-elimination trial is useful. This is where the suspected ingredient(s) is eliminated from the diet for a period of time (usually a minimum of four to six weeks) and the dog is monitored carefully. Sometimes this resolves the issue, and the ingredient is simply avoided in the future. In other cases, the suspected ingredient can be reintroduced at a low level and the dog's response assessed. In some cases of intolerance, a threshold has to be reached before a reaction is seen. For allergies, avoiding the suspected allergen entirely is often the safest choice.

If the adverse reaction is not diet-related, nutritional support in the form of dietary omega-3 fatty acids is often useful in supporting the body's responses. Added provision of antioxidants in the diet can also have benefits in supporting the body's inflammatory responses. For example, vitamins C and E supplementation provides antioxidant support. Minerals such as selenium are also vital as part of the antioxidant defences. Added vitamin A might be beneficial, although it has a limited safe range of supplementation, so more care might be needed in adding this and some other supplements to an otherwise balanced diet.

Digestive Disturbances

Digestive problems can take many forms in our dogs. Sometimes allergies and intolerances create digestive disturbances, which can be managed via dietary changes. In other cases, individual dogs are predisposed to digestive upset as a result of their genetics. Lifestyle, hormonal changes, activity levels and digestive illness can result in either acute or chronic digestive disturbances. Veterinary advice must always be sought when a dog is lethargic and has prolonged vomiting and diarrhoea – trying to cure these situations with diet changes without knowing what the problem is can be dangerous for your dog. In most cases, digestive upset is transient and rectifies itself quickly, but care should always be taken as dehydration is a real risk, especially in very young or older dogs and those with pre-existing conditions.

Pancreatitis

This is an extremely painful condition where the pancreas becomes inflamed. Pancreatitis can be acute and have a sudden onset, often after a 'dietary indiscretion', such as eating high-fat items like butter. It can also be chronic and some breeds, such as cocker spaniels, appear to have a predisposition to developing pancreatitis, not necessarily because of diet. Maintaining a consistent diet is good practice after bouts of pancreatitis and avoiding triggers, such as high-fat food and treats, as well as applying supportive veterinary management. The level of carbohydrate in the diet might also need to be lowered to support the management of pancreatitis – it is good to make nutritional amends with the support of your vet.

Anal Gland Health

Many dogs have problems with their anal gland health, where the glands don't empty naturally. This can cause impaction and infection. In many cases, this is due to the dog's conformation of the anal glands and manual evacuation is needed. However, diet can help. Increasing the amount of insoluble/indigestible fibre in the diet can help to bulk out faeces. A common management technique is to add some bran to your dog's meals, which can help to increase faecal bulk. This helps the 'normal' emptying of the anal glands. However, bran and other forms of dietary fibre can have negative consequences for nutritional health, particularly by affecting the bioavailability of other nutrients. Bran is also unbalanced in its mineral profile, especially the ratio of calcium and phosphorus, so care must be taken if it is used for long periods of time and for dogs with some health conditions. Probiotics and prebiotics might also help digestive health and support normal anal gland health.

Bran is sometimes an easy option to add to your dog's food to bulk out stools and support anal gland emptying.

Exercise-Induced Digestive Upset

Highly active dogs often suffer from digestive upset and loose stools when exercising. This is a result of body movement and rapid transit of digesta, often without being properly digested and absorbed. In many cases this is simply managed through timing of feeding – several hours before intense activity – and reducing the amount fed in meals before active periods. Both of these practices reduce the amount of material moving through the digestive system.

Inflammatory Bowel Disease (IBD) and Other Conditions

There are a number of other diagnosed digestive conditions that diet can support. Often this involves reviewing the composition of the diet, amending levels of specific nutrients, and altering meal timing and amount fed. It is recommended that veterinary support is always combined with dietary changes in managing these conditions, as the individual dog needs specific and personalised support, making generalisations problematic.

Nutrition for a Healthy Skin and Coat

The skin is the largest organ of the body and forms a protective barrier against the external environment. A dog in good health will have a clean, shiny coat that is not excessively greasy, dirty or scurfy. They should feel pleasant to touch, without sores, discharge, evidence of external parasites/infection or unpleasant odour. Know what is 'normal' for your dog's breed/type, including extent and frequency of moulting or shedding of the coat. Moulting is linked to the seasons, with many dogs growing thicker coats in the winter months, but dogs living in centrally heated homes may show less seasonal fluctuation in moulting and shed their coat consistently. Hormonal changes also affect coat condition, especially in entire bitches that will typically moult and change their coat around their seasons. Changes to nutrition can also affect skin and cost quality – often when nutrition is changed, there are transient changes in coat condition especially and shedding may temporarily increase.

Skin and Coat Concerns

The outward appearance and condition of our dogs' skin and coat is one of the most visible ways of gauging their overall health and can give a sign of their nutritional status. Many early signs of nutrient deficiency will appear as changes in skin and/or coat condition, or even the level of pigmentation. When reviewing the overall nutritional health of any dog, a visual and physical assessment of their skin and coat is called for. When reviewing any supportive management to promote skin and coat condition, it is important that a minimum of four weeks is allowed before any real impact is likely to be seen. This also applies to situations where nail growth might need nutritional support. This is because of the growth cycle of the cells and tissues making up the skin, coat and nails. Be very wary of any testimonials that report a miraculous change within days following a nutritional change or supplement introduction.

Nutritional Support for Skin and Coat Condition

Key nutritional pointers for a healthy skin and coat include ensuring that the diet supplies sufficient quality, digestible protein. The skin, coat and nails are all protein-rich. Dietary fat, and especially the omega-3 fatty acids, are important for skin and coat condition. Dogs on high-fat diets will often have better coat appearance and feel than dogs on diets lower in fat. Vitamin E is essential for skin health and supplementation is useful in some cases. Similarly, biotin is important to support skin, coat and nail condition and growth. Supplementation of an otherwise balanced diet should be done with professional help to ensure appropriate provision of nutrients and avoid potential excess.

Other Nutritionally Responsive Conditions

As we learn more about our dogs' health and the management of specific conditions, it is clear that diet and nutrition can be used to support their management. Nutrition alone cannot be used to treat or cure most conditions (with a few rare exceptions), but it can be used as part of overall healthcare and management.

If your dog has been diagnosed with a specific condition, such as diabetes, kidney disease or cancer, you

A healthy skin and coat is supported by good nutrition.

should always make any nutritional changes in consultation with your vet. It is beyond the scope of this book to consider specific nutritional advice for these conditions, as cases are typically highly individual. A referral to a clinical veterinary nutritionist might be useful for health conditions directly linked to food or the digestive system – remember that while non-veterinary nutritionists can be hugely knowledgeable, they cannot diagnose or treat conditions – instead their advice and guidance is supplementary and should be used as such.

Foods that are Potentially Dangerous to Our Dogs

While many dogs can eat all sorts of food with few ill-effects, there are foods and ingredients that are potentially very dangerous for our dogs. Many of these are common human foods and our dogs can eat them by accident or by scavenging. If you think your dog has eaten something potentially dangerous, always seek veterinary advice and don't be tempted to 'wait and see' – this is critical for food such as grapes, raisins and chocolate. All have the potential to cause serious harm to our dogs, but internal damage can occur before outward signs appear. It is always better to be safe than sorry. Other common foods and ingredients to be aware of as potentially dangerous include some artificial sweeteners, such as xylitol (often found in chewing gum and some peanut butter), caffeine, garlic and onions. Many garden plants, including bulbs, are toxic for our dogs, so care should always be taken to limit access and exposure to these.

Diet and Dog Behaviour – Are They Linked?

Nutrition is often thought to be directly linked to behaviour. High protein levels in dog food are often considered to be directly liked to behavioural problems and a food change is often recommended. While this might be the case for some individuals, how nutrition and behaviour are linked is not quite as simple as a single nutrient, or levels of it. Many dog trainers will report that changing diets to lower protein levels, home-prepared, raw, eliminating wheat/other grains and a host of other amends, can alter and improve behaviour. In some cases, this is true, but it might also be due to other variables changing, including the quality of the diet and the caregiver–dog relationship altering.

It is clear that behaviour and nutrition are linked but probably at a much more complex level than usually appreciated. Nutrients such as omega-3 fatty acids support learning and cognition, and there is increasing awareness that gut health, especially, is linked to brain health and behaviour. We are still learning more about these links, but certainly supporting our dogs' digestive microbiomes and ensuring their diet supplies key nutrients are ways by which we can support their behaviour. In most cases, the link between nutrition and behaviour is a very individual one and needs careful exploration to ensure the overall nutrition, training and management of the dog helps them learn and behave in an acceptable way.

Diet Choice for Specific Situations

When feeding for health, remember that every dog is an individual and their situation is also unique. Even when there are specific nutritional requirements to be met for managing particular diseases, there will be individual needs that must also be met. What is important, is ensuring that nutrient provision is adequate and that the diet supplied is acceptable, palatable and digestible.

It could be that a food-elimination trial is needed, to find the culprits of allergies, intolerances, digestive upsets or behavioural concerns. This needs careful management to ensure that no other foods are accidentally fed, which can set back the trial significantly or can simply cause confusion as to what the offending agent actually is. A good example of this is where caregivers think that grains in their dog's food are causing a range of problems. A food-elimination trial is started to investigate this possibility, and the dog's symptoms do not resolve. On further investigation, it is discovered that the dog routinely gets baked dog biscuits or similar, where grains are an integral ingredient. Equally common are situations where an elimination trial resolves a problem, but it later transpires that the dog was being fed the alleged 'offending' ingredient in other treats or snacks, suggesting that something else entirely may have been at work. Accurate dietary records, such as food diaries, are a great way to monitor the impact of diet changes on our dogs and are essential to ensure that we continually feed for health.

Summary

- Nutrition is one way that we can support the lifespan and health span of our dogs.
- Nutrition is a controllable variable that can be amended to help the management of a number of health conditions.
- Weight management, in particular, is essential for the overall health and wellbeing of our dogs.
- Food-elimination trials are a useful way of identifying dietary ingredients that might be linked with digestive or other health problems.
- Diet choice or modification (including supplementation) to support specific health conditions should be done with veterinary advice and on an individual basis.

CHAPTER 14 Feeding for Activity and Performance

The Canine Athlete

Dogs are involved in a range of work, sports and activities. From sled dogs to gundogs, herding dogs to agility dogs, the work and activities our dogs undertake are almost as diverse as their shapes and sizes. Dogs are amazing athletes and they have evolved to have impressive physical, physiological and metabolic adaptations to support athletic activity. For example, dogs have a contractile spleen, which means that they can move large volumes of red blood cells from it both before and during exercise. This improves the oxygen-carrying capacity of the body during activity, as well as aiding the removal of waste materials, such as carbon dioxide.

Selective breeding has further resulted in breeds of dog with adaptations making them suited to particular types of exercise and activity. In training and conditioning the canine athlete, it is necessary to train the entire body in order for adaptive changes to occur. This is done by exposing them to exercise of an intensity, duration and frequency in order to produce adaptive changes. This must be maintained over time to support their performance ability. Rest and recovery are also essential elements of any canine conditioning programme.

Nutrition can support and enhance performance and recovery. Active dogs need fuel, and this can come from stored energy in the form of glycogen and from dietary

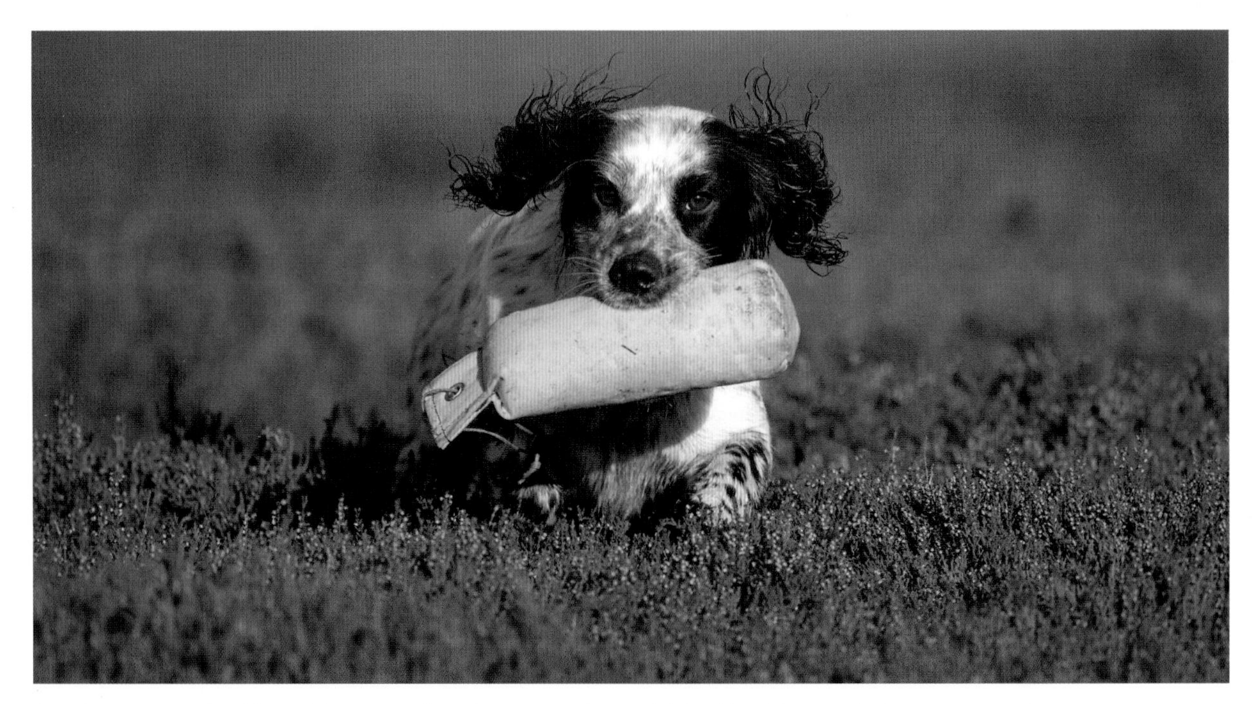

Our dogs are involved in a wide range of work and sporting activities. Nutrition can help support performance and recovery.

energy. Stored glycogen only makes up about 1–2 per cent of an adult dog's bodyweight and cannot sustain prolonged energetic demands. Instead, dogs use dietary fat as their principal energy source. Protein can be used as an energy source, but this may impact on protein being available for repair, regeneration and growth of body tissues after exercise. Equally, carbohydrate can also be used and is important to support sprinting and short-duration activity, as well as the replenishment of muscle glycogen during recovery. Because we can alter what, when and how we feed our dogs, we can make targeted nutritional changes in response to our dog's activity type and level.

Canine Activities

Some dogs are in full-time working or performance/athletic roles. Others are more intermittent in their participation and are effectively active pets. Some canine activities are intense in terms of energy output but are of short duration, such as agility or greyhound racing. Others are low to moderate in terms of intensity but are long in duration – sled dogs or herding and gun dogs, for example. Fundamentally, active dogs have increased metabolic demands to support activity output – resulting in an increased requirement for dietary energy (in the form of kilocalories) but also for water and other nutrients, such as protein and key micronutrients.

Reviewing the frequency, intensity and duration of our dogs' activities can give us an idea of the nutritional and energy requirements of each. This can help us target nutrition specifically for each individual dog's performance output, in combination with appropriate training, physical conditioning and other management strategies to enhance performance. While training and nutrition can help to improve performance output, a dog's fundamental genetics cannot be altered. Genetic limitations cannot be overcome by nutritional interventions, but we can tailor nutrition to meet the demands of activity and performance through food type, amount and delivery to meet an individual's needs.

The Biology of the Canine Athlete

Considering the basic biology of our athletic dogs is important to ensure that we are asking for appropriate output from them and that we can ensure that training, conditioning and nutrition are supportive. While a full review of canine exercise physiology is beyond the scope of this book, there are some key aspects to be aware of. Canine muscles, in particular, consist of different fibre-types, based on their ability to contract and their metabolic function. At the most basic level, muscles are classed as slow-twitch or fast-twitch. Slow-twitch fibres are engaged for long-duration, low-to-moderate intensity exercise and are more dependent upon fat for energy, whereas fast-twitch fibres are predominantly used for short-duration, high-intensity activity and predominantly use carbohydrate as a source of fuel. Greyhounds and sighthounds have more fast-twitch muscle fibres than dogs bred for endurance work, such as fox hounds. Intermediate athletes have a more balanced muscle-fibre composition. Conditioning work can help support your dog's biology to adapt to different forms of activity but, ultimately, muscle composition is a result of genetics and will largely determine what type of activity an individual dog is best suited for.

Exercise and Activity Type

There are broadly three types of exercise our dogs undertake, based on the intensity and duration of the activity – sprinting, intermediate activity and endurance. High-intensity activity is characterised by increased heart and respiration rate. During short-duration activity, the metabolism predominantly uses carbohydrate as a fuel source, but will switch to fat (and occasionally protein) as duration increases, usually beyond thirty minutes. Essentially, short, fast activities benefit from dietary carbohydrate and longer, moderate-intensity activities benefit from fat.

Sprinting is high intensity, short duration. Intermediate exercise includes activities that last for several minutes to a few hours and might be low to moderate intensity. Endurance activities last several hours and are typically low to moderate intensity. Each individual dog's exercise output and frequency of that exercise should be considered in the development of a nutritional strategy (*see* Table). Dogs that are frequently involved in their activity (daily or several times weekly) have increased nutritional requirements compared to those taking part more irregularly or seasonally.

Caregivers need to be critical in their estimation of activity frequency. Distance covered during activity

Different breeds and types of dog have different muscle composition that influences what activities they might be best suited for. Spaniels and fox hounds are intermediate canine athletes.

should also be considered. Short, intense activities have minimal impact on energy requirements, whereas long-distance activity can increase daily energy needs by more than 100 per cent. For example, most agility dogs training or competing once or twice a week will have a very modest increase in their dietary energy requirements, in contrast to a working gundog, hunting and retrieving several times a week or a sled dog covering large distances.

Fuelling for Function – Practical Nutrition for Active Dogs

Feeding dogs for activity and performance is about ensuring optimal nutrition to support and enhance performance and recovery. In contrast to most pet dogs, working dogs and those that participate in energetic activities will have increased nutritional demands. Working in extreme environments further impacts on their requirements for water and other key nutrients. This can be met by ensuring that the diet is highly digestible (certainly greater than 80 per cent digestible) and supplies nutrients at a suitable level. Water must be freely available at all times, except immediately before a sprinting activity, such as racing.

Nutrients for Active Dogs

The physical and metabolic demands of activity increase nutrient requirements. Protein needs to be quality, digestible and increased above maintenance requirements (but only by 5–15 per cent) to support bodily repair and muscle growth. As activity level increases, dietary protein level should increase and approximately 25 per cent of dietary energy coming from protein is a good rule of thumb for most active dogs.

Dietary carbohydrate is not essential for dogs but can benefit active dogs, especially those undertaking short-duration, high-intensity exercise. Racing greyhounds, for example, will benefit from diets where 50 per cent of the kilocalories come from soluble carbohydrates and only about 25 per cent from protein and fat, respectively. Soluble carbohydrate is less important for intermediate and endurance exercise, where fat is key, although when provided as a supportive snack during short exercise breaks or as a recovery aid within thirty to sixty minutes of activity stopping, it can support the replenishment

Examples of canine activities categorised by type of activity/performance based on intensity, frequency, and duration

Type of activity/performance	Examples of activity
Sprinting (high intensity, low duration, mixed frequency – few minutes duration)	Racing – sighthounds, terriers Lure coursing Some agility Some flyball
Intermediate (low to moderate intensity, duration and frequency or moderate to high intensity, duration and frequency – minutes to hours duration)	Obedience Heelwork-to-music Working trials Working gundogs Assistance dogs Scent detection dogs Agility Flyball Field trials and working tests Tracking Guard dogs Search and rescue Canicross Bikejor Scootering
Endurance (low to moderate intensity, long duration and regular frequency – hours, sometimes days duration)	Sled dogs (long distance) Search and rescue Some military/police/patrol dogs

Agility only increases a dog's energy requirements by a modest amount in contrast to longer duration activities.

Water should be freely available at all times for active dogs. Here water is even available during transit and while waiting to work.

of muscle glycogen. This is useful for dogs undertaking activities on successive days.

As intensity and duration of activity increases, a higher proportion of fat in the diet supplies energy in a concentrated and accessible form. Sled dogs participating in long-distance races can expend more than 10,000kcal/day and their diet can consist of 80 per cent kilocalories plus as fat. Dietary fat aids energy intake by increasing the energy density and palatability of food – critical for high-performance dogs where appetite and digestive capacity can be reduced.

Micronutrient requirements for active dogs remain under scrutiny and excess supplementation of individual micronutrients or combinations has not been conclusive. Micronutrient excess could be as damaging as micronutrient deficiency for active dogs. B vitamin requirements are likely to increase as a result of energy expenditure and additional water turnover in the body. Vitamin C might also be lost in this way and might have a useful antioxidant role for dogs undertaking heavy exercise. Indeed, high-fat diets, and especially those rich in polyunsaturated fatty acids (PUFAs), are known to increase oxidative risk. Consequently, the use of antioxidant vitamin supplementation (C and E) might be beneficial for active dogs. The use of a balanced and varied diet for active dogs is likely to supply adequate levels of key micronutrients and any additional supplementation should be undertaken on an individual and evidence-based approach.

Feeding Strategies for Active Dogs

Frequency of feeding and meal size for active dogs is dependent on workload and timing. For many dogs, limiting the amount of digesta in the digestive tract is important to support performance output, but also to ensure that food is effectively digestive and absorbed. For sprint or intermediate canine athletes, reducing the volume consumed (and thus the kilocalories), by around 25 per cent in the 24 hours before activity, is beneficial. Equally, minimising large volumes of food intake within the eight hours prior to prolonged or intense activity is useful to reduce digestive disturbance, the additional weight of digestive bulk and faecal output during activity. However, each individual situation needs assessed, based on volume to be fed, individual preferences and ability to provide required nutrition.

Water and the Active Dog

Water is critical for body structure, function and temperature regulation, especially for the active dog. Dehydration is a significant risk factor for many working and sporting dogs in extreme conditions, and their hydration status determines their endurance capacity. Even mild dehydration significantly affects performance. Water turnover in active dogs depends on the intensity, frequency and duration of activity, as well as ambient temperatures. If dogs are exercising in colder temperatures, their water requirement might be less than for less active dogs in warmer climates, although water should still be freely available. Research has shown that the use of a 'nutrient enhanced' water source can support increased water intake and may support thermoregulation and recovery after exercise. The hydration status of scenting dogs is also important for their olfactory capability and dehydration can seriously impact on their scenting ability.

Many dog handlers will actively 'bait' water with meat juices, gravy or similar, to encourage water intake for high-performance output. Water should be always freely available but, if not possible, it should be offered during breaks and rest periods. Some dogs are reluctant to drink 'different' sources of water, and in these situations, carrying bottles of their usual water is a sensible precaution to avoid voluntary reduced water intake.

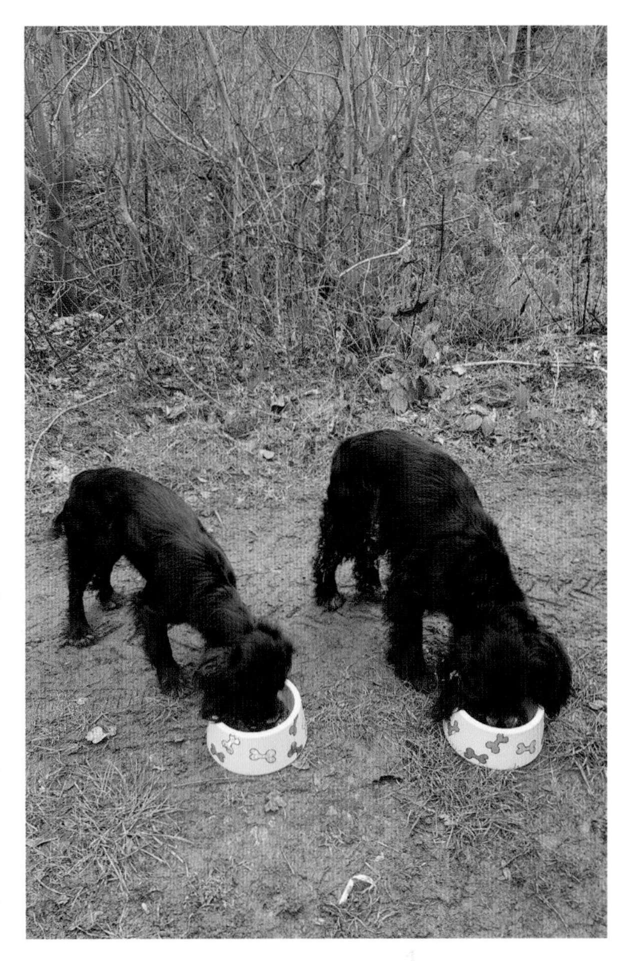

When to feed is important for active dogs to minimise digestive disturbance and support performance. Sometimes meals are useful during a busy working day however, as for these working gundogs during their lunchtime break.

Water and Temperature Regulation

Water has useful temperature-regulation properties, and our dogs use water to regulate their body temperature. Many animals sweat to cool their body down, but dogs have a more limited capacity to sweat than horses or humans, for example. Sweating works by water evaporating from the body surface and drawing heat away from the animal. Evaporative cooling in this fashion is an effective cooling mechanism, but dogs tend to use other cooling strategies. Dogs do have some sweating capabilities, notably via their paw pads, but panting is more commonly observed as a response to cool down, and water is essential for this. Panting is where breathing is shallow and rapid, promoting water loss from the respiratory system and excess heat is carried with that water.

For dogs exposed to warm environments or for dogs that have been exercising hard, fresh, clean drinking water is essential for cooling. Dehydrated dogs have a very limited cooling ability, which can be fatal in extreme cases. While a hot, panting dog should not be allowed to drink excess amounts of water in a single go, water should be available before, sometimes during and after exercise. Avoid offering a dog that is panting rapidly large amounts of water in a single serving – they can often be sick and rapid, excessive consumption may lead to water intoxication. Regular water-intake through diet and drinking can help to manage this. Allowing breathing rates to steady after hard exercise and before drinking is also a sensible precaution. Many dogs will choose to immerse themselves in water after activity as a cooling mechanism, and will often drink while cooling their bodies down at the same time. A note of caution – there is a very real risk of water intoxication, especially for dogs immersing themselves repeatedly in water and retrieving items from water; this should be managed carefully.

Dogs use panting as a major cooling mechanism and their ability to sweat for cooling is extremely limited.

Should I Use Electrolytes?

The use of electrolytes to support performance and recovery in other species is common, but exercising dogs tend to lose more water than electrolytes because their capacity to sweat is much lower. This means that water replacement is likely to be more important for the highly active dog than the provision of electrolytes. However, there is some evidence that electrolyte solutions are safe, acceptable and can potentially aid heat-tolerance in exercising dogs.

Are 'Snacks' and 'Energy Supplements' Needed?

The use of snacks and energy supplements for active dogs can create debate. Many feel that a dog fed a suitable diet should not need any additional snacks or supplements, whereas other handlers routinely use them and are convinced that they help their dogs. A number of commercial or homemade options are available and intended for use either before, during or after activity, to support performance and/or recovery. If a dog is fed a nutritionally adequate diet, then additional or extra nutrition is not necessarily needed. However, as anyone who is a long-distance runner or endurance athlete will testify, prolonged activity, especially in difficult conditions, typically needs additional fuel in the form of energy-dense, highly digestible food. Equally, short bursts of activity may benefit from nutritional support for recovery.

If an active dog is lacking in energy and/or losing body condition or performance is affected, they should have a vet check to rule out any health concerns. Their diet should then be audited to check that it is supplying enough energy to support the activity they are undertaking. Energy snacks and supplements might be useful, providing concentrated and targeted supply of extra kilocalories or other nutrients, such as protein, some specific amino acids, antioxidants and micronutrients such as taurine and carnitine that may support performance and recovery. Many such supplements are provided as fluids, so also help hydration.

Some supplements and snacks formulated for active dogs provide a balanced supply of protein and carbohydrate. Protein can help support tissue repair and recovery after activity. Carbohydrate, specifically soluble forms,

Dogs will often enjoy cooling themselves down by immersing in water.

can help replenish muscle stores of glycogen depleted after activity – this is especially useful for dogs undertaking strenuous activity on consecutive days. To aid the replacement of muscle glycogen in this way, such snacks are best fed within twenty minutes of exercise finishing, and certainly within an hour, as this is when the cells and metabolism are primed to use nutrients in this way. Many handlers will also use post-activity snacks as a suitable reward for 'work well done'. If the snack is also nutritionally valuable to support recovery, then a dual benefit is obtained.

Dietary supplements and functional foods might have a role in the nutrition of active dogs, but the evidence of their value, and even level of supplementation required, is limited. Limited trial and clinical data mean that, despite the supplement market being large, definitive value is difficult to assess. Joint health is a particular concern for active and working dogs and to date, omega-3 fatty acid supplementation has the most evidence of efficacy, to support natural anti-inflammatory processes in the body.

Summary

- Our dogs' energy requirements will change based on activity level, intensity, frequency and duration.
- Highly active, and especially endurance, canine athletes benefit from diets with increased energy supply from dietary fat.
- Carbohydrate and protein are also important for active dogs but at levels suitable for activity type.
- Hydration status of active dogs is critical to support their health and performance output.
- Electrolytes, snacks and supplements might be useful for active dogs but should be used on an individual and evidence-based basis.

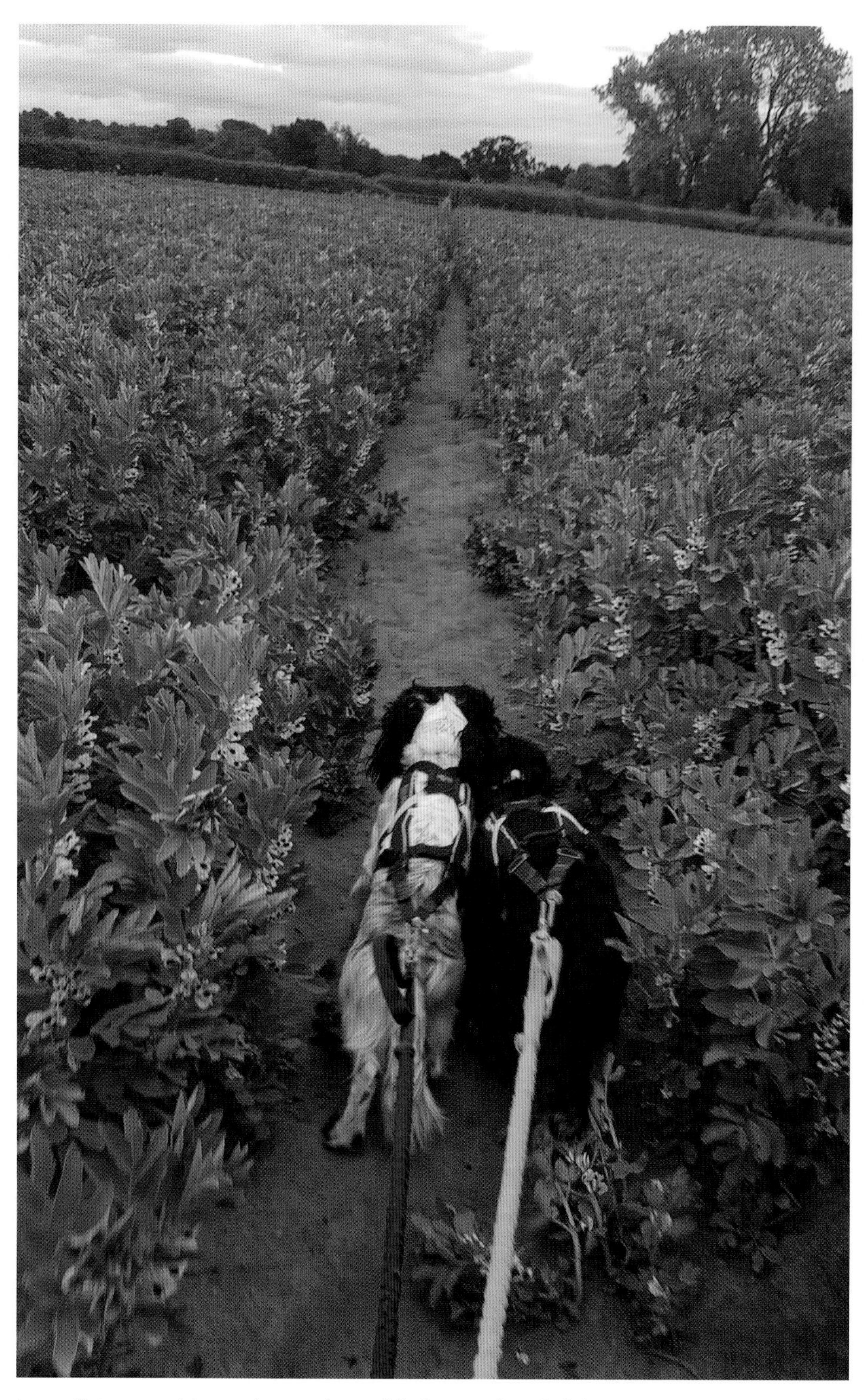

Long-distance activity, such as canicross, bikejor or other sled dog sports, might mean that targeted use of functional snacks supports performance and recovery.

Conclusion

The Essentials of Canine Nutrition

Nutrition is critical to ensure that our dogs survive and thrive. We are all obliged to ensure that our dogs are free from hunger and thirst. Indeed, this constitutes one of the five domains of animal welfare, highlighting its importance in overall care and management. So, at the very least we all have a duty to make sure that our dogs have appropriate access to food and water. However, nutrition can be taken further – it can be altered, amended and reformulated. Food can be presented in different ways, amounts and forms. Ingredients can be supplied in different ways and food can be processed to different extents, or sometimes not at all. Nutrition is one of the few variables that we can have direct control over and that we can use to support our dogs' health, wellbeing and, sometimes, even performance. We can also tailor our dogs' nutrition for our benefit – convenience, cost and lifestyle can all impact.

The Promise of Nutrition

Nutrition is often thought to be a magic bullet – one thing that we can all have significant control over to make positive changes for our dogs' health, wellbeing, behaviour and longevity. Yes, nutrition is important for all these aspects of our dogs' lives, but it is not the only thing. Equally, sometimes nutritional changes and amends have no direct effect at all, and other approaches must be considered and implemented.

Throughout this book, we have explored the essentials of nutrition that can help us navigate our way through the world of canine nutrition. A key theme has been that each and every one of our dogs is unique, and this applies as much to their nutritional requirements as to their personality. Science provides us with a solid, but evolving evidence-base. We can use it as the foundation of our nutrition knowledge and understanding, to make great choices for our dogs, as well as ourselves, while being open to developments in knowledge and understanding, and practical nutrition strategies.

You Do You – You Do Your Dog

Whatever and however you decide to feed your dog, as long as it is nutritionally balanced, provides sufficient energy, is safe, acceptable and palatable for your dog, then you are meeting their essential nutritional needs. You will also need to consider aspects of your lifestyle that might also have an impact. Specific diet choices, food types, use of supplements and feeding for enhanced activity might even mean that you exceed your dog's essential requirements. Indeed, nutritional guidelines are based on minimum nutritional requirements, and

Nutrition is central to our care and management of our dogs. We need to balance nutritional science with our emotional connection with our dogs.

Feed them well and it shows in their enthusiasm for life and work.

nutrition to thrive is as important as it is to survive. Providing this is not damaging to your dog's health (e.g. excess energy) or has significant sustainability impacts, then it is entirely your choice and may even have some additional benefits for your dog.

In a world where everyone can comment and sometimes judge, it is more important than ever to be comfortable and happy with the choices we make for ourselves, and our dogs. I hope this book has helped you to have confidence in your current choices, perhaps helped you to make some evidence-based choices going forwards or even to explore some different ideas.

Your dog doesn't care how beautiful or handsome you are. They don't care what your IQ is. They don't even care how much money you have in the bank (except maybe enough to be able to care for them). Instead, in return for care, compassion and connection, our dogs give us joy, loyalty and companionship. They are our exercise partners, work colleagues and family members. They are our therapists and friends.

Feed your dog well, keep them active and help them to keep a lean bodyweight and body condition, and they will hopefully have a long and happy life with you. When it comes to canine nutrition and feeding, use nutritional science as your starting point and then you do what is right for your dog and you – that might be using a commercial diet only, including some fresh ingredients, home-cooking or feeding raw, all have their value for individual situations.

As we learn more about the biology of dogs, the human–dog relationship and even how our dogs have evolved over the past few thousand years, we gain more knowledge about helping them live long, healthy lives. Nutrition is integral to this.

Feed them well and keep them well. Enjoy your dogs and every moment you get to spend with them.

Do what is right for your dog and you when it comes to nutrition and feeding.

Summary

- Nutrition is important but it needs to be considered as part of our dogs' overall lifestyle and management.
- Remember that every dog and their caregiver (i.e. you) have individual situations and circumstances – good nutrition takes account of this.
- Nutrition should always be evidence-based but each individual dog and caregiver's situation must be acknowledged.
- Nutrition-wise, you do what's right for your dog and you.

Bibliography and Further Reading

Ahlstrøm, Ø. *et al.* (2011). Energy expenditure and water turnover in hunting dogs in winter conditions. *The British Journal of Nutrition, 106 Suppl. 1*, S158–S161.

Ahmed, F. *et al.* (2021). Raw meat-based diet (RMBD) for household pets as potential door opener to parasitic load of domestic and urban environment. Revival of understated zoonotic hazards? A review. *One Health (Amsterdam, Netherlands), 13*, 100327.

Albizuri, S. *et al.* (2021). Dogs that ate plants: changes in the canine diet during the late Bronze Age and the First Iron Age in the Northeast Iberian Peninsula. *Journal of World Prehistory 34*, 75–119.

Arendt, M. *et al.* (2016). Diet adaptation in dog reflects spread of prehistoric agriculture. *Heredity, 117*(5), 301–306.

Avis, S. P. (1999). Dog pack attack: hunting humans. *The American Journal of Forensic Medicine and Pathology, 20*(3), 243–246.

Axelsson, E. *et al.* (2013). The genomic signature of dog domestication reveals adaptation to a starch-rich diet. *Nature, 495*(7441), 360–364.

Beasley, D. E. *et al.* (2015). The evolution of stomach acidity and its relevance to the human microbiome. *PloS one, 10*(7), e0134116.

Bermingham, E. N. *et al.* (2014). Energy requirements of adult dogs: a meta-analysis. *PloS one, 9*(10), e109681.

Bischoff, K. & Rumbeiha, W. K. (2018). Pet food recalls and pet food contaminants in small animals: an update. *The Veterinary Clinics of North America. Small Animal Practice, 48*(6), 917–931.

Bjone, S. J. *et al.* (2007). Grass eating patterns in the domestic dog, *Canis familiaris. Recent Advances in Animal Nutrition in Australia, 16*, 45–49.

Boyd, J. (2020). Canine diet. In: Vonk J., Shackelford T. (eds) *Encyclopedia of Animal Cognition and Behavior*. Springer, Cham.

Bray, E. E. *et al.* (2022). Once-daily feeding is associated with better health in companion dogs: results from the Dog Aging Project. *GeroScience*, 10.1007/s11357-022-00575-7.

Case, L. P. *et al.* (2011). *Canine and Feline Nutrition*, 3rd edn. Mosby.

Case, L.P. (2014). *Dog Food Logic*. Dogwise Publishing.

Cavett, C. L. (2021). Consistency of faecal scoring using two canine faecal scoring systems. *The Journal of Small Animal Practice, 62*(3), 167–173.

Center, S. A. *et al.* (2021). Is it time to reconsider current guidelines for copper content in commercial dog-foods? *Journal of the American Veterinary Medical Association, 258*(4), 357–364.

Cobb, M. L. *et al.* (2021). The animal welfare science of working dogs: current perspectives on recent advances and future directions. *Frontiers in Veterinary Science, 8*, 666898.

Craig, J. M. (2021). Additives in pet food: are they safe? *The Journal of Small Animal Practice, 62*(8), 624–635.

Davis, M. S. *et al.* (2008). Effects of training and strenuous exercise on hematologic values and peripheral blood leukocyte subsets in racing sled dogs. *Journal of the American Veterinary Medical Association, 232*(6), 873–878.

Di Cerbo, A. *et al.* (2017). Functional foods in pet nutrition: focus on dogs and cats. *Research in Veterinary Science, 112*, 161–166.

Ferrell, F. (1984). Preference for sugars and non-nutritive sweeteners in young beagles. *Neuroscience and Biobehavioral Reviews, 8*(2), 199–203.

Finarelli, J. A. (2007). Mechanisms behind active trends in body size evolution of the Canidae (Carnivora: Mammalia). *The American Naturalist, 170*(6), 876–885.

Freel, T. A. *et al.* (2021). Digestibility and safety of dry black soldier fly larvae meal and black soldier fly larvae oil in dogs. *Journal of Animal Science, 99*(3), skab047.

Gal, A. *et al.* (2021). Less is more? Ultra-low carbohydrate diet and working dogs' performance. *PLoS One. 16*(12): e0261506.

Garamszegi, L. Z. *et al.* (2020). The role of common ancestry and gene flow in the evolution of human-directed play behaviour in dogs. *Journal of Evolutionary Biology, 33*(3), 318–328.

Golder, C. *et al.* (2020). Cats have increased protein digestibility as compared to dogs and improve their ability to absorb protein as dietary protein intake shifts from animal to plant sources. *Animals: An Open Access Journal from MDPI, 10*(3), 541.

Gordon, D. S. *et al.* (2020). Vitamin C in health and disease: a companion animal focus. *Topics in Companion Animal Medicine, 39*, 100432.

Hart, B. L. *et al.* (2018). The paradox of canine conspecific coprophagy. *Veterinary Medicine and Science, 4*(2), 106–114.

Hart, B. L., & Hart, L. A. (2018). How mammals stay healthy in nature: the evolution of behaviours to avoid parasites and pathogens. *Philosophical Transactions of the Royal Society of London. Series B, Biological Sciences, 373*(1751), 20170205.

Hill, R. C. *et al.* (2011). Water content of faeces is higher in the afternoon than in the morning in morning-fed dogs fed diets containing texturised vegetable protein from soya. *The British Journal of Nutrition, 106 Suppl. 1*, S202–S205.

Jimenez, A. G. (2021). Plasma concentration of advanced glycation end-products from wild canids and domestic dogs does not change with age or across body masses. *Frontiers in Veterinary Science, 8*, 637132.

Kaminski, J. *et al.* (2019). Evolution of facial muscle anatomy in dogs. *Proceedings of the National Academy of Sciences of the United States of America, 116*(29), 14677–14681.

Klein, C. *et al.* (2019). Metabolisable energy intake and growth of privately owned growing dogs in comparison with official recommendations on the growth curve and energy supply. *Journal of Animal Physiology and Animal Nutrition, 103*(6), 1952–1958.

Laflamme, D. P. (2008). Pet food safety: dietary protein. *Topics in Companion Animal Medicine, 23*(3), 154–157.

Lahtinen, M. *et al.* (2021). Excess protein enabled dog domestication during severe Ice Age winters. *Scientific reports, 11*(1), 7.

Luisana, E. *et al.* (2022). Survey evaluation of dog owners' feeding practices and dog bowls' hygiene assessment in domestic settings. *PloS one, 17*(4), e0259478.

Lupfer-Johnson, G. & Ross, J. (2007). Dogs acquire food preferences from interacting with recently fed conspecifics. *Behavioural Processes, 74*(1), 104–106.

Lyu, Y. *et al.* (2022). Differences in metabolic profiles of healthy dogs fed a high-fat vs. a high-starch diet. *Frontiers in Veterinary Science, 9*, 801863.

Machado, F. A. (2020). Selection and constraints in the ecomorphological adaptive evolution of the skull of living Canidae (Carnivora, Mammalia). *The American Naturalist, 196*(2), 197–215.

Mankowska, M. *et al.* (2017). Confirmation that a deletion in the POMC gene is associated with body-weight of Labrador retriever dogs. *Research in Veterinary Science, 112*, 116–118.

Meineri, G., *et al.* (2021). Effects of 'fresh mechanically deboned meat' inclusion on nutritional value, palatability, shelf-life microbiological risk and digestibility in dry dog-food. *PloS one, 16*(4), e0250351.

Mendez, A. D. & Hall, N. J. (2021). Evaluating and re-evaluating intra- and inter-species social transmission of food preferences in domestic dogs. *Behavioural Processes, 191*, 104471.

Miller, H. C., & Bender, C. (2012). The breakfast effect: dogs (*Canis familiaris*) search more accurately when they are less hungry. *Behavioural Processes, 91*(3), 313–317.

Morelli, G *et al.* (2020). A survey of dog owners' attitudes toward treats. *Journal of Applied Animal Welfare Science: JAAWS, 23*(1), 1–9.

Morelli, G. *et al.* (2021). A survey among dog and cat owners on pet food storage and preservation in the households. *Animals: An Open Access Journal from MDPI, 11*(2), 273.

Mullen, K. M. *et al.* (2020). The pathophysiology of small intestinal foreign body obstruction and intraoperative assessment of tissue viability in dogs: a review. *Topics in Companion Animal Medicine, 40*, 100438.

National Research Council (2006). *Nutrient Requirements of Dogs and Cats.* Washington, DC: National Academies Press

Oberbauer, A. M. & Larsen, J. A. (2021). Amino acids in dog nutrition and health. *Advances in Experimental Medicine and Biology, 1285*, 199–216.

Otto, C. M. *et al.* (2017). Evaluation of three hydration strategies in detection dogs working in a hot environment. *Frontiers in Veterinary Science, 4*, 174.

Palaseweenun, P. *et al.* (2021). Urinary excretion of advanced glycation end products in dogs and cats. *Journal of Animal Physiology and Animal Nutrition, 105*(1), 149–156.

Penell, J. C. *et al.* (2019). Bodyweight at 10 years of age and change in body composition between 8 and 10 years of age were related to survival in a longitudinal study of 39 Labrador retriever dogs. *Acta Veterinaria Scandinavica, 61*(1), 42.

Pereira, A. M. *et al.* (2021). Zinc in Dog Nutrition, Health and Disease: A Review. *Animals: an open access journal from MDPI, 11*(4), 978.

Perri, A. R. *et al.* (2021). Dog domestication and the dual dispersal of people and dogs into the Americas. *Proceedings of the National Academy of Sciences of the United States of America, 118*(6), e2010083118.

Raffan, E. *et al.* (2016). A deletion in the canine POMC gene is associated with weight and appetite in obesity-prone Labrador retriever dogs. *Cell Metabolism, 23*(5), 893–900.

Rankovic, A. *et al.* (2019). Role of carbohydrates in the health of dogs. *Journal of the American Veterinary Medical Association, 255*(5), 546–554.

Reiter, T. *et al.* (2016). Dietary variation and evolution of gene copy number among dog breeds. *PloS one, 11*(2), e0148899.

Reynolds, A. J. *et al.* (1999). Effect of protein intake during training on biochemical and performance variables in sled dogs. *American Journal of Veterinary Research, 60*(7), 789–795.

Samant, S. S. *et al.* (2021). Dry pet food flavor enhancers and their impact on palatability: a review. *Foods (Basel, Switzerland), 10*(11), 2599.

Schäfer, W. & Hankel, J. (2020). Energy consumption of young military working dogs in pre-training in Germany. *Animals: An Open Access Journal from MDPI, 10*(10), 1753.

Su, D. K. *et al.* (2019). Impact of feeding method on overall activity of indoor, client-owned dogs. *The Journal of Small Animal Practice, 60*(7), 438–443.

Sueda, K. L. C. *et al.* (2008). Characterisation of plant eating in dogs. *Applied Animal Behaviour Science*, 111, 120–132.

Sumner, R. N. *et al.* (2019). Independent and combined effects of diethylhexyl phthalate and polychlorinated biphenyl 153 on sperm quality in the human and dog. *Scientific Reports, 9*(1), 3409.

Sumner, R. N. *et al.* (2020). The dog as a sentinel species for environmental effects on human fertility. *Reproduction (Cambridge, England), 159*(6), R265–R276.

Sumner, R. N. *et al.* (2021). Environmental chemicals in dog testes reflect their geographical source and may be associated with altered pathology. *Scientific Reports, 11*(1), 7361.

Thes, M. *et al.* (2016). Metabolizable energy intake of client-owned adult dogs. *Journal of Animal Physiology and Animal Nutrition, 100*(5), 813–819.

Tseng, Z. J. & Wang, X. (2010). Cranial functional morphology of fossil dogs and adaptation for durophagy in Borophagus and Epicyon (Carnivora, Mammalia). *Journal of Morphology, 271*(11), 1386–1398.

Uribarri, J. *et al.* (2010). Advanced glycation end products in foods and a practical guide to their reduction in the diet. *Journal of the American Dietetic Association, 110*(6), 911–16. e12.

van De Sluis, B. *et al.* (2002). Identification of a new copper metabolism gene by positional cloning in a purebred dog population. *Human Molecular Genetics, 11*(2), 165–173.

Weber, M. P. *et al.* (2017). Digestive sensitivity varies according to size of dogs: a review. *Journal of Animal Physiology and Animal Nutrition, 101*(1), 1–9.

Zanghi, B. M. *et al.* (2018). Working dogs drinking a nutrient-enriched water maintain cooler body temperature and improved pulse rate recovery after exercise. *Frontiers in Veterinary Science, 5*, 202.

Zanghi, B. M. & Gardner, C. L. (2018). Total water intake and urine measures of hydration in adult dogs drinking tap water or a nutrient-enriched water. *Frontiers in Veterinary Science, 5*, 317.

Zhang, Z. *et al.* (2020). Deciphering the puzzles of dog domestication. *Zoological Research, 41*(2), 97–104.

Zoran, D. L. (2021). Nutrition of working dogs: feeding for optimal performance and health. *The Veterinary Clinics of North America. Small Animal Practice, 51*(4), 803–819.

seful Resources

FEDIAF (2019). *Code of Good Labelling Practice.* Available at https://www.fediaf.org/self-regulation/labelling.html

FEDIAF (2021). *Nutritional Guidelines for Complete and Complementary Food for Cats and Dogs.* Available at https://fediaf.org/self-regulation/nutrition

Pug BCS chart is available at www.vet.cam.ac.uk/files/media/Pug_health_scheme_BCS_v2.jpg

Dog BCS chart from the WSAVA – https://wsava.org/wp-content/uploads/2020/01/Body-Condition-Score-Dog.pdf

Index

Related Titles from Crowood

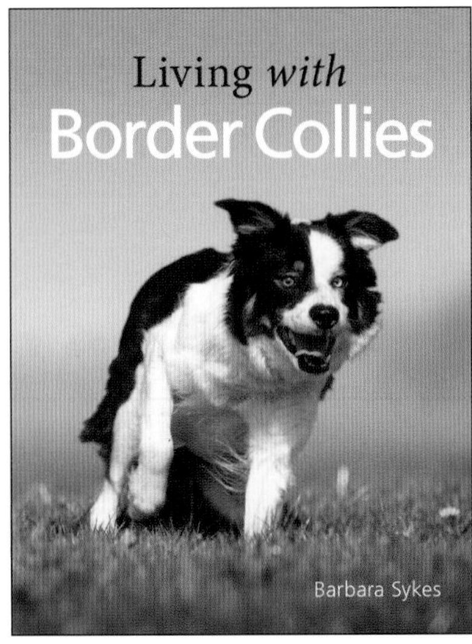

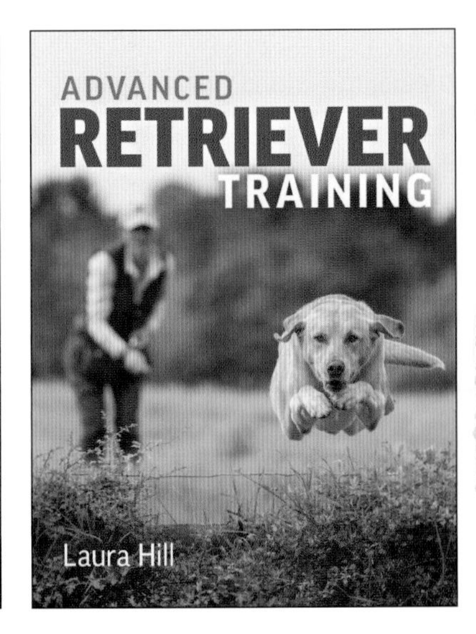